W0050205

Game India

Game India

Seven Strategic Advantages
That Can Steer India to Wealth

R.N. BHASKAR

PENGUIN
BUSINESS

An imprint of Penguin Random House

PENGUIN BUSINESS

USA | Canada | UK | Ireland | Australia
New Zealand | India | South Africa | China | Singapore

Portfolio is part of the Penguin Random House group of companies
whose addresses can be found at global.penguinrandomhouse.com

Published by Penguin Random House India Pvt. Ltd
4th Floor, Capital Tower 1, MG Road,
Gurugram 122 002, Haryana, India

First published in Portfolio by Penguin Random House India 2019
This edition published in Penguin Business by Penguin Random House India 2024

Copyright © R.N. Bhaskar 2019

All rights reserved

10 9 8 7 6 5 4 3 2

The views and opinions expressed in this book are the author's own and the
facts are as reported by him, which have been verified to the extent possible,
and the publishers are not in any way liable for the same.

ISBN 9780670090884

Typeset in Sabon by Manipal Digital Systems, Manipal
Printed at Replika Press Pvt. Ltd, India

This book is sold subject to the condition that it shall not, by way of trade
or otherwise, be lent, resold, hired out, or otherwise circulated without the
publisher's prior consent in any form of binding or cover other than that in
which it is published and without a similar condition including this condition
being imposed on the subsequent purchaser.

www.penguin.co.in

This is a legitimate digitally printed version of the book and therefore might not
have certain extra finishing on the cover.

Dedicated to a fond hope of a resplendent India

Contents

Prologue

Everybody likes stories. They are what we grew up with, what we turn to when in doubt. Stories are the beginning of all thought.

One of the triggers for this book too lies in a story, narrated to a large gathering by the late Nani Palkhivala—eminent jurist, management guru and tax consultant.

* * *

For those who were young in the 1980s, Nani Palkhivala was iconic. He was such a lofty legal luminary, he was almost an institution. But he was renowned for yet another unique contribution. Every year, about a week after the budget papers were presented to Parliament, he would deliver a much awaited, much eulogized speech—his critique on the budget.

This was a time when there were no private television networks in India. Doordarshan, the sole master of the airwaves, was reluctant to telecast views critical of government policy. So those who wished to benefit from Palkhivala's views, had no choice but to attend his public discourse.

Palkhivala would pore over every clause and sub-clause of the budget and deliver his appraisal of the government's plans and intentions. His views were revered; almost every corporate baron, tax consultant, finance manager from all over India— even students—thronged to listen to him. Such was his hold over people's imagination that most flights from all major Indian cities to Mumbai (it was Bombay then) were filled to capacity a couple of days before and after the date that Palkhivala had chosen for the delivery of his evaluation. Palkhivala continued this 'free' contribution to the nation year after year till the late 1990s when age made him give up this practice.

That he made a deep impression on me would be an understatement. I owe a great deal of my understanding of India's economy as well as my vision for the country to his thoughts and analyses. That is why it is not surprising that the inspiration for this book comes from one of the ubiquitous tales he told in the course of one of his speeches, a story that is as relevant today as when he first narrated it.

* * *

When God decided to create man—a version goes—He made a clay image of Himself and then put it into the oven to bake. Impatient, yet excited about creating this creature, God took the clay model out of the oven rather quickly, for fear that it would get burnt. He was in for a shock. The creature was half-baked! Yet conscious that He couldn't undo what He had already created, He breathed life into the clay model. And man was born. Not exactly as God might have wished him to be, but marvellous nonetheless.

So God gave his creative efforts a second chance. He made another clay model of Himself and put it into the oven to bake. Now, He told himself to be patient, to wait. Finally, after a great deal of time, He pulled the creature out. This time, the being was burnt ebony black—extremely beautiful, but still not quite what God had in mind. As before, the Lord imparted breath to this creature as well.

Then, God decided to make one final attempt. He crafted a third clay model of Himself. This time He took care that it would bake for neither too long nor too brief a period. At the precise moment when He believed that it was perfectly done, God extracted this model. Glowing a rich brown, it looked stunning—and exactly as God had hoped he would be!

So thrilled was God that He began bestowing qualities on His latest creation. 'You shall be wise, creative, adventurous, hard-working . . .' A few more adjectives were just waiting to trip off his tongue, but before he could utter them, the white and the black creatures rose in unison and shouted, 'God, stop!' God looked at them incredulously. Pointing accusing fingers, the two castigated Him roundly. 'A God is supposed to be impartial. He has to be fair. He should bestow His gifts on all.'

Realization struck God. They were right. Instead of being balanced and just, which was His essential nature, He had got carried away. But, what could He do? He could not take back what He had already given. As He wondered and worried about just how to right this wrong, an idea struck him. 'I know,' God said, 'if I cannot erase what I have already given the brown man, let me at least restrict him with a handicap.'

Then he broke into a twisted smile and softly murmured, 'I shall give him the Indian government.'

* * *

This brings me to three questions:
1. Is the Indian government really a handicap?

2. Who are the visionaries who have risen above every
   constraint the government or its laws might have imposed?
3. What can we learn from them to propel the Indian growth
   story forward?

It was in trying to answer these questions that this book
was born. In it, I have analysed how, for years, our nation's
rulers have been blind to the key strategic advantages this
country has, and yet how, because of our inherent potential
and possibilities, we, as Indians, can still hew a path to a
financially more viable and vibrant India.

My vision for India is drawn from many sources. While
I will certainly be presenting statistics and tables to back my
assertions, I will also source case studies from within the
country and across the world to highlight what has been
done to exploit certain strengths, what potential specific ideas
hold, and how they could redefine the game for this country.

The book therefore aims not to condemn past policies
nor castigate people or political parties, but to depict a future
of hope and prosperity and to bring to light the wealth and
promises that lie within this vast, versatile and divergent nation.

ONE

The Land of Milk and Money

Milk and Wealth Creation in Gujarat

It was in 1995 that I really got to understand the vision of Dr Verghese Kurien, the man who ushered in what is known today as the milk revolution. I sought an appointment with him, flew to Baroda (now Vadodara), and then took a long ride to Anand, where the company that manages the Amul brand of products—Gujarat Cooperative Milk Marketing Federation (GCMMF)—is headquartered. The National Dairy Development Board (NDDB) was nearby. Dr Kurien supervised both, but from NDDB he took only a token salary of Rs 1 per month.

The day in Anand was spent visiting one dairy plant after another. I was taken first to the milk collection centres in the village. Then came the pasteurization plants, and the processing plants from where exotic products like ghee (clarified butter), shrikhand (sweetened yoghurt), cheese and curd were produced, packed and shipped all over India.

At 6 p.m., I was escorted to Kurien's house. With typical warmth and amiability, he asked me to accompany him to his

1

office, where he normally stayed till 9 p.m. He had a hectic schedule and was often travelling around the country, and sometimes the globe. But he had made the time for reminiscing and nostalgia.

This man, whose very name had become synonymous with milk, began with the most unexpected remark. 'My entry into the milk business was entirely accidental.' I must have looked amazed. And so, eyes twinkling, he went back in time. 'Do you know, I was an abandoned child? I was found and brought up by missionaries.' By now, I was listening to every word. He went on to narrate how his ability to speak English, along with a letter of recommendation from the missionary, got him a job with the British government in Bombay. His task had been to keep detailed records of the volumes of milk that came to the city from Kaira (now Kheda or Khera) district in Gujarat, and were then sent to soldiers who were gearing up for the Second World War.

Soon, he was offered a scholarship to study pasteurization in the UK. The British wanted this plant so that the milk for the soldiers could get a longer shelf life. The study would enable him to set up a pasteurization plant in Gujarat for the milk that came from there. But his heart and mind rebelled. He did not want to study pasteurization. His interests lay in a different direction altogether—in the field of nuclear physics. So, without telling anyone, he jumped ship at Aden, and went to the US to study nuclear physics. He timed his return in such a manner that everybody in Bombay thought he had returned after completing his course in pasteurization.

But fate had other plans for Kurien. When he returned to Bombay, he was packed off to Kaira to build a pasteurization plant. He tried to protest, but was warned against telling the truth about his change in course, lest he be court-martialled for wasting Her Majesty's time and money.

Kurien talked to me about the difficulties he faced while living in Kaira. 'Apart from the fact that I wasn't suitably qualified, I was a Christian in a predominantly Hindu village. And I was a bachelor. No family would agree to take me in as a tenant, and when I finally found accommodation, it was in a cowshed.'

He had to approach multinational corporations for help in building a milk pasteurizer, but each time, he was rebuffed. One expatriate manager of a company shooed him away with the words, 'You monkeys will never learn how to build a pasteurizer!' Kurien was incensed and promptly began using the skills he had acquired as a student of nuclear physics to design a pasteurizer himself. What happened next should come as no surprise—he succeeded.

Then events caught up with him. Local milk producers went on a warpath demanding higher prices for their milk; they wanted to bypass the local procurement agent and form a cooperative. The British administration relented. Permission granted, the producers faced their first roadblock—they did not know how to manage a cooperative. It was then that one of the local leaders, Seth Tribhuvandas, urged the milk producers to approach Kurien to manage the cooperative for them. By then, Kurien's meticulousness in keeping records, his administrative skills, his knowledge of English, his ability to interpret the laws and his ability to design a pasteurizer had all impressed Tribhuvandas immensely.

That cooperative became the Kaira District Cooperative Milk Producers Union. Like Kaira were other milk cooperatives as well dotting the landscape of Gujarat. These had to be brought under a structure. All these were coordinated by Gujarat Cooperative Milk Marketing Federation or GCMMF. Today, it is India's largest food product marketing organisation with annual turnover (2017–18) US$4.5 billion.

Its daily milk procurement is approximately 18 million litres per day from 18,554 village milk cooperative societies, eighteen member unions covering thirty-three districts and 3.6 million milk producer members[1]. It became the hub for India's milk revolution. This, in turn, took charge of the Amul brand, making it one of the most valuable brands in India.[2]

Kurien's work was so spectacularly successful that the then prime minister of India, Lal Bahadur Shastri, decided to see the plant for himself in October 1964. A trip was organized, and he was taken around Kaira. Shastri was overwhelmed. On his return, he promptly wrote[3] to the governors and chief ministers of all the states, and to all the cabinet ministers of the central government, 'As you are perhaps aware, I visited the Kaira District Co-operative Milk Producers' Union, Anand (Gujarat), better known as "Amul" in the end of October last with a view to inaugurating their new cattle feed compound factory. Through this letter, I propose to share with you what I saw there and its importance in the context of the programme envisaged for the establishment of co-operative dairies all over the country during the Fourth Plan.'

Shastri promptly took two decisions. First, that the milk cooperative movement would become a national priority. Second, that the National Dairy Development Board (NDDB) would be put under Kurien's charge. This would eventually become the basis of a national dairy development policy. On this foundation was built the Milk Revolution—the result and realization of Kurien's vision.

---

[1] www.amul.com/m/organisation

[2] See Amul <http://www.amul.com/m/about-us>, accessed on 31 October 2015.

[3] http://www.amuldairy.com/index.php/white-revolution

The GCMMF website explains:

> He [Shastri] understood that the success of Amul could be attributed to four important factors. The farmers owned the dairy, their elected representatives managed the village societies and the district union, they employed professionals to operate the dairy and manage its business. Most importantly, the co-operatives were sensitive to the needs of farmers and responsive to their demands.[4]

That evening while the two of us sat together chatting, Kurien explained the driving force behind his vision. 'I predict that within the next decade India will become the world's largest milk producer,' he declared. I nodded politely, aware that India was struggling to even retain its place as the sixth largest producer of milk.

Kurien suddenly exclaimed, 'Don't just sit there nodding like a fool. Ask me why!'

Obediently, I asked him the question.

Kurien's eyes lit up with the glow of a visionary. 'What is India's population?' he asked.

'Around 800 to 850 million,' I said, which was the figure at that time.

'Correct!' said Kurien. 'And what is the staple diet of most Indians?'

'Mainly rice and wheat,' I said, a bit uncertainly because I was not sure what Kurien was getting at.

'Exactly,' he declared. 'And this is where India has the biggest advantage in the world.'

---

[4] See Amul, http://www.amul.com/m/about-us, accessed on 31 October 2015.

I looked at him quizzically, shook my head and said, 'I don't quite understand.'

Kurien was triumphant. 'You see, most Indians consume rice and wheat. For every kilo of rice or wheat that is consumed, there are three to four kilos of chaff. That chaff is consumed by cattle. Food for cattle is a natural byproduct. In almost every other country, farmers have to grow food for cattle. In India, it comes free. Thus India is bound to remain the lowest cost producer of milk in the world. Since the first job of any government is to feed its people, there will always be rice and wheat production. Hence, there will always be food available at a marginal cost for cattle.'

'But doesn't China have the same advantage?' I asked.

'Aha! That is where god has been kind to India. China also consumes rice. But most Chinese people cannot digest milk. You cannot become a global power of a product easily if you do not have a large enough market at home. China has the opportunity, but will not become the world's largest producer precisely because its population won't let it!'

This was one of my first major lessons in understanding the natural strategic advantages that countries must recognize and then exploit. Kurien was doing just that. He had discovered in milk what very few people had discovered so far.

'But,' added Kurien, 'this advantage has to be protected and nurtured. You have to ensure that India's competitors do not destroy this advantage.'

'But how would they?' I asked, beginning to realize that I was being given a glimpse of something I had not even anticipated.

'By dumping cheap surplus milk in India,' he said. 'That is why I have persuaded the government to transfer to NDDB all milk and milk products coming from overseas. Most of them are gifts or come in as aid, and could queer the pitch for milk prices in the market. If you do not protect milk prices for the farmer, why will he produce milk?'

								Table 1
Milk production across the globe								
								million tonnes
Country	1996	2001	2006	2011	2016	5-year CAGR (%)	10-year CAGR (%)	20-year CAGR (%)
India	68.6	83.6	100.5	128.1	159.4	4.5	4.7	4.3
United States of America	69.9	75	82.5	89.1	96.4	1.6	1.6	1.6
China	10.2	14.5	36.5	41.8	42	0.1	1.4	7.3
Pakistan	23	26.3	31.2	36.7	39.7	1.6	2.4	2.8
Brazil	19.3	21.4	26.4	32.4	33.9	0.9	2.5	2.9
Germany	28.8	28.2	28	30.4	32.7	1.5	1.6	0.6
Russian Federation	35.8	32.9	31.4	31.6	30.8	-0.6	-0.2	-0.8
France	23.8	23.8	23.5	25.3	25.4	0.1	0.8	0.3
New Zealand	10	13.1	15.2	17.3	21.7	4.6	3.6	3.9
United Kingdom	14.8	14.7	14.3	13.8	14.9	1.5	0.4	0
Rest of the world	243.6	257	279.9	296.2	301.8	0.4	0.8	1.1
Total	**547.7**	**590.6**	**669.4**	**742.7**	**798.5**	**1.5**	**1.8**	**1.9**
Sources: FAOSTAT (accessed on 1 October 2018) and NDDB								

I learnt that since much of the milk came to India as aid—hence, free of cost—the entire market price of the milk sold through NDDB became profit. This profit was used to create a market development fund, and the money was used to promote weaker cooperatives and help them become strong. Kurien had turned 'dumped' milk and 'aid' milk into an amazing market development opportunity! This was done without any recourse to the government for funding support. NDDB was thus an organization that was funded by the industry and for the industry. Hence, technically, it did not even violate any World Trade Organization (WTO) norms as no government subsidies were sought.

Kurien's vision for making India a milk production hub did come to pass. By 2000, India had become the world's largest (and cheapest) producer of milk (see Table 1).

Game India

However, with the European Union (EU) becoming one region, it displaced India as the biggest producer. But, according to Amul's managers and India's policymakers, India should overtake the EU as well by the end of this decade (see Table 2).

Table 2

Top global milk producers—India could re-emerge the leader by 2020

figures in million tonnes, except where stated otherwise

	2012	2013	2014	2015	2016	2017	2018	2019-E	2020-E	2016–20 estimated growth (%)
EU	156	157	161	163	166	169	172	175	177	1.6
India	134	138	145	151	157	164	170	178	185	4.2
USA	91	91	94	96	97	99	100	102	104	1.7
China	45	45	45	45	46	46	46	46	47	0.5
Pakistan	38	39	39	39	40	40	41	41	42	1.2
Brazil	33	33	34	35	36	37	37	38	39	2
Others	270	270	274	281	287	293	298	303	308	1.8
Total	766	773	792	810	829	847	865	883	901	2.1

Notes: E=Estimated

Sources: IMARC report, Edelweiss Research, NDDB

Today, milk production in India is increasing at a compounded annual growth rate (CAGR) of 5 per cent compared to 1 per cent for the world. Many global research companies have said that the growth of milk production in India is only 4.5 per cent and that demand is outstripping supply. But the truth is quite the opposite. It would appear that many of these stories are aimed at creating a scare among India's policymakers so that they allow milk imports, even without canalizing it through the NDDB. Fortunately, thanks to the efforts of India's large milk players, and some savvy policymakers, such stories have been discounted.

A recent report from Edelweiss (India Dairy, Crème de la crème: Milking the value chain, 1 December 2017) states:

India's dairy sector is a very white, bright and freely flowing opportunity. It's got size (INR 5.4trn), leadership (largest milk producer globally, 160 million metric tonnes) and growth – 15% CAGR over 2016–20E. We believe this scale and underlying momentum will throw up even more possibilities, and the organized market will grow even more rapidly at 20% p.a., doubling into a INR 2.5trn market by 2020. This should be driven by a mix of underlying structural trends led by:

1. A huge unorganized market (~78%) led by fresh dairy products;
2. A consumption and market shift to high-margin emerging VADP [value-added dairy products]; 2.5x over FY16-20E and;
3. Large vegetarian population (31%), which has sub-standard protein consumption. This mix has been the backbone of India's dairy market growth over the years, and it's set to accelerate.

Today, India produces milk at 18 US cents a kilo compared to 28–35 cents for Europe and the US. With the reduction of subsidies under the WTO rules, milk from the US and Europe will become increasingly expensive. This can be an advantage for India. The country could move on to become the world's biggest supplier of milk and milk products, but only if government policies do not destroy this natural advantage.

Kurien also changed the way business could be done in India. He taught the country that the best way to augment the production of agro-produce was by ensuring that the farmer got a better price. Previously, the government had subsidized agricultural produce, so that industry got its raw material at a low cost. It had ignored the farmers' right to get remunerative prices. The government's glib justification for this has been that agriculture got subsidies, and that it has to look at the interests of industry as well. This philosophy began changing only after the 1990s.

Today, milk is the only product in India where the farmer gets anywhere between 70–85 per cent of the market price. Of course, there are farmers who do not belong to the cooperative movement—often with the connivance of state government officials. They remain exploited and get barely 30–50 per cent of the market price. For most other products, both in India and overseas, the producer is lucky to get even 30 per cent of the market price. At times it can be just 10 per cent.

Kurien fashioned a structure where the cooperative pays farmers *daily* for the milk they sell. He thus created a benchmark for paying back farmers, and even today all milk cooperatives pay the farmers within ten days. 'The farmer is a small player. He cannot wait for his cash to come in a month or two later. He needs to be paid immediately,' is what Kurien would often say.

Not surprisingly, the most exploited milk producers in the country are usually in areas where the cooperative movement has not really taken off, especially in north and northeast India.

Kurien also showed the business community that it was possible to contain processing, packaging, distribution and marketing costs at under 20 per cent of the market price for milk. Globally, one-third of the market price goes to the producer (the farmer or the cattle farm), roughly one-third goes to the processor, and the rest is retained by the trade (the distributor, wholesaler, marketer and retailer). Kurien changed this global model.

The entire processing, packaging, marketing and distribution of Amul's range of products is managed so efficiently that costs are kept to under 20 per cent of the price of milk. Kurien's experiment made it clear that the fastest way out from rural poverty was to encourage milk production (more on that a little later) and support it through a cooperative movement, which took care of the procurement, processing, distribution and marketing of this perishable product. The world stood astounded. Nobody had even imagined that such a management model would be possible, let alone feasible and sustainable.

Milk production also improved rural nutrition because milk producers would normally consume milk themselves before selling the rest to the cooperative.

Today, Kurien has left behind the Amul brand and an industry that continues to grow.

Milk and Wealth Creation in Karnataka

While Kurien discovered the power of generating wealth through milk in Gujarat, another man chanced upon the same route, rather serendipitously down south in Udupi. Both of them understood a management mantra popularized almost five decades later—that there was huge wealth potential at the bottom of the pyramid.

A young boy, Tonse Madhav Anant Pai, returned home a qualified doctor after completing his education. His relatives were proud of him; he was, after all, the first doctor in the family. Madhav wanted to go to Hong Kong, pursue further studies, and even set up practice there. But his strong-willed mother would not hear of it. 'You must stay with us,' was her exhortation. 'You must serve people in your own country; be of use to your kith and kin.'[5]

Madhav could not argue with her. So began his career as a doctor, in a little clinic in an unknown corner of India. That

---

[5] Selden Menefee, *The Pais of Manipal* (Manipal: The Academy of General Education, 1984), p. 29.

corner was called Malpe. It had nothing to claim to its credit. It was just another fishing village among the thousands that dot the coast of India and the banks of its rivers.

For this restless young man of medicine, his fledging practice was far from engaging. Confronted with routine complaints revolving around childhood infections and adult coughs and colds, Madhav's intelligence was seldom challenged. Nor did his learning curve show promise of improvement. In short, Madhav was bored. He flailed about, yearning for better opportunities. But constrained by his mother's wishes, he felt trapped.

It was in the midst of this turmoil that Madhav suddenly had his 'eureka' moment. He realized that his inability to grow was linked to the condition of his people; *they* had not grown! Could he alter their story? Could he create opportunities for their progress?

He looked objectively at the life of his community. Men went out into the waters to fish. They returned with their catch, handed this over to their wives and made their way to the local liquor dens to drink away what remained of the day. It was the women who cleaned the fish, sold it and used the proceeds thriftily to run their houses and keep their children healthy. Madhav saw that these women were, in fact, the backbone of society. With this realization, Madhav was ready, within a few weeks, to put Plan A into action.

He began, in his gentle way, telling mothers that money ought to be saved for their children so that they did not end up the way their fathers had—getting drunk every night. The women were delighted to have a sympathetic ear, but invariably scoffed at his suggestion that they salt away cash. The response usually was, 'Where is the money to save? Does my husband leave me any?'

Soon, anticipating their response, Madhav came armed with another question: 'How much money do you now have?'

Invariably, the mothers would undo the knot at the end of their saris and pull out the coins that had been tied within. They would display the coins and tell him that this was all they had. Calmly, Madhav would take a 25-paise coin and, holding it up to the sun, ask them, 'Can you save this?'

The amount was too small to fight over. Inwardly most women smiled at the foolishness of the doctor, who thought that the 25-paise coin could help them build a fortune. But Madhav insisted, 'No, this is all that I want!'

Considering that even banks back then required a minimum of five rupees to open a savings account, the 25-paise coin seemed like an embarrassingly small sum. But for Madhav, it was sufficient. 'I shall send my compounder to your house every day,' explained the doctor. 'Whenever you have a 25-paise coin that you can hide from your husband's eyes, give it to my man. He will then enter the details in two notebooks. One you will keep for your records, the other will be for my reference.'

Week after week, tirelessly, Madhav sent his compounder to each house in the village to find out if the women had a 25-paise coin that they could hand over to add to their savings. Within a few years, Madhav found that the 25-paise coins from so many households had become a few thousand rupees! In those days, it was a tidy fortune. Now that he had the money, he had to work on ways to make that money sweat. He had promised the village folk that he would even give them interest on their deposits, if they kept the money with him for three years. He needed an enterprise to earn some money on what he had collected.

Now was the time to move to Plan B.

Madhav began instigating the mothers once again. 'Your daughter has been falling sick very often because she needs nourishment,' he would tell one mother. To another, he would say, 'Your son needs to play, but doesn't get the right kind of food. Fish and rice aren't enough!' Gradually, he began to toy with the concept that the diet the children received was inadequate. He then began telling the mothers that the best way to improve the health of the children was to give them milk.

'Where can we get the milk?' was the usual retort. 'We can't even pay for the food that we eat, and this doctor wants us to give our kids milk. Milk costs money, you know!'

Madhav would smile indulgently, and then quietly explain that it was time for them to purchase a cow.

'We cannot afford milk, and he wants us to buy a cow!' the women would scoff. 'And who will pay for the cow?'

That was when Madhav would coax them by promising to advance the money to buy a cow.

And how were they to repay the cost of the cow?

'Simple,' Madhav would explain. 'Give the first glass of milk to your child. I will purchase the rest of the milk from you. And from the money you get from the milk, I shall take some towards repayment.'

The scheme sounded much too simple. Many thought it to be a con. But when the first woman agreed to Madhav's suggestion, and when others actually saw the family making money from the sale of milk even after making the necessary repayment, more families rushed to borrow money from Madhav to purchase cows.

That was when Madhav faced his first major crisis. Purchasing the milk produced by two or three cows was easy. But when the number increased to fifty, then hundred, then five hundred, a new method would have to be introduced.

That led Madhav to Plan C. He, too, decided to form a milk cooperative. Intuitively, he knew that the fastest way to sustainable incomes and wealth accumulation was through backyard cattle ownership. He had stumbled onto the same realization that Kurien had arrived at earlier.

Milk created wealth, and thus more money began being saved with Madhav. To manage this larger flow of money, he started the Canara Industrial and Banking Syndicate Ltd, which later came to be known as Syndicate Bank.

It was milk that catalysed wealth generation for the entire village. Soon, more villages joined in. Madhav realized that trade in milk itself would not be enough. Education had to be the foundation of the future. And thus was born the Academy of General Education, which in turn began sponsoring schools and colleges. It was this cluster of schools and colleges that later became the Manipal Educational Complex.[6]

---

[6] Madhav's life is replete with fascinating anecdotes. During the 1960s, when Madhav was travelling across the length and breadth of India in order to find creditworthy borrowers, he chanced upon a trader who wanted working capital to finance the import of yarn, which he planned to sell in India. As the borrowed amounts began growing larger with each transaction cycle, Madhav became interested in this trader's business acumen; he asked him, 'If it is so profitable to sell yarn in India, why don't you manufacture it in the country yourself?' The trader said he needed a licence. Madhav knew some people in the government who could help him with this. A few trips to Delhi, and the trader got his licence for making yarn in India. Not even Madhav could imagine that this trader would one day become one of the largest industrialists in the country—Dhirubhai Ambani. It could also explain why someone from the Pai family enjoyed a position on the board of Reliance Industries till recently.

When Indira Gandhi decided to nationalize banks—claiming that banks back then did not serve the needs of rural communities—the story of Syndicate Bank proved her claim to be a lie. Here was India's only bank that was headquartered in a rural area and had its roots among low income people!

Stories of this variety prove that nothing cures and eradicates rural prosperity the way that milk and milk cooperatives do. Today, village-level cooperatives account for nearly 3.6 million milk farmers and procure close to 12 million tonnes of milk each year. Together they add up to almost half the organized sector's output of milk, though in terms of the national market for milk their share would be close to 9 per cent.

So immense has the influence of cooperatives been in India that even the best private sector milk producers prefer to adopt the effective practices embraced by cooperatives. They pay the farmers anywhere between 70–80 per cent of the price that the end customer pays. Like Amul, they not only collect milk from the producers, but also train them to adopt good milking practices, advise them regarding cattle nutrition, and tell them how to better feed cattle, opt for cattle vaccination, and get high-grade cattle sperm. This in turn ensures that farmers remain loyal suppliers to the marketing and distribution networks they have built.

Consider, for instance, Nestlé, which adopted the models set up by Kurien in Moga, Haryana, from where it sources much of its milk. Consider too, two very large players, Hatsun Agro Products and Heritage Foods, which have replicated Kurien and Pai's vision.

In just over four decades, Hatsun has become India's largest private sector company in the dairy industry. (Mother Dairy may be larger, but it is a wholly owned subsidiary of NDDB, which is more of a government-owned entity after Kurien demitted office.) Hatsun collects milk from fine quality cows belonging to over three lakh farmers spread over 8500 villages in Tamil Nadu. It has dairies in ten locations, with state-of-the-art facilities, international knowhow and personnel—thus ensuring health and hygiene and products of excellent quality. Hatsun's dairy products are exported to thirty-eight countries in North America, the Middle East and Southeast Asia.

Heritage too has done quite well for itself. It is run by the family of Chandrababu Naidu, currently chief minister of Andhra Pradesh, and so enjoys political patronage. It could be coincidental that the state's own milk brand Vijaya has suffered a decline in fortunes ever since Naidu began propping up the fortunes of Heritage. If one ignores the political reasons behind the venture, one begins to see how this enterprise has empowered village communities, especially women. Milk is one industry which invariably empowers women. In most villages, it is women who do the milking and taking care of the cattle.

Milk along with other extension programmes Andhra Pradesh has introduced for agriculture in general have made its farmers one of the most progressive in the country.

Maharashtra and Milk

Cooperatives are excellent vehicles for wooing an electorate, as politician-sponsored milk cooperatives in Maharashtra have shown.

In Maharashtra, most cooperatives are run by politicians. Most began as sugar cooperatives, but almost all of them have diversified into dairy farming and cooperative banking. Unfortunately, in Maharashtra at least, both milk cooperatives and cooperative banking have been exploited to enrich the promoters rather than the members of the cooperative.[7]

---

[7] https://www.freepressjournal.in/analysis/is-maharashtra-abetting-drought-farmer-distress/1392278

What is well known to most people is the siphoning of money from cooperative banks. Politicians love cooperative banks. True, they have to bring in 10 per cent of the funds themselves, but that is usually provided by the state in Maharashtra, without even insisting on a seat on the bank's board of directors. The remaining funds come from depositors. And if media reports are anything to go by, as many as 165 such banks have been shut down in Maharashtra in the past thirty years.[8] The depositors got barely 10–20 per cent of their money back. The most memorable case was that of Maharashtra Cooperative Bank. In May 2011, Reserve Bank of India (RBI) had to dissolve its board because by 2010 the bank had notched up (conservatively) non-performing assets of 7.6 per cent of advances (its deposit base at that time was Rs 18,998 crore). However, within three years of its politician-appointed board being replaced by professionals, the bank became profitable. Criminal cases against the directors of this bank are still waiting completion.

What is not known is the way these cooperatives used the milk industry to fleece hapless farmers. While Gujarat was paying the farmers as much as Rs 30 a litre of milk, and Tamil Nadu and Andhra over Rs 26, Maharashtra's cooperatives were paying them just Rs 18. Thanks to a government circular, the minimum support price for milk in Maharashtra has now been raised to Rs 25 a litre. But the powerful cooperatives have managed to get the state to provide Rs 5 of this amount as a subsidy to the farmers. Thus common taxpayers will pay Rs 5 per litre, while the cooperatives will pay only Rs 20.[9]

---

[8] http://www.moneylife.in/article/continuing-failures-in-cooperative-banks/46157.html

[9] http://www.freepressjournal.in/analysis/rn-bhaskar-energy-prices-favour-india-may-be-not-opec/1085442

Such instances of exploitation caused the share of agriculture in Maharashtra's gross state domestic product (GSDP) to be only around 7 per cent even as late as 2014. The current government—in sync with strategies being pursued by the central government—wants to provide better returns to farmers. It has already increased the share of agriculture in its GSDP to 12 per cent. This has a double advantage. First, it improves the wealth of the countryside. Second, it endears the present political party to rural folk who have now begun to realize how they were being exploited by the politicians who had set up the cooperatives.

In August 2016, the government of Maharashtra entered into an agreement with NDDB to set up milk processing facilities and a cooperative dairy farm headquartered in Nagpur (the home of the current chief minister Devendra Fadnavis and the union minister Nitin Gadkari). By March 2017, this milk cooperative began paying Rs 26 per litre of milk to farmers who had joined the cooperative movement. The new cooperative then started spreading its collection catchment area to those areas controlled by politicians from the Congress and the Nationalist Congress Party (NCP). By August 2017, the government moved a step further and came out with an order giving milk procurement a minimum support price (MSP) of Rs 27 a litre. Ajit Pawar (nephew of Sharad Pawar who controls the fortunes of the NCP) was livid. In an interview[10] he claimed that this would cause cooperatives a loss of Rs 9 per litre of milk each day, which could mean huge hardships for milk cooperatives in the state.

---

[10] http://indianexpress.com/article/india/curb-your-expenses-cm-fadnavis-urges-states-dairy-farmers-4981806/

The government's pincer move of setting up its own cooperative and issuing the order to fix the MSP of milk at Rs 27 a litre has put the cooperatives of both the Congress and the NCP in a fix. That in turn helps the government in three ways. First, it can now boast of a higher GSDP. Second, it builds a vote bank among farmers, which could prove to be immensely useful at the hustings in 2019 when general elections are due. Third, it cuts down the political funding that was being used by both the Congress and the NCP, who control most of the cooperatives in the state.

At the same time, there is no denying that the fastest route to rural poverty alleviation is through milk. In Maharashtra, this is playing out brilliantly.

In a way, this strategy of using milk to boost agricultural incomes was also adopted by Prime Minister Narendra Modi to woo farmers in Uttar Pradesh (UP, a very important state politically because it accounts for the highest number of seats in Parliament). Even while he was chief minister of Gujarat—where GCMMF and NDDB are headquartered—he was aware of the marginalization of cooperatives in UP, the largest milk producing state in India. When Kurien was alive, he tried to start cooperatives in UP. They survived till he stepped down from the management of both GCMMF and NDDB. Politicians began calling the shots, and the entire cooperative movement was allowed to wither away. Milk from cattle owners slipped into the hands of middlemen.

When Modi became prime minister, his office is believed to have nudged NDDB into permitting Gujarat's cooperatives to set up milk processing and collection centres on the outskirts of Delhi, but aimed at wooing milk producers of UP. For almost two decades, middlemen in UP had been exploiting small farmers, at times compelling them to sell their milk at as low a price as Rs 14 a litre. Ironically, even

Mother Dairy, a wholly owned subsidiary of NDDB, began purchasing milk through these middlemen and not through cooperatives. Legally, since NDDB—its parent company—allows cooperative milk federations to purchase milk only from cooperatives, this move on the part of Mother Dairy (of purchasing milk from middlemen) was extremely curious.

Then, in 2015, NDDB sent out an order to Mother Dairy to begin purchase and collections only from milk cooperatives and to reduce collection and purchase from middlemen. Suddenly, there was support for cooperatives from the central government. Mother Dairy was reluctant to support middlemen, and Gujarat's cooperatives began collecting milk from farmers in UP at Rs 26 a litre. The writing on the wall was quite clear. By 2016, belatedly, even the Mulayam Singh government began talking about the need to promote milk cooperatives. But it was too late. Farmers had already begun to look on Modi as their messiah. Giving farmers a higher price for milk was one major factor in helping the BJP win by huge victory margins in the state elections in UP. Milk once again proved its usefulness both as the fastest route to rural prosperity and in creating a vote bank among farmers.

Where Calculations Go Wrong

That is why it was ironic to see the central government actually pushing for a total ban on the slaughter of cows. The losses that such a ban caused were huge (see Table 3). True, many states already had laws discouraging cow slaughter. But in most states, these laws were seldom enforced. With a wink and a nod, most farmers would sell their nulls and non-lactating cows to middlemen who would then sell them to slaughterhouses. Even Prime Minister Modi, while he was chief minister of Gujarat—the second largest milk producing state in the country (see Table 4)—did nothing to prevent farmers from selling their infertile cows and bulls to middlemen.

Table 3
Total bovine slaughter loss potential
(figures in lakh, except where stated otherwise)

	For India
Cow population	1,909
Buffalo population	1,087
Total bovine population	2,996
Cattle deaths (assuming a 5% mortality)	149.8
Average price at which a non-lactating bovine is sold	15,000
Estimated loss (in Rs crore)	**22,470**
Assuming 60% of states enforce this ban (loss, Rs crore)	**13,482**
Notes: Old cattle used to be sold at around Rs 20,000 a head in Maharashtra, Gujarat and Punjab. We have estimated the average to be Rs 15,000	
Sources: 19th Livestock Census, 2012	

If you go to Anand, the epicentre of the milk movement and headquarters of both GCMMF and NDDB, you will discover that most milk producers are Hindus—mostly Vaishnavites, or followers of Vishnu. Talk to them privately, and they too will admit that they had always sold their bulls and infertile cows to tradesmen, preferring not to know what happened to them thereafter.

It was quite possibly electoral compulsions that caused the prime minister to turn a blind eye to vigilantes who took up the enforcement of the cow slaughter ban. But the move was to have disastrous consequences. UP was the largest beef exporter in India. It was also a large centre for the leather industry. Both industries suffered (see Table 3 for estimates of bovine related losses). Some have moved shop to West Bengal in the east and to Tamil Nadu and Andhra Pradesh in the south where political support for a total ban on cow slaughter does not exist. Expect both the beef and leather industries to gradually migrate to these states.

	Cows	203.70	Buffalo % share	Cow, Bull (% share)	Ratio (Cow: Buffalo)
Uttar Pradesh	195.57	306.25	61.03	38.97	0.64
Madhya Pradesh	196.02	81.88	29.46	70.54	2.39
Rajasthan	133.24	129.76	49.34	50.66	1.03
Maharashtra	154.54	55.94	26.54	73.46	2.76
Gujarat	99.84	103.86	50.99	49.01	0.96
Andhra Pradesh	95.96	106.23	52.54	47.46	0.90
Bihar	122.32	75.67	38.22	61.78	1.62
West Bengal	165.14	5.97	3.49	96.51	27.66
Assam & Northeast	132.90	5.79	4.08	95.92	22.95
Karnataka	95.16	34.71	26.72	73.28	2.74
Odisha	116.21	7.26	5.88	94.12	16.01
Chhattisgarh	98.15	13.91	12.41	87.59	7.06
Jharkhand	87.30	11.86	11.96	88.04	7.36
Tamil Nadu	88.14	7.80	8.13	91.87	11.30
Haryana	18.08	60.85	77.09	22.91	0.30
Punjab	24.28	51.60	68.00	32.00	0.47
Jammu & Kashmir	27.98	7.39	20.57	79.43	3.79
Himachal Pradesh	21.49	7.16	24.96	75.04	3.00
Uttarakhand	20.06	9.88	32.99	67.01	2.03
Kerala	13.29	1.02	7.15	92.85	13.03
All India	**1,909.04**	**1,087.02**	**36.24**	**63.76**	**1.76**

Table 4

Statewise bovine population

figures in lakh

Notes: Highlighted areas are for states where the cow ratio has slipped below 0.75
Sources: 19th Livestock Census, 2012

What is unfortunate is that the government was not even mindful of the fact that the leather industry creates around seven jobs for each lakh rupee of investment.

In fact, one of the reasons why this government has begun to lose popularity is because the cattle slaughter ban—including prohibiting sale and movement of buffaloes meant for slaughter—actually drove the backward classes to find common ground with the Muslims in their disenchantment. Both communities consume beef and participate in the leather trade. Muslims are also active in the business of slaughterhouses and in exporting meat. The ban hit them hard. Not surprisingly, they have become wary of this government.

It is possible that the population of cows will also decline in these states. But if the ban is enforced rigorously, expect the country to see a farmer loss of around Rs 13,500 crore each year (see Table 3). Expect farmers to protest with their votes. Or else, expect the milk industry to shift to other states.

Overcoming Religious Predilections

The roots of the cow slaughter ban were beginning to be perceived even in the 1950s. The call for the ban was muted, but it was always around.

Cow slaughter did not really bother many till the mid-1950s or even the 1960s. All along, as in Anand, almost all cow owners in the western belt of India sold their cattle off to traders when they became too old to procreate and generate milk. While these cow owners did not slaughter cows themselves, they were not squeamish about letting the traders do the job for them.

Somewhere along the way, many of the cow owners were told by their community leaders that the cow was sacred. They were reminded of their sinful ways, especially when they sold their cattle to traders. Political players, taking advantage of a situation that offered a vote bank, also began promoting the cause of cow protection.

This resulted in two parallel developments. First, many erstwhile cattle owners—having been made increasingly wary about cow slaughter—began shying away from what used to be their traditional profession. Since business abhors a vacuum, communities (especially Muslims) that were less fastidious about cattle slaughter took on the task of owning cows. What followed was a lopsided demographic, where entire communities, constrained by religious dogma, were reduced to becoming carriers of milk—no more—while a few groups, unsentimental about cows, became cattle owners.

Another development was the shift of the entire veterinary trade from Hindu families to Muslims. Since Muslims began owning more cattle than the Hindus in these parts, trade in chemicals used for producing medicines for animals also slipped into Muslim hands. The seeds were sown for major fault lines, which could be easily exploited or stoked by unscrupulous politicians.

Equally, with commerce-savvy states like Gujarat banning cow slaughter, some erstwhile cow owners opted for buffaloes instead. Not only was the care of buffaloes not burdened with religious sentiment, these animals also produced milk with higher fat content. Since most cooperatives paid for milk depending on the amount of fat it possessed, buffalo milk meant more money!

The consequence of this is even more worrying. As the latest census of cattle shows, the population of cows has begun dropping alarmingly in the very states where the cow slaughter ban is being enforced strictly. Gradually, it won't be surprising if the cow itself becomes an endangered species in the very land that wants to promote the animal (see Table 4 on state-wise bovine population).

Read the table closely. Look for the states where the ratio of cows to buffaloes has dipped below 0.75. These are the states where the ban on cow slaughter could actually drive cows out of the region. More worrisome is the fact that the two largest milk producing states, Uttar Pradesh and Gujarat, have a ratio that is less than 1, though not as low at those sported by Haryana and Punjab.

Today, the highest margins for milk producers can be found in states that are more benign about cow slaughter. It is because of this that Tamil Nadu and Andhra Pradesh have seen more growth in the leather and milk businesses than most other states have in the past two decades.

Religious chauvinism has the capacity to affect both domestic and international business. We must bear in mind that the beef export market alone is worth Rs 30,000 crore. It is a big employer as well, as is the leather industry.

The warning signs are there. If India has to grow, it would be unwise to allow religion to dictate commerce. It is bad for business and also for national harmony.

Encouraging Milk Production in the East and Northeast

There are states that have vehemently opposed the ban on cattle slaughter. Possibly under pressure from the centre, some of the governments of the north-eastern states tried to push through a similar law banning cattle slaughter. The reaction was so hostile that all attempts to push through or even suggest the enforcement of this law had to be scuttled. Proponents of the cow slaughter ban were compelled to take a back seat.

The north-eastern states can be expected to do extremely well in the cattle business in the coming decades for several reasons. NDDB has begun work on a milk cooperative and processing plant in Guwahati in Assam. The entire northeast region has a milk deficit. Once milk collection infrastructure and a processing plant are set up there, the cow population in the region can be expected to grow phenomenally. The absence of a ban on cattle slaughter can also result in the meat and leather industries flourishing there. With multiple revenue streams, this region should do very well.

It will be sad to see the milk industry move away from UP and Gujarat—the states from where Lord Krishna once led his cattle herder tribesmen—will lose their age-old advantage to other states. But when you have aberrational practices, the business consequences too become aberrational.

There are several factors that make the development of business in the northeast an imperative for the Indian government.

First is the military imperative. The army had once advocated for the development of the milk industry in Kashmir and the northeast. The easy availability of locals who were willing to take up backyard farming and the availability of water and fodder made these areas perfect for nurturing this industry. What is equally interesting is that just by changing the cattle feed mix for even animals that do not produce much milk, the economics of the dairy industry can be improved substantially (see Table 5).

Moreover, commercial linkages and asset ownership would help blunt the lure of terrorism or insurrection. But such plans are yet to find fulfilment. Some of the army's funding for them was suddenly withdrawn. The retirement of a key general who wanted this done was another setback.

The absence of political will is a third factor. Many politicians in the east and northeast made huge amounts of money through illegal mining. Illegal mining thrives in areas where local populations can be exploited. Usually, such people are poor and will do anything for a little money that they could earn. Bringing prosperity to the farmlands of the Northeast would make availability of cheap labour a problem. It would also embolden farmers to complain to the authorities about such activities which cause significant damage to the environment. In

				Table 5

Old feeding system for cow giving 7 litres of milk per day

	Dry Matter (DM) (kgs)	Cost/kg DM (Rs)	Total Cost (Rs)	Crude Protien (Gms)
20 kg Green Fodder	4	1	4	400
3 kg Paddy Straw	2.4	5	12	70
4 kg Rice Bran	3.6	11.1	39.96	320
1 kg GNC	0.9	35.6	32.04	360
1 kg Branded Feed	0.9	16.1	14.49	180
	11.8		102.49	1330

Notes: DM = dry matter; gms = grams; Kg = kilogram

INCOME (Rs) 7 litres *Rs 20/litre = Rs 140 less feeding cost Rs 102.5

Profit: Rs 37.5 per cow per day

New feeding system allowing the cow to give 10 litres of milk per day

	DM (kgs)	Cost/kg DM (Rs)	Total cost (Rs)	Crude Protien (Gms)
40 kg Green Fodder	8	1	8	800
5 kg Desmanthus	1	1.5	1.5	200
400 grams Branded Feed/litre milk	3.6	16.1	57.96	720
1 kg Branded Feed for body maintenance	0.9	16.1	14.49	180
	13.5		81.95	1900

Notes

Income (Rs) : 10 litres *Rs 20/litre = Rs 200 less feeding cost Rs 82

Profit: Rs 118 per cow per day

Difference: Rs 118-Rs 37.5 = Rs 80.5; or Rs 8 per litre of milk saving in feeding costs alone

Sources: Industry

fact, the army's thinking was right. Research has consistently proven that terrorism works best in a soil of disaffection and arises from a feeling of alienation and being exploited.[11]

The need for developing dairy farming in the north and the northeast is obvious. Such a move would give locals a good source of income, without uprooting them or forcing a significant change in their lifestyles. Once locals have a stake in their territory, and are also in touch with processing units and marketing networks, affluence and commercial ties only grow.

Second is the national imperative. The northeast has been left to fend for itself for too long. It is time to integrate these states into the national mainstream of business and commerce. Failing to do so could create conditions ripe for insurrection. Most north-easterners believe that they have been exploited. The scourge of illegal mining in the hills has benefited many politicians, and they were happy to keep these states independent of the purview of central economic planners.

The third reason is commercial. Both the east and the northeast are rich in fodder and in water. Homestead cattle breeding there can be a big catalyst for rural wealth generation. Besides, both regions are agnostic (even disdainful) about cattle slaughter.

Finally, the countries that border these states—Myanmar, Bangladesh and China—experience a terrible milk deficit. There is thus an export market too, which beckons cattle owners, provided someone is willing to set up a collection system and create marketing and distribution channels.

---

[11] In fact, when General Ata Hasnain tried to create new jobs in Jammu & Kashmir (he even tried to promote dairy farming there, and this author was involved briefly with such efforts), disenchanted and disheartened youth were weaned away from terrorist activities. However, with General Hasnain's retirement from active service in J&K, nobody has carried forth his plan.

Given the right support, the milk, leather and meat industries can be expected to grow at a rapid pace in these regions.

In fact, two other states are likely to benefit from this new vision of developing the northeast (and the east) as the future milk production centres. NDDB is now determined to make the milk cooperative movement flourish in both West Bengal and Orissa. Both states have lots of water, plenty of foliage and abject poverty. Both states have seen politicians making more money from the illegal sale of forest produce and mining output. Hopefully, the milk industry can catalyse economic growth in these regions as well.

Both Cooperatives and the Private Sector Embrace Milk

It is a fact that milk by and large generates wealth.

The largest player in the country remains Amul (see Table 6), managed by the GCMMF. Today, this brand accounts for sales of over Rs 24,000 crore, making it the largest food processing company in India, and possibly even in Asia. Its value added milk processing capacity (curd, butter, lassi, ice cream, sweets, etc.) has been growing at 16 per cent CAGR over financial years (FY) 2011–17 to 30 million litres a day. Further, its target is to expand it to 38 million litres per day and to generate revenues of Rs 50,000 crore by the turn of this decade. It is on its way to becoming the largest fast-moving consumer goods (FMCG) company in India.

The other notable player is Hatsun—the largest private sector player in the country. True, Mother Dairy is bigger, but it is a subsidiary of NDDB, and has special facilities granted to it by governments, which is not possible for stand-alone private sector players. Hatsun today accounts for sales of Rs 4200 crore and sells its products under various brands (see Table 7). One of them is Arokya (launched in 1995 as a

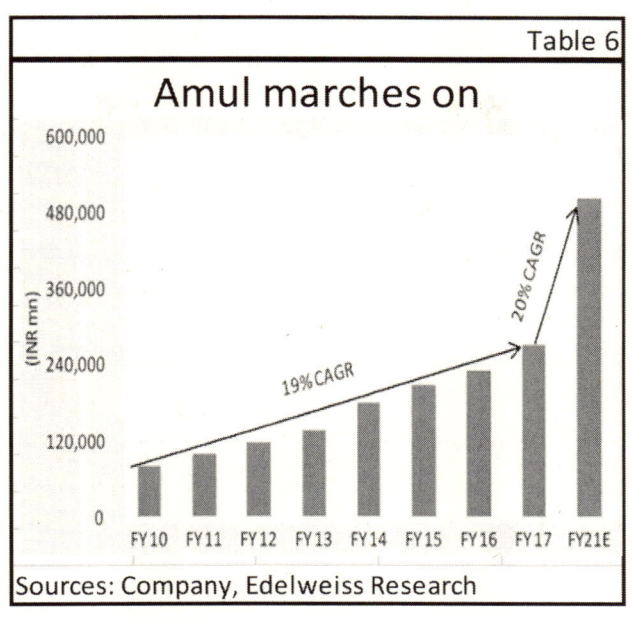

Table 6

Amul marches on

Sources: Company, Edelweiss Research

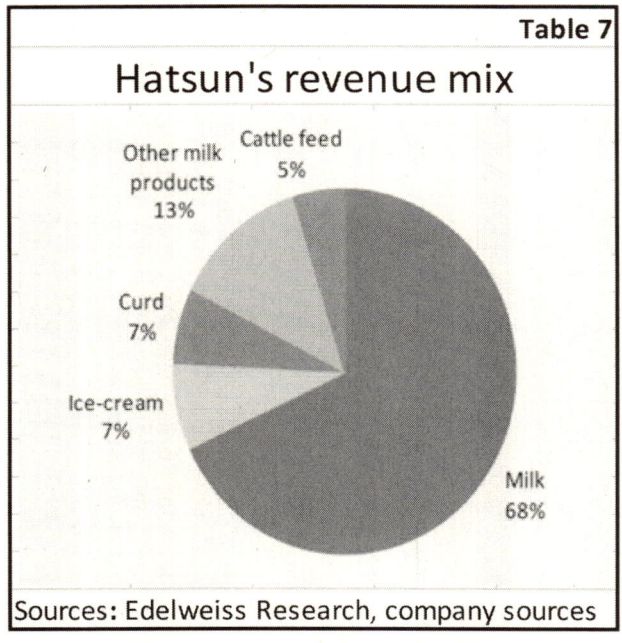

Table 7

Hatsun's revenue mix

Sources: Edelweiss Research, company sources

popular milk brand and now available in both the southern and northern parts of India). Another brand is Arun Ice Creams, its first product. Ibaco is another brand it sells its ice creams under. And then there is Hatsun, the brand under which it sells most of its dairy products—curd, paneer, ghee, butter, milk powders, buttermilk, lassi, etc. Finally, there is Santosa, under which it sells 12,000 tonnes of cattle feed a year (it hopes to add another 10,000 tonnes to this capacity).

The industry has been profitable for many players. As more players enter the field, the biggest beneficiary will remain the farmer, who will be assured of a steady offtake and reasonably firm prices. One only hopes that the government uses this model to ease the distress that India's farmers have been facing.

For the farmer, a cow or a buffalo is a money-spinner. It also adds to the nutrition intake of the entire family. And for the dairy industry, selling milk as liquid milk is immensely profitable, because it involves little processing and has a ready domestic market. But this is one industry that needs excellent logistics, because milk has a very short shelf life.

Production by Masses

During Kurien's tenure, the cooperative sector grabbed the limelight. With his ability to focus on production by the masses rather than mass production, Kurien singlehandedly made the milk cooperative sector a wealth generator. He knew that the most profitable route for milk production was when households had three to ten cows in their backyard, when a family could tend to the cows themselves without paying for outside labour, and when feed was managed judiciously, so the family could increase milk production and earn a net surplus of around Rs 100 per cow per day (for around three hundred days a year because the cow could be expected to go dry for around sixty-five days per annum). Thus a family that owned five cows could earn Rs 500 a day (see Table 5). This was in addition to any other farming income that could be earned. In any case, Rs 500 a day can go a long way in rural areas where the cost of living can be quite low.

There is another reason to believe that the potential for growth in this industry is high. Given the poor logistics in India, only 14 per cent of the milk market in India belongs to the organized sector (see Table 8). In any case, almost 54 per cent of the milk produced is consumed at home by the family. This is one of the main sources of nutrition. But of the marketable surplus, the share of the organized sector is just 14 per cent.

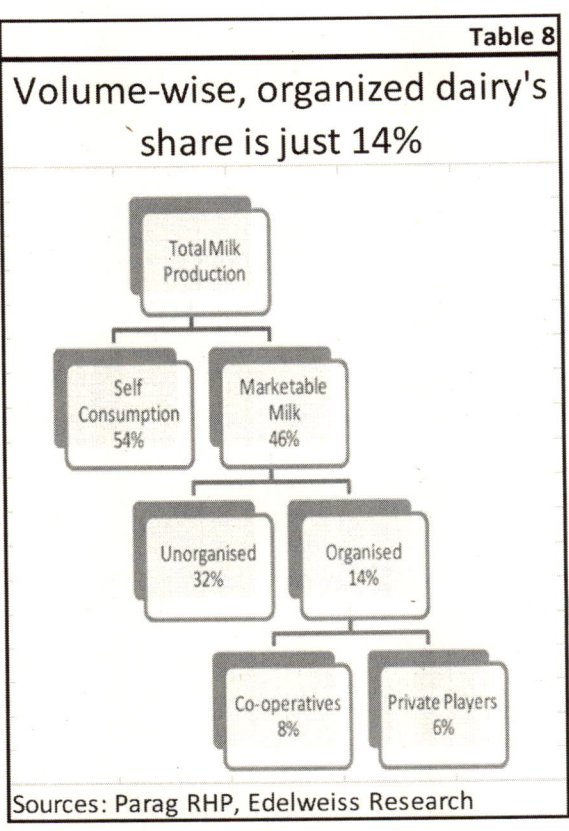

Table 8

Volume-wise, organized dairy's share is just 14%

Total Milk Production

Self Consumption 54%

Marketable Milk 46%

Unorganised 32%

Organised 14%

Co-operatives 8%

Private Players 6%

Sources: Parag RHP, Edelweiss Research

This share is bound to increase. And along with this expect farm incomes to increase as well, creating additional purchasing power for the country. Then add the additional jobs of distributors and procurement centres that could come up. The milk industry has a lot of oomph left. It would be unwise for the government to meddle with it.

Following Kurien's footsteps, state governments also moved in, with each state creating its own milk brand. Some like Tamil Nadu (which had Aavin) have fared quite well. Others like Maharashtra (which had Aarey) trundled along, while still others like Milkfed in Kerala performed poorly. Then there are states like Andhra Pradesh where a state brand—Vijaya—was allowed to lose market share.

The private sector, on its part, chose the best management practices of the cooperative sector. Except for the ownership pattern, few could distinguish between the two sectors. And both have tried to ensure that the farmer is left with a profit of at least Rs 100 per cow per day for three hundred days a year. Lately, like the Pais of Manipal, both the cooperative and the private sector have been engaged in upgrading the educational standards of people in their catchment areas as well. An educated farmer is a lot more dependable when it comes to following written instructions, whether sent through SMS or as printed literature.

The question that naturally emerges is this: why is it important for cooperatives to keep pace with private players, and for parity to exist across all sectors? The answer is quite simple: if the private sector begins to marginalize the cooperatives, then one can expect it to return to its old rapacious ways of exploiting the producer. This could lead to an unhealthy cycle of booms and busts on milk markets and milk production.

While competition in the marketplace is good, it is the cooperatives that will maintain the benchmark for ensuring that almost three-fourths of the consumer price for milk goes back to the farmer. If the cooperative movement is allowed to falter, then, as in any other industry, the milk producer's share in the market price will fall. That is not good for the farmer, nor is it good for the industry. Homestead cattle farming employs millions in India. It creates a decent cash flow; it improves nutrition for the poorest of the people. Therefore, the small producer can survive only if the cooperative movement is strengthened, which in turn will make even the private milk industry respect the milk producer a lot more than would otherwise be the case. The beauty about production by the masses is that the surplus a farmer gets to keep includes his income as well. Dairies that purchase cattle have to employ people to look after and to milk the animals. This becomes an additional cost. When a farmer looks after the milk production, the labour he puts into this activity has been blended into the price at which he sells the milk. That is why the Amul-Hatsun-Heritage model suits India because the ownership of cattle is decentralised, the cost of labour is also kept low, and the profit for the milk plus labour costs go to the farmer. That is one more reason why Kurien's legacy has survived. It is peculiar to India. It is meant for India. And it will serve India well, as long as the government does not do anything foolish like a ban on cattle slaughter, or allowing imports and thus disrupting farm prices.

Thus, in a post-Kurien world, it would be interesting to put down a few points that would help ensure this strategic industry to remains vibrant.

1. The government needs to allow someone with Kurien's drive and dedication to emerge, without looking at cooperatives merely as a means to further its political interests. This won't be easy, because the temptation to

use cooperatives as vote banks is far too great. But if that were to happen, the primary motive to run a cooperative will be politics, not the welfare of farmers.

2. The government should actually auction prime outlets for milk distribution to the highest bidder, and not just to quasi-government owned enterprises like Mother Dairy or Aarey. This would help create a level field.

3. The country's policies must allow large purchasers of milk and milk products—such as the army or public sector units—to place orders strictly on the basis of price and quality. Today, certain sectors are allowed to purchase milk and milk products only from cooperatives, which means that not every sector is given an equal chance to succeed.

4. Each state needs to be encouraged to come out with an MSP for milk. That should deter unscrupulous traders from shortchanging farmers.

5. Finally, it is imperative to ensure that all sectors—cooperative, government owned and private—observe the principle of transparency. They should mention procurement prices and volumes every month.

Managing EXIM Policies

Kurien was right. No milk policy can succeed if the government does not play a supportive role. Such support can be measured by the government's export-import (EXIM) policies.

If India is to have a vibrant milk industry—and this is critical, since the milk sector is important for India's poverty alleviation programmes and also for its nutritional needs—it is imperative that nobody is allowed to flood the market with imported milk that may be purchased at subsidized prices. India's policymakers will have to work out a strategy which allows for a mechanism that will prevent producer prices from being adversely affected. While it was possible to channelize all imports through NDDB in the past, WTO rules may make such a structure difficult. So, in today's world, we might need to have anti-dumping duties, or other import tariffs, to ensure that imported milk (or milk products) does not queer the market pricing, which will eventually hurt milk producers.

Savvy market-men may remember how the duty-free import of milk was allowed by the government some years ago, which caused a glut in the market, resulting in a sharp dip in prices. This, in turn, allowed the price of milk procurement by middlemen in north India to fall to almost Rs 14 per litre (as against Rs 25–28 a litre), causing milk producers in these regions to march onto the streets and pour their milk on the roads. Such poor policymaking must be discouraged.

The government must also stop its on-again-off-again export policy for milk and milk products. They hurt the market. Exports must be allowed. Yes, there is a danger that reduced supplies in the domestic markets (caused by goods being diverted for export) could result in a price hike. That is politically undesirable. But this is where the government must use the powers it has to keep prices stable without curbing exports. Obviously, any such operation will have to come under constant public scrutiny to ensure that no malpractice takes place.

Encouraging Transparency

Another thing that the government must ensure is greater transparency. Mother Dairy, for instance, is a wholly owned subsidiary of NDDB, a government owned company, formed under a separate Act of Parliament. Yet ever since it was incorporated, it has not bothered to share its unabridged annual reports with its suppliers or even with the media. It used to claim that since it provides copies of its annual report to members of the Parliament, it was not obliged to share its annual reports with anyone else. This is quite unlike what Kurien used to do. He would call a press meet each year, and share all accounts and operational details with the media. This, in turn, would compel milk cooperatives to be careful about how money was being used because of the threat of tremendous public scrutiny. There is nothing like transparency to ensure fair business practices. Happily, the old practices were modified a couple of years ago. NDDB is a lot more transparent today, and so is Mother Dairy.

In fact, Mother Dairy had previously refused to share the details of its procurement cost and volumes. At least two judgments went against Mother Dairy,[12] and a Delhi High Court order dated 27 January 2010 ruled that even Mother Dairy's parent organization, NDDB, is obliged to open itself to scrutiny by the Comptroller Auditor General (CAG).

Fortunately, as mentioned earlier, both organizations have become a lot more transparent during the past few years. One hopes that this will continue. The health of these organizations is crucial to the health of the dairy industry. And the health of this industry is of crucial significance to India.

The Future of Milk = the Future of India

Fortunately for India, milk production has been growing healthily at around 4.5 per cent per annum, though the growth

---

[12] Central Information Commission, Complaint No.CIC/SS/C/2010/000594 , 000595 & CIC/SS/C/2011/000006 Dated 07.03.2011, Right to Information Act, 2005-Section 18–Date of Decision: 15.04.2011.

of the organized sector has been at over 15 per cent (see Table 9). This means more milk from the unorganized sectors will move into the organized fold. It could mean higher prices for farmers. This could mean more purchasing power, which could translate into healthy GDP growth.

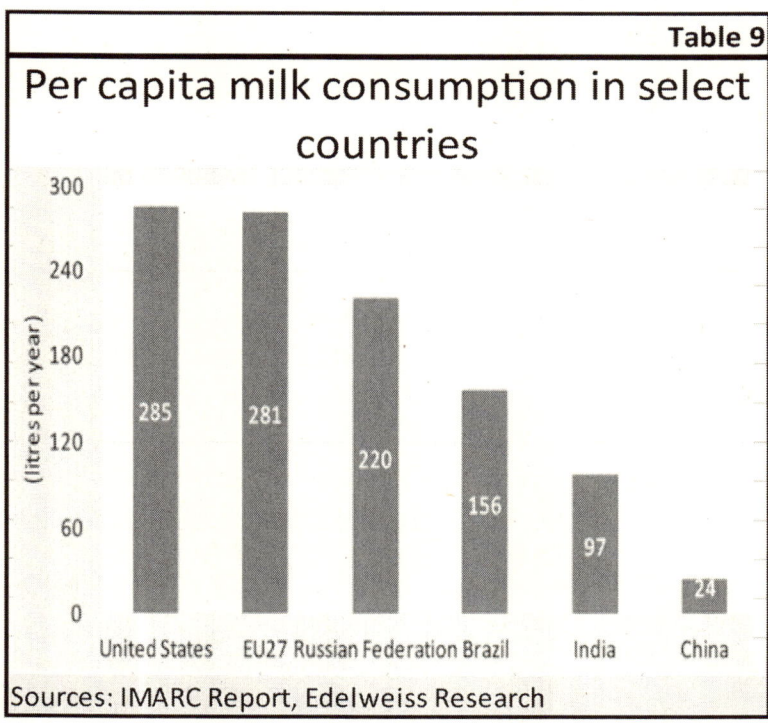

Table 9

Per capita milk consumption in select countries

Sources: IMARC Report, Edelweiss Research

Global experience tells us that as people move from poverty to middle income levels, their focus on food changes from consuming merely cereals, to consuming other types of food that provide more nutrition. India will witness similar trends for the next two decades or so. That is why India's demand for milk can only be expected to grow (see milk consumption table).

At a time when the government is confronted with a need to create more jobs and to increase purchasing power, milk could be the short-term answer to some of these goals. The milk industry creates self-employment on a massive scale, besides supporting ancillary industries like transportation, refrigeration and distribution. Each of these is a force multiplier in the unorganized market for employment. On the one hand, encouraging the milk industry could slow down the pace of urbanization (thus allowing rural folk to become wealthier on their own lands, and allowing their territories to blossom and grow organically). On the other, it can help (and *has* helped) eradicate poverty and improve nutrition.

It is therefore imperative for us, as a nation, to move quickly and enable the growth of this most vital industry. Only then will it be game, set and match India.

Catalysing Growth in the Milk Industry

Kurien, Tonse Madhav Anant Pai, R.G. Chandramogan (managing director and chief promoter of Hatsun) and Chandrababu Naidu understood the enormous potential of milk to galvanize rural wealth generation. Yet, there are developments that could make this industry curdle. And they all have their origin in the handicap mentioned by Nani Palkhiwala—the Indian government.

However, can these handicaps be remedied in the future? My belief is, yes, they can, and if the right effort is made, enormous wealth can be generated for India.

But the legacy of Kurien and Pai needs a more focused approach. There are measures that the government has taken that can only endanger the milk movement. If one were to list the blundering steps of the government within the milk industry, one would arrive at five key issues:

1. the harm caused by religious myopia;
2. the failure to encourage milk production in the north and northeast of India;
3. the need for a level playing field for both private and cooperative players;
4. the need to insulate milk from politics; and
5. the need to educate policymakers about why protecting domestic prices of milk for Indian farmers is crucial for India's very survival.

During his later years, Kurien wanted to extend his milk model to other agricultural produce as well. He began working on promoting Safal (a combination of sabzi and fal—vegetables and fruits). He began by selling frozen peas and other vegetables. But he could not create a national movement like he had done with milk. There were several reasons for this. Unlike milk, where he could bring in standardization, fruits and vegetables did not lend themselves to standardization very easily.

Sorting and grading were the solution. But Kurien found himself battling with state governments which had erected artificial marketing monopolies, often under the Agricultural Produce Market Committees or APMCs. These APMCs were set up with the idea of providing to farmers a marketplace where they would get a fair price for their crop, all round the year. Most APMCs had their own food storage facilities too. But gradually, these became extortionate monopolies. Middlemen would collect the produce from farmers at prices as low as 10 per cent of the marketplace, sell them to the APMCs, who in turn would sell them to licensed traders who then sold them to the open markets. Unlike Kurien's plan— where 80 per cent of the market price went to farmers, state governments abetted a system that allowed 90 per cent to go to the trade.

It is only in the recent years that Modi started addressing this problem, with the abolishing of APMCs in Gujarat when he was chief minister there. Many more governments have followed suit. But the marketing infrastructure hasn't been developed, leaving farmers at the mercy of middlemen even now.

The government's solution is doubling farm incomes. But doubling a meagre 10 per cent of the market price to 20 per cent is no solution. The benchmark should be 50 per cent of the market price.[13]

The solution lies in creating an NDDB-like structure for each crop, and moving the government out of procurement and patronage. But the government treats farmers as a vote bank, and also a big source for political funds. It is unlikely to adopt the Verghese Kurien model easily. The Kurien model empowers farmers. It leaves little scope for politicians to make money. The current model for agriculture is for the farmer to be exploited, and for the politician to take the spoils. This must change.

On the milk front, it appears that notwithstanding the bitterness created by the ban on cattle slaughter, wiser counsels have begun to prevail. The Supreme Court of India has frowned upon the inability of the government machinery to keep cattle vigilantes at bay, and has questioned the logic behind the ban on trade of cattle (including buffaloes). In November 2017 the apex court even suspended the ban on cattle slaughter.[14] All this suggests that the policy blunders relating to cattle slaughter might get redressed. The milk industry could resume its growth tempo.

It looks like Kurien's dream will not go unfulfilled.

---

[13] https://www.firstpost.com/business/farmers-on-the-war-path-solution-lies-not-in-msp-but-in-giving-farmers-a-share-in-the-revenue-5313951.html

[14] https://www.bbc.com/news/world-asia-india-40565457

TWO

Look Up, India! The Sun Is Shining

In 2008, energy analysts were stunned to see the writing on the website of Desertec,[1] an organization that sought to promote solar power – especially from the world's largest deserts. A single line on its home page read, 'Within six hours deserts receive more energy from the sun than humankind consumes within a year.' (See image 1)

Desertec wanted to harness the power of the sun from the vast expanses of the desert in Africa. Setting up a project in the Sahara desert was found to be economically viable and even feasible. All that was needed was to first stitch up contracts with countries that comprise the Sahara[2] —Those were the days when the Middle East was not yet convulsed with regime changes, plots and counter plots, and even invasions. The language of 'If you are not with us, you are against us' was something that the world never thought it would have to reckon with.

---

[1] http://www.desertec.org
[2] https://www.sporcle.com/blog/2018/03/a-list-of-the-sahara-desert-countries/

Within 6 hours deserts receive more energy from the sun

than humankind consumes within a year.

Dr. Gerhard Knies

The red square represents the total surface needed
to provide the worlds total electricity demand.

In reality numerous CSP-Plants will be spread in the deserts all around the globe.

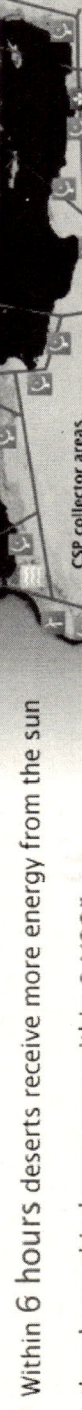

CSP collector areas
for electricity

World 2005

EU-25 2005

MENA 2005

TRANS-CSP Mix EUMENA 2050

In the mid-2000s, many experts were convinced that it would be possible to harness the power of the sun from the Sahara and carry the electricity through high voltage direct current (HVDC) lines across North Africa and into Europe. This, they thought, would allow European nations to protect themselves from the gas supply stranglehold that Russia enjoyed. Almost everyone involved in the power sector decided to become part of a consortium to make this project feasible. To protect themselves against project finance (and political) risks, they agreed to work under the umbrella of Desertec with Munich Re—the reinsurer—as the consortium leader.

Munich Re announced the signing of a memorandum of understanding in Munich to establish the Desertec Industrial Initiative (DII), headquartered in Hamburg. DII was to 'analyse and develop the technical, economic, political, social and ecological framework for carbon-free power generation in the deserts of North Africa'. Signatories to the DII included the best of blue-blooded names in the energy sector: ABB, Abengoa Solar, Cevital, Deutsche Bank, E-ON, HSH Nordbank, MAN Solar Millennium, Münchener Rück, M+W Zander, RWE, Schott Solar and Siemens. This project, once the feasibility study was completed by the end of 2008, was expected to lead to the setting up of a solar power generation facility to generate a whopping 80,000 megawatts (MW) of power.

But soon the blazing fury of geopolitics that continues to this day put a stop to these plans. However, Desertec remains a pious hope even now. While Desertec is still a dream people remember, most non-Germans have forgotten the contribution of one person, without whom the growth of solar power in the world, and even the lofty plans that Desertec.org cherished, would not have been possible. That man was Hermann Scheer.

Scheer (29 April 1944–14 October 2010) was a Social Democrat (popularly referred to as the Green Party) member of the German government. He was also president of Eurostar (European Association for Renewable Energy) and general chairman of the World Council for Renewable Energy. In 1999, Scheer was awarded the Right Livelihood Award for his 'indefatigable work for the promotion of solar energy worldwide'.

Scheer was an electrical engineer. He believed that if solar power was given just 1 per cent of the subsidies and incentives that the oil and coal industries had received for a hundred years, he could transform energy patterns in the world. He was convinced that the continuation of the current patterns of energy supply and use would not be environmentally, socially, economically and politically desirable. He believed that renewable energy, particularly solar energy, was the only realistic alternative. Scheer concluded that it was technically and environmentally feasible to harness enough solar radiation to achieve a total replacement of the 'foclear' (fossil/nuclear) energy system. The main obstacle to such a change was seen to be not technical or economic, but political (the US and OPEC, along with Russia, continue to be the key drivers of the hydrocarbon economy).

Scheer engineered this transition by Germany (of reducing dependence on hydrocarbons and instead opting for solar power) by adopting a revolutionary strategy that few could imagine. Both his strategy and his vision have been wonderfully explained in a forty-eight-minute TV programme that can be viewed on YouTube.[3] It was largely on account of his efforts that, by 2014, 31 per cent of Germany's energy capacity was

---

[3] http://www.youtube.com/watch?v=mLHBFyfvK8A

accounted for by renewables (see Table 2). Almost 90 per cent of the renewables came from solar.

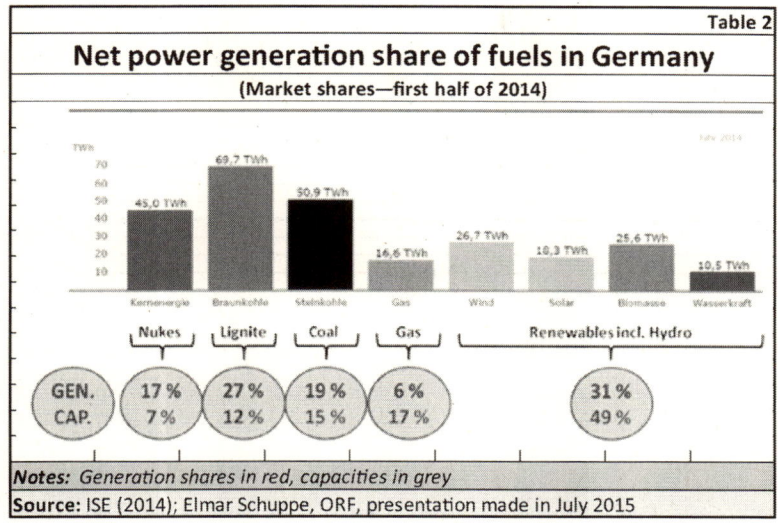

Table 2

Net power generation share of fuels in Germany
(Market shares—first half of 2014)

Notes: *Generation shares in red, capacities in grey*
Source: ISE (2014); Elmar Schuppe, ORF, presentation made in July 2015

So what was Scheer's strategy? He introduced an ingenious policy to encourage solar power and in particular rooftop solar power. He focused on houses that had roofs aligned north-south rather than east-west, as the north-south roofs could capture sunlight both in the morning and the evening.

Aware that most people would not take the trouble of installing and maintaining solar panels on their rooftops, Scheer introduced laws that would allow for the emergence of a middle layer. This middle layer comprised agents who put up the solar panels on rooftops, financed almost entirely by the government. The homeowner got the benefit of using the solar power produced from his rooftop free of cost. If the production exceeded consumption, the homeowner could sell the surplus power to the agent and make some money himself. Thus, homeowners had a double benefit. They could use the solar power free of cost, and they were also paid for the surplus energy produced by the panels on their respective rooftops.

The agent therefore played three roles: he was the installer, he maintained and serviced the solar panels, and, equally important, he played the role of aggregator—collecting minuscule amounts of power from individual houses, 'smoothening' out the inconsistencies in energy flow (because of the intermittence factor) and then selling the 'clean stream of consolidated power' to the grid.

In turn, the agent received a volume-based commission, attractive enough to cover his costs for installation and maintenance and also leave him with reasonable surpluses. This did mean that the price paid for solar power was high, and those who invested in solar power were guaranteed this high price for twenty years. Each year, the new contracted prices became lower (once again for twenty years). Thus, even today, Germany pays a high price for solar power because of the old contracts. The tapering off effect will begin manifesting by the turn of this decade (see Table 3). By the end of the 2020s, solar pricing in Germany will be able to compete with grid prices. True, the state incurred losses initially from the higher tariff paid for solar, but it will win eventually, more so if the costs of dealing with pollution—and attendant health costs—are also taken into account. Starting from 2023, Germany will see the surcharge customers pay for encouraging investment in solar fall steadily until 2035. At the same time, the share of renewables in the power mix will rise to 60 per cent (wind, not solar, may take a larger share of this pie).

The aggregator thus became the market-maker. In order to make more profits, he encouraged his team to come up with innovations that could generate much more (and cheaper) solar power. That is how plastic reflectors to focus weak sunlight on rooftops were invented. Sun reflectors soon

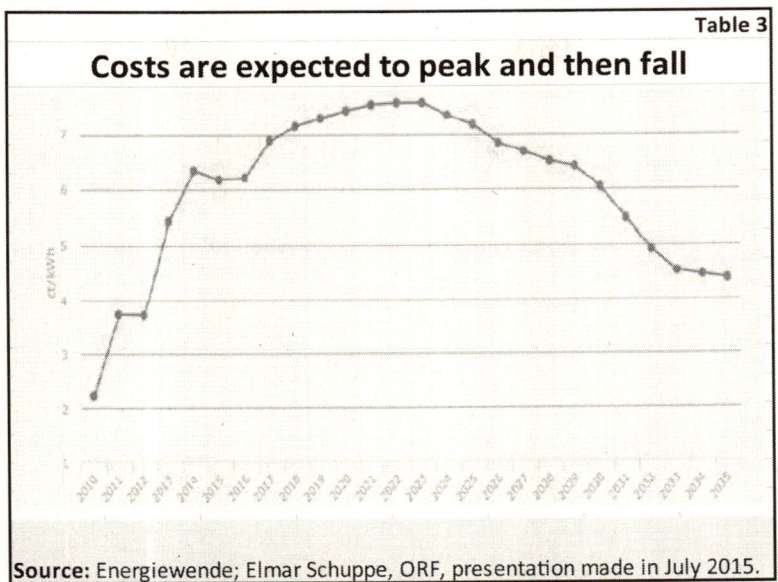

Source: Energiewende; Elmar Schuppe, ORF, presentation made in July 2015.

became both popular and cheap. This generated volumes, which created markets that allowed for more innovations in fields related to solar energy (see Table 4).

The plan worked. In just eight years, prices of solar panels plummeted. And it was then that people began to realize that the solar power industry in Germany had begun employing more people than the automobile and engineering sectors.

The other (unintended) consequence was that Germany generated a huge demand for solar panels, which got the Chinese interested, leading them to set up huge manufacturing capacities for solar photovoltaic (PV). Together, both Germany and China (and then the US and other countries thereafter) helped push down the cost of PV, which tumbled from over $75 per watt of installed capacity to under $0.5 (see Table 4). Globally prices tumbled below $0.3 per Watt. These prices continue to fall.

	Table 4
Solar modules: prices tumble and volumes soar	
US module shipments 2006–17	

Year	Avg value ($ per peak watt)	Annual shipment (peak kiloWatt)
2006	$3.50	320,208
2007	$3.37	494,148
2008	$3.49	920,693
2009	$2.79	1,188,879
2010	$1.96	2,644,498
2011	$1.59	3,772,075
2012	$1.15	4,655,005
2013	$0.75	4,984,881
2014	$0.87	6,237,524
2015	$0.71	9,942,978
2016	$0.72	13,451,187
2017	$0.48	10,864,545

Note: Dollars are not adjusted for inflation.
Sources: EIA; US Energy Information Administration, Form EIA-63B, 'Annual and Monthly Photovoltaic Module Shipments Report';
https://www.eia.gov/renewable/annual/solar_photo/xls/pv_table3.xlsx
https://www.eia.gov/renewable/annual/solar_photo/xls/pv_table4.xlsx

More significantly, as mentioned earlier, by 2008, Germany saw more people employed in the solar sector than in the automobile sector.

Another contribution made by Scheer was the concept of feed-in tariffs (or FIT). This was the tariff that was paid to agents (and through them to householders) for feeding electricity into the grid. This (initially) expensive solar power got pooled with the electricity generated from other sources (thermal, gas, nuclear, wind and hydro). This ensured that the end price paid by the customer did not matter too much to consumers. The initial high costs of solar were dampened by the larger pool of conventional power. As solar power costs tumbled, and its share in the energy basket grew, the average pooled cost of power would also come down.

As a result, by 2009, FIT policies were enacted in around sixty-three jurisdictions around the world, including in Australia, much of Europe, Iran, the Republic of Ireland, Israel, the Republic of Korea, South Africa, Thailand, Turkey and several states of the US, while gaining momentum in China, India and Mongolia.

But the biggest advantage was that the Scheer model allowed each household to become a power generator.

India Enters the Picture

Now cut to India. This author had been lobbying—since 2009, through his columns—for India to opt for solar power as an alternative source of energy. Hence, it was heartening to see the Manmohan Singh government announce its decision to promote solar power.

On 11 January 2010, the government launched the Jawaharlal Nehru National Solar Mission, also known as the National Solar Mission. It had a target of generating 20 gigawatts (GW) by 2022. This target was subsequently increased to 100 GW by the Narendra Modi government in the 2015 Union Budget.

India thus increased its solar power generation capacity by nearly five times from 2650 MW on 26 May 2014 to 12,288.83 MW on 31 March 2017. The country added 5525.98 MW in 2016–17, the highest in any year. According to the Central Electricity Authority (CEA), the country saw total solar power installed capacity swell to 21,631 MW.[4] However, even 21.7 GW of achievement against a target of 100 GW is still far short of the mark.

								Table 5
Year-wise Targets (in MW)								
Category	2015–16	2016–17	2017–18	2018–19	2019–20	2020–21	2021–22	Total
Rooftop Solar	200	4,800	5,000	6,000	7,000	8,000	9,000	40,000
Ground-mounted solar projects	1,800	7,200	10,000	10,000	10,000	9,500	8,500	57,000
Total	2,000	12,000	15,000	16,000	17,000	17,500	17,500	97,000
Notes: To meet the scaled-up target of 1,00,000 MW, MNRE has proposed to achieve it through 60 GW of large- and medium-scale solar projects, and 40 GW through rooftop solar projects.								
Sources: Kapoor, Tarun (1 July 2015). 'Scaling up of Grid-Connected Solar Power Projects', Ministry of New and Renewable Energy, archived from the original (PDF) on 26 February 2017.								

The good thing is that as in Germany, reverse auctions helped push down the price of solar power in India year after year. Thus from a high tariff of Rs 10.95 per kilowatt-hour (kWh), competitive bidding saw these tariffs tumble to Rs 2.44 a unit, and prices continue to slide (see Table 6).

While some have lauded the government on its ability to bring tariffs down, others say that such low tariffs are just not viable, and that this sector too will be witness to huge non-performing assets (NPAs). The truth will be known within a few years.

---

[4]   http://www.cea.nic.in/reports/monthly/installedcapacity/2018/installed_capacity-03.pdf

Table 6	
Solar Tariffs: Milestones	
Month/Year	**Rs/kWh**
Dec-10	10.95
Dec 2011	7.49
Dec 2012	7.28
Aug-13	5.50
Nov 2014	6.46
Sep 2015	5.09
Dec 2015	5.00
May 2016	4.66
Jul 2016	4.34
May 2017	2.44
May 2018	2.44

Notes: The lowest tariff finalized through reverse bidding was on 2 July 2018 at an SECI auction.

In August 2018, the National Solar Mision recommended to the Solar Energy Corporation of India (SECI) that India's solar power tariffs be capped at Rs 2.5 and Rs 2.68 per unit for developers using domestic and imported solar cells and modules, respectively. A policy announcement is now awaited.

Sources: CEA and media reports.

If these tariffs are for real, it means that India could set up the residual 88 GW of solar capacity at prices that even the thermal power sector cannot match. This would mean lower project costs for the country, and a cleaner energy source for its people. And considering the speed with which China is setting up solar power—10 GW[5] in the first quarter of this year alone—it does appear that demand for hydrocarbons will soon begin declining.

While this is something one cannot comment upon at the moment, there are many other aspects that have certainly gone wrong.

Where India Lost the Plot

Unfortunately, India did not learn some of the best lessons from Germany. In fact, it even ignored some of the political imperatives that ought to have been considered when planning for solar in India. Broadly speaking, these sins of omission and commission can be categorized under five heads:

---

[5] https://mercomindia.com/china-solar-10gw-q1-2018/

1. Rooftop solar versus land grab
2. RPO (renewable purchase obligation) games
3. Honouring contracts
4. Cozy deals
5. Rural focus lost

Rooftop Solar Ignored

First, it is evident that India enjoys huge advantages over Germany. After all, it receives more sunlight than Germany. Look at the maps that show the irradiation potential for both Europe and Germany (see Table 7). Compare them with the maps for India. They reconfirm that India has a goldmine of an opportunity.

India is endowed with rich solar energy resource. The average intensity of solar radiation showered on India is 200 MW per square kilometre. With a geographical area of 3.29 million square kilometres, this amounts to 657.4 million MW (see Table 8).

Furthermore, India has more people compared to Germany. More people translates into more homes. And even if one discounts 40 per cent of the households that may not have proper homes, the residual number is large enough to promote solar power on a massive scale.

Some planners argue that the cost of setting up rooftop solar is still too high, and that most rural houses don't have good rooftops. But that is an excuse. By just putting up a pole outside each hut with a solar panel atop it, the rooftop and the cost problems can be addressed. Many of the sturdiest solar panels for households in Africa are of this type. As far as battery costs are concerned, instead of opting for lithium-ion batteries, even simple (through primitive) lead acid batteries could act as storage devices. This too has gained popularity in several regions in Africa. The batteries are robust and do not take much maintenance either.

Table 7

India has more sunlight, more land mass and more rooftops than Germany

Global horizontal irradiation · Europe

Average annual sum (4/2004 - 3/2010)

< 700   900   1100   1300   1500   1700   1900 > kWh/m²

0   250   500 km

© 2011 GeoModel Solar s.r.o.

India Solar Resource
Global Horizontal Irradiance - Annual Average

Sources:
https://www.google.co.in/im
gres?imgurl=https://www.nre
l.gov/international/images/in
dia_ghi_annual.jpg&imgrefurl
=https://www.nrel.gov/intern
ational/ra_india.html&h=3300
&w=2550&tbnid=jVWY3lMArp
bpHM:&tbnh=160&tbnw=123
&usg=__ILJ73wh8M-
Y3gKEZS2SJmr4RT2Q%3D&vet
=1&docid=bXAIFP-
wnUgrnM&client=firefox-
b&sa=X&ved=0ahUKEwiCht_z
75DYAhUr9YMKHSh6C-
AQ9QEILDAA_
https://en.wikipedia.org/wiki
/File:SolarGIS-Solar-map-
Europe-en.png

	Table 8

Solar could shape India's destiny

State-wise Solar Power Potential (estimate)		Installed capacity (GW) of all power sources	
States & the nation	**GWp**	**Source**	**Capacity**
Andhra Pradesh	38.44	Coal	185.24
Arunachal Pradesh	8.65	Gas	24.51
Assam	13.76	Diesel	0.92
Bihar	11.20	**Total Thermal**	**211.67**
Chhattisgarh	18.27	Nuclear	5.80
Delhi	2.05	Hydro	42.78
Goa	0.88	Small hydro	4.27
Gujarat	35.77	Wind	26.87
Haryana	4.56	Bio-mass#	4.95
Himachal Pradesh	33.84	Solar	6.76
Jammu & Kashmir	111.05	**Total:Renewables**	**42.85**
Jharkhand	18.18	**Total for India**	**303.08**
Karnataka	24.70	Notes: Data as of 31 May	
Kerala	6.11	2016; Bio power includes	
Madhya Pradesh	61.66	biomass power generation	
Maharashtra	64.32	and co-generation (4.83 GW)	
Manipur	10.63	and waste-to-energy (0.83	
Meghalaya	5.86	GW); Data includes private	
Mizoram	9.09	power generation capacity.	
Nagaland	7.29	Source: CEA	
Orissa	25.78	(http://www.cea.nic.in/month	
Punjab	2.81	lyinstalledcapacity.html)	
Rajasthan	142.31	Solar Potential Source: MNRE,	
Sikkim	4.94	Govt of Indiia, 2015	
Tamil Nadu	17.67	Notes: GWp = Gigawatt peak;	
Telangana	20.41	National Institute of Solar	
Tripura	2.08	Energy (NISE) carried out this	
Uttar Pradesh	22.83	exercise taking data from	
Uttarakhand	16.80	Census 2011 and from the	
West Bengal	6.26	India Waste Land Atlas 2010,	
Union Territories	0.79	Ministry of Rural	
India Total	**748.98**	Development.	

Batteries are important because solar power can be captured only during the day. If one needs power at night, one needs to store the power. There is another reason why batteries become extremely important. Solar power can be intermittent. A bit of cloud blocking the sun can cause solar power capture rates to plummet. The battery collects the intermittent power and then sends it out for consumption at a steady rate. That is why, the cost of batteries is crucially important.

That explains why, after accounting for the time when the sun is not visible, and the conversion losses arising from heat being turned into electricity, the throughput is only around 17 per cent of the installed capacity. To overcome the problem of intermittent solar power supply, one needs batteries or inverters to take the power, store it and allow it to go out in a steady supply of energy. The battery storage also allows people to use solar power when the sun is not shining. Fortunately, recent research into solar cells allows them to generate solar power even when there are clouds, though the amount generated is not as much as when the sun is shining.

Unfortunately, the government of India chooses to impose high import duty rates on batteries and battery components as well.

The figures that talk about the solar power potential in India show that of the 749 GW bonanza that India could reap, its planners had kept targets for just 100 GW.

Advantage India, but . . .

As luck would have it, the timing for India's entry into the solar sector couldn't have been more propitious. India was beginning to adopt solar power when prices of solar panels and batteries had already begun crashing. The dropping prices of solar panels and the sharp drop in battery storage prices meant huge advantages for the solar industry in particular and for India in general. During the last five years, battery prices have already crashed by more than 70 per cent. And these prices are likely to fall by another 70 per cent by 2025 according to research conducted by BNEF.[6]

In other words, India ought to be reaping the harvest of benefits that Germany, China and the rest of the world have brought to the solar landscape. A chart by BNEF illustrates the situation quite aptly.[7] The number of installations across the world continues to soar. At the same time, prices of solar installations continue to fall.

Thus, even while India did adopt rooftop solar eventually— from 2016–18 (see Table 3)—the pace of adoption of this route has been painfully slow. Instead, it continues clearing mega projects that required large tracts of land. Even seven years later, when India did decide to embrace rooftop solar (in February 2016), it did so almost grudgingly. This was after several reminders.[8]

---

[6] http://www.dnaindia.com/analysis/standpoint-policy-watch-a-dirge-for-fossil-fuels-2093414
    http://www.asiaconverge.com/2015/06/battery-a-dirge-for-fossil-fuels/

[7] BNEF, annual presentation made in New York on 6 May 2016– the image can be found at http://www.asiaconverge.com/wpcontent/uploads/2016/10/2016-09-22_2-Firstpost-BNEF-solarcosts-capacity.jpg

[8] http://www.asiaconverge.com/2015/10/indias-expensive-solarpower-birth-pangs/
    http://www.asiaconverge.com/2016/09/adani-solar-project-is-good-but-rooftop-solar-is-better/
    http://www.asiaconverge.com/2016/04/india-not-learn-germanyshermann-scheer-solar-power-model/

Off with the Blinkers

The government finally woke up to the need for promoting rooftop solar first in February 2016 and second in 2018 when it began promoting floating solar as well.[9] Unfortunately, even then, the government did not set up a middle layer of people who could install, maintain and aggregate minuscule amounts of power from rooftop solar. As a result, the government paid lip service to solar power, without using the potential of this sector to create jobs. And this was a government that wanted to create jobs. India's planners were looking a gift horse in the mouth.

This is where the folly of India's planners becomes obvious. The combined advantage of sunshine, people and houses should have made the planners plump for rooftop solar right from the start.

RPO Games

More time was spent by the planners in trying to work out renewable power repurchase obligation schemes (often referred to as REC or renewable energy certificates or RPOs). The concept sounded good. It was meant to work like carbon credits, except that the regulator was in India, the arbiter was the power ministry and the players were often speculators—

---

http://www.dnaindia.com/money/report-of-hermann-scheer-and-his-german-model-that-sperfect-for-india-1508960

http://www.dnaindia.com/analysis/column-policy-watch-solar-wobbles-ahead-2057224

[9] http://www.asiaconverge.com/2016/06/solar-power-the-agony-and-the-ecstacy/

http://www.freepressjournal.in/fpj-imc-forum/spotlight-on-solar-energy/871958

many of them having the same strategies that the infamous Enron had once adopted.

The concept was based on the government's decision that solar power would account for a share of 8 per cent in a state utility's total energy pool. The idea was to push state governments into adopting solar power. And if they faced a shortfall in solar power purchase (either from captive units or merchant purchases, preferably through power purchase agreements or PPAs), the erring states would have to make good the difference by purchasing RPOs instead. The greater the shortfall with state distribution companies (discoms), the higher would be the demand. The greater the demand, the higher the market price for these solar certificates. Thus solar certificate owners would be able to profit enormously, in case state discoms did not meet their minimum solar commitments annually.

There were three flies in the ointment.

First, there was no guarantee that the solar power producer could always find buyers for the power he had promised to generate. Many states had PPAs with solar producers, which they did not honour (more on this later).

Second, it did not take long for big players to persuade select discoms to go slow in meeting their solar obligations, thus guaranteeing an excellent return on their solar certificates. This was by adopting the same strategy that Enron did.[10] Just when energy markets were deregulated in California, power generation plants began closing down, one after another. The cited causes were either an accident, or maintenance, or fuel supply shortage. A scarcity was created, energy prices began climbing, and power consumers and state grids paid the

---

[10] The story can be found in the video, *The Smartest Guys in the Room: The Amazing Rise and Scandalous Fall of Enron*, by Bethany McLean and Peter Elkind.

price because they were compelled to purchase power from independent merchant producers at astronomical prices.

Third, there was no regulatory mechanism whereby a discom head would be personally pulled up for not meeting the solar obligation targets.

It was a recipe for a scam. Some states saw the dangers and immediately decided to set up captive solar power generation units, thus avoiding cozy relationships either with solar power producers, or with speculators. But such states were few in number.

Thus while the solar mission scheme had lofty ideals, the underpinnings of governance were missing.

Honouring Contracts

A big flaw with the solar mission plan was that even though Indian state governments entered into PPAs with solar power producers for purchase of power at newly discovered prices, these PPAs were not always honoured.[11] Some states refused to pick up power from solar power generation stations unless the PPAs, which were legally binding and irrevocable, were renegotiated.

Ostensibly, these states wanted to save the taxpayers' money by renegotiating high tariff PPAs and working out agreements with lower prices. The argument was specious.

They forgot that before any new technology becomes popular, the first rates quoted are always high. Then reverse bidding pushes it down, year after year. Since these tariffs had been guaranteed for fifteen to twenty years, that guarantee

---

11 http://www.business-standard.com/article/economy-policy/ solar-power-some-bright-spots-many-clouds-117123000718_1. html

should have been honoured. This is what the best of countries did. They honoured contracts. This is what Germany, which had binding contracts for twenty years, did too.

Unfortunately, ever since India broke a Parliamentary oath to the erstwhile princes, in 1971, to pay them a certain sum year after year for agreeing to amalgamate their respective kingdoms into the newly formed country called India, some politicians [mistakenly] believe that the court of the people is superior to the legal courts or even the Constitution.[12] Not

---

[12] When India won independence, almost a third of its territory was still governed as independent princely states. Prior to independence, while the British had enjoyed suzerainty over them, they were still sovereign states. In 1947, there were 555 princely states accounting for around 48 per cent of pre-independence India (and had 28 per cent of its population). Under the Indian Independence Act of 1947 the British left the rulers to decide if they wished to accede to India or Pakistan or remain fully independent. It was the diplomacy of Vallabhbhai Patel, a Congress leader, that persuaded almost all princes to accede to India. In turn, the government promised them privy purses and privileges based on the status and revenues of each kingdom. This tax-free privy purse was guaranteed to them and their successors under Article 291 of the Indian Constitution. They would be charged to the Consolidated Fund of India.

In 1969, many elected representatives of the Swatantra Party were erstwhile princes. They began to pose a political threat to the Congress Party, which was in power. That could explain why politicians (mostly from the then undivided Congress) decided to push for a motion through Parliament (in 1969) to abolish privy purses in India, and the official recognition of titles. The motion failed in the lower house by one vote.

Prime Minister Indira Gandhi then decided to propose the motion once again in 1971, and got it successfully passed as the 26th Amendment to the Constitution of India. Indira Gandhi defended her motion on the grounds of pushing for equal rights

surprisingly, some states thought that they could challenge the original PPAs on the grounds that the payment terms were too high especially in light of the declining prices of solar equipment. In many cases, the disputes are pending before the courts. In some, the central government has prevailed on the state governments to honour contracts. But many solar power producers are in dire straits because the interest clock keeps ticking and their interest burden therefore swells. With no cash flow and soaring interest costs, some have declared bankruptcy. This matter too is pending before Indian courts.

Once again, Indian legislators overlooked the cardinal principle of doing business—that contracts have to be respected, unless an element of deceit is proved. This unwillingness to honour contracts has made the government one of the biggest litigants in cases before the Supreme Court.

Cozy Deals

Badly drafted policy guidelines, the unwillingness to honour contracts and a business opportunity that was quite visible to astute businessmen made some of them enter into cozy deals with state governments. Obviously, details of the deals are not available. But the manner in which deals were struck at higher prices even after a low price had been discovered through the reverse auction process made it abundantly clear that many businessmen had adopted the cozy relationship route for doing business in the solar power sector.

---

for all citizens and the need to reduce the government's revenue deficit. By then she had ensured that the judges of the Supreme Court were people who supported her causes. The legal challenge to this amendment failed, and India threw out one of its key constitutional guarantees.

Rural Focus Lost

The most painful outcome of the gaps in the solar policy was that the rural focus for solar power was lost. This was despite the government being committed to 'power for all' by 2022. In fact, one of the biggest beneficiaries of solar power could have been the rural sector. But for doing that, the government would have needed to adopt a decentralized cluster power distribution model (more on this later). This was something that the government-owned REC had already advocated more than 15 years ago. But this was forgotten. There is only one brief mention of a decentralized cluster methane based power generation facility in Purnea in Bihar.[13]

Instead of promoting decentralized cluster based (solar) power generation and distribution models, the government ordered all solar power generated to be sold to the grid.

The decision to feed all solar power into the grid was sensible from one point of view. Given India's size, having a uniform network for power made sense. But stretching long electricity lines to reach the remotest hut in the remotest village depending on the grid might not be such a good idea.

But cluster based power generation and distribution was how one could synergize Germany's rooftop idea and India's village needs. This is another strategy that India's planners overlooked.[14]

There are five reasons why the rural sector should not be overlooked when we think of solar.

---

[13] Page 113 of the REC annual report for 2016-18 which can be downloaded from http://www.recindia.nic.in/uploads/files/ar-2016-17.pdf

[14] http://www.moneycontrol.com/news/business/dear-pm-modi-heres-how-bureaucrats-are-planning-to-scuttle-your-rooftop-solar-employment-plans-2468501.html

First, rural connectivity with the grid is an expensive proposition. That fact is that given the remoteness of villages, while it costs barely Rs 5 to provide an urban dweller with an electricity connection, it can cost Rs 20,000 or more to connect a house in a remote area. Hence having a local generator, with short lines of distribution, makes more sense. But electricity from a generator costs at least three to six times more than grid power. It adds to pollution as well, and the fumes it generates are dangerous for the respiratory tract. That is why the decentralized, cluster approach is the most sensible one for India.

Second, the longer the distribution lines, the greater are the technical losses. However, rooftop solar has the shortest transmission line—from the rooftop to the consumer below. That is why solar rooftops are more effective when the focus is on reducing transmission losses.

Third, long transmission lines provide unscrupulous people the temptation to hook into overhead wires and steal electricity. At times, even the cables that carry electricity are stolen. Hence, once again, the circumstances favour decentralized clusters. A caveat is required here. Local mafia bodies exist even in villages, and entrepreneurs have to learn to make adjustments with them. That is unfortunately the price India has to pay because it has not allowed a robust law enforcement and dispute redressal system to grow.

Fourth, when a decentralized cluster power generation module is given to a private entrepreneur, he keeps a beady eye on any kind of theft that could take place, or any tinkering with the meters that measure power consumption. However, many powerful people in rural India do not like such a set-up. There are villages in Maharashtra where vested interests have not allowed the authorities to even install electricity meters. Any attempt to cut off power supplies to the region is met with a political threat of a whiplash by common people. Over the years, the regime of subsidies, mollycoddling powerful vested interests and bureaucratic collusion have together created an environment where the state grid comes very close to being dysfunctional. Once again, the answer will lie in decentralized cluster-based power generation systems.

The fifth reason is the most crucial. If India had adopted the German system of rooftop solar it could have created many more jobs.[15] It is worth recalling how Germany, quite accidentally, discovered that in just eight years, it had created more jobs in the solar sector than in the automobile engineering sector. India has more sunlight, more land, more people and hence more rooftops.

If only (as an illustration) 100 villages were to be treated as a cluster, India's six lakh villages could become 6000 clusters. Each cluster would have a private promoter who could set up the solar power system with appropriate battery storage. This could be done for forests areas as well, because the Indian Forest Act allows for a small clearing for power generation. Thus tribal living in forest areas could also benefit from decentralized solar power clusters.

Each private sector entrepreneur would be interested in getting his captive area to consume more electricity. He would therefore become a catalyst for encouraging rural folk to start some business or the other—welding, lathe machine operation, smelting using electric arc furnaces etc. The list is endless.

As more enterprises come up in villages, the solar power producer-entrepreneur would earn more money and his

---

[15] http://www.moneycontrol.com/news/business/economy/the-electrifying-plan-that-would-create-83-million-jobs-from-solar-energy-2410301.html

captive area would spawn more businesses, which could uplift the village. Our estimates show that in this way, at least 83 million jobs could be created within two to three years (see Table 9). In fact, such an approach would also allow the present government to meet its promise of jobs for India's teeming millions. Given that India needs to create at least 12 million jobs every year, and the fact that India has not created many jobs for the past five years, this should be music to any economic planner's ears.

Table 9	
Rooftop solar and the employment	
Jobs created during 2009–2011	800,000–1,250,000
Jobs created in 2015	155,000
Jobs created in 2016	122,000
New jobs required each year in India	12–16 million
Number of villages	640,867
Number of people living in them	833,100,000
Villages with a population of 10,000+	3,976
Recommended village cluster solar and methane centres	6,500
Employment potential	
Each cluster employment potential	10
Cluster employment potential	65,000
Each metropolis solar employment potential	10,000
Number of metropolises	30
Solar power support staff for 30 metropolises	300,000
Fresh employment generation through village electrification @ 5 per village	3,204,335
Employment potential in 2–3 years @10% of rural population which create business units	83,310,000
Notes: Each cluster has around 100 small villages; each village of 10,000 people can be a cluster by itself.	
Sources: Government statistics, media reports and Census 2011	

The decentralized rooftop solar power exercise could kick off a process of economic revival in rural areas. A more prosperous and economically vibrant rural sector would slow down the process of urbanization, which could reduce overcrowding in cities. Rural prosperity would allow almost 50 per cent of India's population to expand the consumption market considerably, which in turn would make the wheels of industry move faster. It would also allow India's planners to develop new roads connecting villages and cities and plan another round of upgrading villages into towns and towns into newly emerging smart cities. That will allow the government to cope with the inevitable urbanization of India without its painful accompaniment of large-scale migration.

Three caveats need to be put in place here. First, as mentioned earlier, the local mafia, which wants to steal power, will always be around. Even while there may be a private entrepreneur who may not want to allow theft of power, he will still have to make peace with the local mafia because the current law and order situation may not be able to insulate the entrepreneur (more on this in Chapter V, 'The promotion of vulnerability').

Second, batteries are still quite expensive. It is better to use solar in conjunction with methane generated from local agro waste or forest waste or human and animal waste (more on this in Chapter III, 'People matter').

Third, wherever the grid reaches a village, even grid power may be used. This could be of help during the rainy season when sunlight is poor for several days at a stretch. At such times, a bit of power from the grid may be of help. But as technologies advance, and microgrid technology begins to get implemented, these new grids will find solutions on how to link up with each other and ensure that power from the main grid may not be needed. But the distribution part of the decentralized cluster power generation model business must lie with a private entrepreneur, subject to the rules the state may lay down. You need the private entrepreneur to become a catalyst for promoting new businesses in each cluster.

Meeting Peak Power Demand

There is one more important issue that governments will have to take note of: using the limited battery storage used by decentralized clusters of solar power to meet peak demand for electricity. Peak time electricity is the most expensive form of power because the generation plants that are set up are typically used for just two to three hours during a twenty-four-hour period, when demand for power peaks. Thus, interest and other costs are paid for a twenty-four-hour period, but the facility is used for only two to three hours. This makes peaking power extremely expensive. If this peak is met through battery storage, the average cost of power will automatically come down.

Studies in many cities have shown that as even cars become electric vehicles, parking slots can be connected to the grid, and car batteries can also be used to meet peaking demand. Clearly, power planners have to rethink the entire range of possibilities when decentralized cluster power and batteries become ubiquitous. There will be a greater demand for micro grids and grid intelligence than ever before.

Where Is the Money?

How will such a scheme of decentralized cluster solar power in rural areas be financed? Simple: the private entrepreneur can get the money to finance the cluster rooftop solar module from banks.

The banks can receive refinancing from an arm of the government.

And how will the government get the money? Our proposal is that each state government takes the total quantum of subsidies and losses it incurs each year on the power distribution front. The subsidies include power that was stolen but was misdeclared as subsidized power.[16] Together, they represent the black hole from which the government will first have to emerge.

This subsidy-cum-losses amount should then be capitalized for ten years and transferred to another company, where it is bundled as an asset. The company can then float bonds against these amounts. These bonds should be offered to the public, which may want to invest in long-term government securities that offer a decent discount rate. This bond issuing company will then play the same refinancing role for the rural power sector that India's National Bank for Agriculture and Rural Development (NABARD) does for agriculture.

The money lent out by the bank must be to a private entrepreneur, not to a government entity. This is because when dealing with subsidies and losses, a government entity is not to be trusted. It can continue pouring good money over bad and then pass on the bill to taxpayers. It will always be subject to pressures to take decisions that are politically expedient. Of course, doing this will also require an efficient dispute resolution mechanism.

In this context, the anecdote involving Torrent Power is relevant. Torrent was invited to deal with the losses incurred

---

[16] For instance, the state of Maharashtra has more pump sets per acre of rural land than is the norm. Clearly, some smart person in the state bureaucracy has tried to pass off power theft as agricultural pump set consumption.

in the Bhiwandi industrial belt in Maharashtra.[17] What the state could not do for almost three decades, Torrent managed to achieve in just three years. The Bhiwandi cluster became profitable, and Torrent earned a percentage of the money it had recovered. Today this is a case study taught in most management schools in this country. But even Torrent could not wipe out the losses and the leakages entirely. The reason: elementary. The local mafia had to be accounted for. In the absence of an effective law enforcement and dispute resolution mechanism, the cost of doing business always goes up. Secondly, the concession term should be for longer periods. We believe it should be for twenty-five years at least, so that the entrepreneur can plan his strategies even with subsidized power initially. A longer-term franchise allows him to plan for a longer term for amortization of costs and for making decent returns.

To make the scheme politically acceptable, it is proposed that each rural household gets subsidized power of up to 100 to 200 units a month. Any consumption beyond this level will invite market rate tariffs. Since state discoms are viable at Rs 4.50 a unit, without subsidies, the solar power producer can make profits by selling the additional power at Rs 5.50 a unit. The difference between the cost of production of solar power (around Rs 3 a unit or kWh) and Rs 5.50 will be the entrepreneur's margin from which he services the subsidy, interest, depreciation and operational costs.

That price benchmark then becomes the tariff for the entire state, irrespective of whether it is for household, slum, commercial or industrial consumption. Today, households

---

[17] http://www.pmanifold.com/knowledge/blog/performance-analysis-of-distribution-franchisee-bhiwandi-case-study-by-torrent-power-limited/

generally pay around Rs 6–7 a unit. Industries pay around Rs 8 a unit, commercial establishments pay around Rs 10–12 a unit, while hoardings, advertisements, malls and displays could pay up to Rs 14 a unit. The new tariff structure should be good news for everyone (but for those who specialize in power theft).

Catalysing Entrepreneurship

Since the entrepreneur has to make money from families that use more than 100 units, he also plays the role of catalyst to promote small business enterprises in the cluster. If the commercial venture is successful, the farmer makes money, but so does the solar power producer-distributor. As a businessman, the solar power entrepreneur will employ a small army of people to help with the installation and maintenance of the solar rooftop units and the batteries. He employs bright young people who then encourage farmers to use more electricity. For instance, a well-off farmer could be encouraged to install refrigerators and air conditioners in his house. A poor farmer could be persuaded to buy a lathe machine, or a semi-automatic rudimentary harvester, or a sewing machine. The household may opt to set up an oven for making bread for the community. Another farmer could be persuaded to invest in a tractor, which could take the produce of the entire village to the nearest rural marketplace. The list is endless. Once power is made available, local imagination and enterprise will come up with ideas that can generate money in that region.

When decentralized individuals begin to work innovatively, the collective result is often greater than the sum of all parts put together. This is what Kurien discovered when he began focusing on 'production by the masses and not mass production'. This has been India's way all along, and there is no reason to believe that it should be different in the future as well.

The distributed cluster solar power model is acutely dependent on the entrepreneur. He would play the same role that the middle layer did in Germany. Obviously, the local power generation entrepreneur would have to be more careful (than collusive state government officials) about people who try to beat the system. A clever way to cheat governments of subsidy amounts is by breaking up family units into more households. This way, each household gets the subsidized free power quota of 100 units. So, if a medium-sized family were to break up into three households, it could use 300 units of free subsidized power. This is precisely what has happened with slums. While the population in slums declined, the number of households went up. Anyone familiar with the linking of subsidy with households would easily recognize the motivating factor for splitting up existing families into smaller units.[18]

The results that one could get from promoting the decentralized cluster solar power model could be electrifying (pun intended). Each cluster could create jobs for at least ten people. That alone should create over 65,000 jobs within eight months (maybe even six months). Business development in villages could see incremental employment within the first year itself. That could mean 3.2 million rural jobs. Both roofs and walls could be enabled with solar panels in cities with dense populations. The potential is mind-boggling.

---

[18] http://www.dnaindia.com/money/report-policy-watch-the-emerging-pattern-in-slum-demographics-1970216
http://www.asiaconverge.com/2014/03/caste-politics-of-slums-their-effects-on-cities/

Within two to three years, one can expect at least 10 per cent of the rural population to get jobs or start small businesses, or augment their earnings. That should translate into a staggering 83 million additional jobs. Even if one discounts the number by 50 per cent, it would still leave the country enough headroom to meet the annual job demand of 12 million each year.

Overnight, this model could bring electricity to all village households, create jobs in rural areas, reduce the pace of urbanization and push up India's GDP.

Moreover, the more one uses solar, the less one needs to import oil and coal. Kerala's experiments with solar boats are a great example to bear in mind. Operational costs drop to less than 10 per cent. The government's own experiments with solar/compressed natural gas (CNG) operated cargo ships, which can navigate even shallow stretches, are another example of how solar can complement transportation.[19] It is only a matter of time before the electric cars and trucks that India wants to see on its roads are also recharged using solar. The result: less pollution, reduced import of oil and gas, a healthier current account deficit and a more vibrant India.

Add to this methane digestors, but more on that later.[20] They could replace smoke-filled fireplaces based on firewood with cooking gas stoves. This in turn could help reduce

[19] http://www.firstpost.com/business/find-out-how-indias-vastly-unexplored-7500-km-coastline-can-generate-millions-of-jobs-3170668.html
http://www.asiaconverge.com/2016/12/coastline-and-waterways-mean-jobs/

[20] http://www.freepressjournal.in/editorspick/solar-methane-await-better-days-r-n-bhaskar/889111
http://www.asiaconverge.com/2016/07/solar-methane-better-days-ahead/

deforestation and improve air quality. And it could save India millions on healthcare as well.[21] According to the Economic Survey, coal combustion has a negative impact on the respiratory system and is linked to cardiovascular diseases, neurological effects, etc. This is in addition to the health impacts on coal miners, who are at a higher risk of chronic bronchitis and other lung diseases. The annual number of deaths linked to coal-based power plant pollution is estimated to be around 115,000 and the total monetary cost is around $4.6 billion a year.

Dovetail the rooftop solar models, the methane generation plans with floating solar plants[22]—the type that the government has now started encouraging—and you will be generating solar power without the use of land and also reduce evaporation of water. The ideal locations are dams and lakes. The Tatas began experimenting with floating solar plants in 2011, but both the Indian government and the world have begun catching on to this only recently. The government has already announced plans to set up at least ten such projects.[23] Countries like Indonesia and Thailand have also begun looking favourably at floating solar projects. The new solutions are safer, more robust and immensely beneficial to the environment (provided care is taken that the floating solar plants are not executed badly and end up suffocating the fish and other water-based organisms).

---

[21] Economic Survey of India 2016-17, Vol 2, p. 126, para 5.22.

[22] http://www.dnaindia.com/business/report-solar-power-over-water-an-interesting-bet-at-tata-1562042
http://www.asiaconverge.com/2011/07/floating-solar-makes-its-debut/

[23] https://www.moneycontrol.com/news/business/comment-floating-solar-set-to-make-a-splash-2560037.html
http://www.asiaconverge.com/2018/04/floating-solar-gains-allure/

Why Did India Not Emulate Germany?

Logically speaking, India should have promoted rooftop solar, floating solar and decentralized rural clusters instead of large solar farms. The latter involves the cost of land acquisition. In rooftop solar (or solar panels fixed on the top of a pole next to a dwelling place), there is no cost related to land acquisition.

There could be two possible explanations for this reluctance to adopt the decentralized cluster and rooftop solar power model.

The first could be that the government was under pressure from large industry players to promote large-scale solar farms. In India, larger project costs invariably allow for large amounts of money to be skimmed away by allowing for the padding of project costs and tariffs. It also permits the possibility of land grab. This is precisely what happened to the Special Economic Zones (SEZs) concept, which the previous government (and P.C. Chidambaram, former finance minister) touted so aggressively. More than three-fourths of these SEZs eventually became nothing but real estate development ploys. The real estate sector is reckoned to use and generate the largest amount of unaccounted cash often referred to as black money in India.

But the second explanation is more insidious. It has to do with the nature of power subsidies, which is closely intertwined with politics and theft.

In India, power is not supplied to all at a uniform price. It is supplied to farmers (and to slum dwellers) at highly subsidized prices. Since the price of agricultural power varies from state to state, it would be safe to say that these power tariffs are normally around Rs 1 per unit (kWh). Common consumers and households pay a tariff of around Rs 6 per kWh. Industry pays around Rs 8 while malls and hoardings pay around Rs 14. Depending on the state, the average cost of power (which is the average of the pooled cost of generation, power purchase, transmission, distribution and losses) is around Rs 4–5 per kWh. Obviously, the subsidy to the farm sector is possible only by charging higher tariffs to all other sectors because the rural sector accounts for almost 50 per cent of India's population, even though its contribution to national GDP is only around 14 per cent.

And this is where the games begin.

Because agricultural power is priced at such low levels, many powerful farmers (which also include those who are close to politicians) use this power for industrial purposes. In the books, this consumption continues to be classified as agricultural power. Additionally, states are unwilling to admit that they have allowed power theft to take place. So, savvy states like Maharashtra club theft too as agricultural power consumption. That could explain why this state has, on an average, more pump sets per acre than any other state in spite of agriculture contributing to just 12 per cent of state GDP (GSDP) (it used to be 7 per cent till a few years ago). So subsidy, diversion, theft and misdeclaration cause the losses to mount. Thus total losses, after dipping in 2013–14, continue to remain at high levels (see Table 10).

What does this have to do with solar power? A great deal. With solar costs falling below Rs 3 a unit, every household or factor that decides to use solar power means that much additional money not reaching the government to cross-subsidize the agricultural sector (and slum dwellers). That would increase the state deficit on the one hand, and reduce the ability of powerful interests to divert cheap power for their business purposes on the other. That could also explain why a crucial document like the Economic Survey 2017 tried to show solar power as being more expensive than other forms of power. Nothing could be further from the truth.[24]

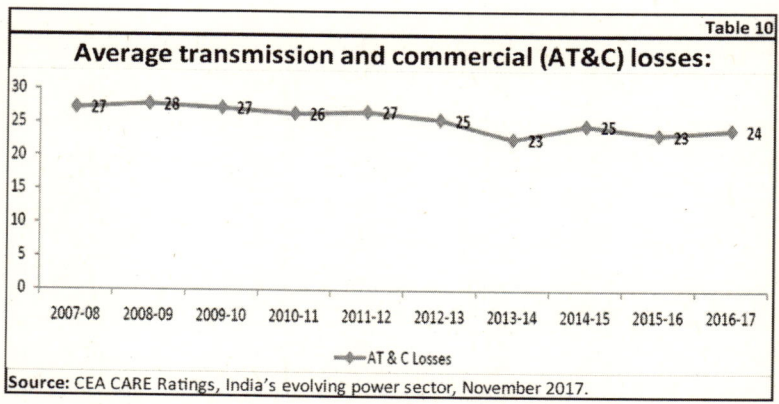

Table 10

Average transmission and commercial (AT&C) losses:

Source: CEA CARE Ratings, India's evolving power sector, November 2017.

Solar Does Not Need Lip Service

That is why in spite of lip service being paid to solar power, most states are reluctant to encourage either factory or household rooftop power. Instead, many state governments have slapped something called 'standby power' charges for any commercial user who decides to make use of solar power. These additional levies have been kept so high that they effectively neutralize any benefit a person would get from the use of solar power.

Moreover, one major fact that many people overlook is that solar tariffs have climbed down with hardly any subsidy benefits (see Table 11). This is not the case with wind, which still needs subsidies in order to be viable.

---

[24] http://www.moneycontrol.com/news/business/economy/why-the-economic-survey-is-wrong-about-renewables-2390283.html

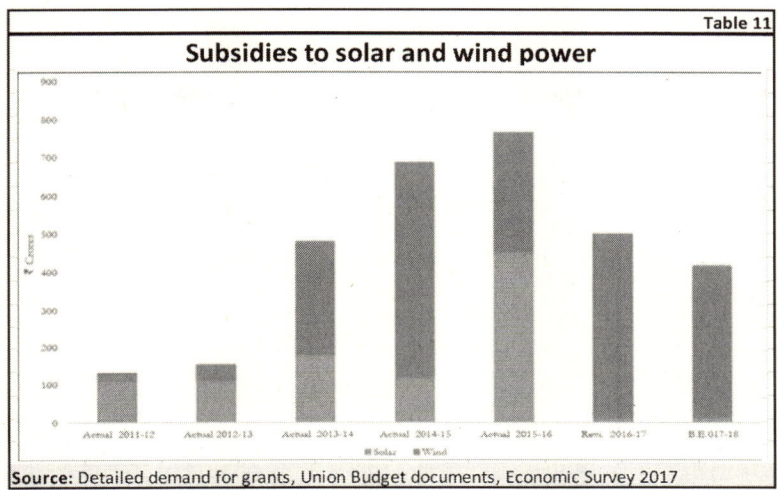

Table 11

Subsidies to solar and wind power

Source: Detailed demand for grants, Union Budget documents, Economic Survey 2017

The result is simple. Large solar plants continue to get promoted over rooftop projects. Large solar plants sell power to the grid. Thus, they do not destabilize the current regime of cross-subsidization of power tariffs. Rooftop solar would primarily help self-consumption, thereby reducing offtake of expensive power from the state grid.

As a result, India has lost an amazing opportunity to reduce its import bills, which swell because of oil and gas. It has lost an opportunity to improve health of its people by reducing pollution caused by the chimney output from coal based power plants. But more importantly, India appears to have lost an opportunity to create jobs. According to this author's calculations, India could create as many as 83 million jobs in a couple of years if only it gets its solar policies and practices right.[25]

[25] http://www.moneycontrol.com/news/business/economy/the-electrifying-plan-that-would-create-83-million-jobs-from-solar-energy-2410301.html

Grim Realities on the Job Front

First let us understand the grim realities confronting the government. India has a very large population (1.3 billion). And if one takes both the size of the population and the fact that this population has been growing at an average rate of around 2 per cent a year, it is safe to assume that India's population will grow by around 26 million each year.

Assuming half of the population will not enter the job market (housewives, self-employed businessmen), the country will still have to create 12–13 million jobs each year. Add to this the backlog of poor job creation for at least four years by the previous government (2010–2017), and the urgency assigned to job creation is immense.

In fact, the Modi government came to power on the promise of employment generation. But reality has been harsher than the rosy picture conjured up earlier. According to the government's own estimates, during 2015 and 2016, India created just 2,77,000 jobs. This was lower than the number of jobs created in 2009 to 2011, and certainly less than the 12 million jobs that are required to be created each year.

That is why it is surprising that the prime minister's advisors have not alerted him to the potential for job creation that the solar power industry offers, but only if a middle layer is created and the decentralized cluster power generation model is adopted.

How to Create Jobs and Economic Wealth

The solution to the job crisis is obvious. Look at what Germany did. When the late Hermann Scheer (energy minister

---

http://www.asiaconverge.com/2017/10/solar-power-could-trigger-employment-generation/

of Germany in 2000) decided to push for solar power in his country, he adopted three strategies.[26] One was creating a middle layer, the second was providing subsidies for solar power generation during the formative years and the third was introducing a power buyback policy that later came to be known as the FIT (feed-in tariff).

As mentioned earlier, his decision to focus on the development of a middle layer of installers, maintainers and aggregators inadvertently increased employment opportunities in the solar power sector.

Remember, Germany has less sunlight and fewer people than India. So India, with more people (hence more houses) and much more sunlight, should have more rooftop solar units. If the solar power exercise was successful in Germany, it should be doubly successful in India. This country could make the middle layer that much more profitable and vibrant. It could be an excellent solution to India's need to create jobs.

But how does one tackle the subsidy problem? If a solution cannot be made politically acceptable, it could run the risk of running aground.

The first step is to create village clusters. One effective way is to use 100 villages or so as one cluster. Villages that have population densities of more than 10,000 should be treated as independent clusters (the Census 2011 puts the number of such villages at 597,464).

Each of these clusters should be given to entrepreneurs who then approach the banks with the requisite bank guarantees and agreements that compel them to follow a

---

[26] http://www.firstpost.com/business/what-india-could-not-learn-from-germanys-hermann-scheer-solar-power-model-2749400.html
http://www.asiaconverge.com/2016/04/india-not-learn-germanys-hermann-scheer-solar-power-model/

certain process. The process that has to be followed has been discussed elsewhere.[27]

To make decentralized cluster solar power generation acceptable, rural households may be promised 100 units of subsidized power each month. Some people may ask why a rural household will agree to pay for power that he generates on his own rooftop. The reason is that otherwise, he would have to incur the capital costs, which are now being borne by the installer, aggregator and distributor. Second, he would have to maintain the power apparatus, the invertors, and the battery link himself. Third, he would not be licensed to link his household to any other as that licence would vest with the cluster power generation entrepreneur. Lastly, there will be no guarantee of standby power, because he would have to go back to the local entrepreneur who is the decentralised cluster licence holder.

That is how one can ensure that any additional consumption would invite payment of market prices. To ensure that the villagers do not arbitrage between stolen grid power and paid-for solar power, it is also essential that all connections to the grid are completely cut off.

What about standby power when the sun isn't shining? To tackle this issue, standby batteries with storage capacities of 24–48 hours should be installed for each household, but against a bank guarantee (refinanced by the state government). The bank guarantee would ensure that entrepreneurs do not just borrow money from the government, pocket the amount, and do not supply power to the villages after the money has come in.

---

[27] http://www.moneycontrol.com/news/business/economy/the-radical-power-for-all-solution-that-the-government-should-adopt-2396605.html

The amortization of the battery cost along with the cost of the solar power installation and the decentralized distribution network is borne by the cluster entrepreneur. If for any reason there is need for additional power, the entrepreneur may resort to the use of a genset. At no time must the grid connection be restored.[28]

With batteries that guarantee standby power, as well as aided by a methane-based power supply, the grid may not be needed at all, though most villages that already have access to grid power could use a hybrid system. That again could be set in motion by the local cluster entrepreneur.

The grid now does not need to subsidize agriculture. In fact, agriculture gets its other subsidies (fertilizer, nutrients, etc). But what is important is that the rural sector is given a whiff of better times to come by gently prodding it towards enterprise and small-scale industries. A small incentive in rural areas carries more bang for the buck than in urban areas. In fact, small-scale industries will remain the biggest employment generator in the coming decades (see Table 12).[29]

Managing small clusters and the grids will require more smart grids to be put into place. But that is an exercise that can be taken up sector by sector. The transformation of the power sector by making rural areas almost entirely dependent on cluster (solar) power generation must be allowed to go ahead.

---

[28] http://www.moneycontrol.com/news/business/economy/the-radical-power-for-all-solution-that-the-government-should-adopt-2396605.html
http://www.asiaconverge.com/2017/09/radical-power-solution-government-should-adopt/
[29] 'Future of Jobs in India: A 2022 Perspective', 15 September 2017.

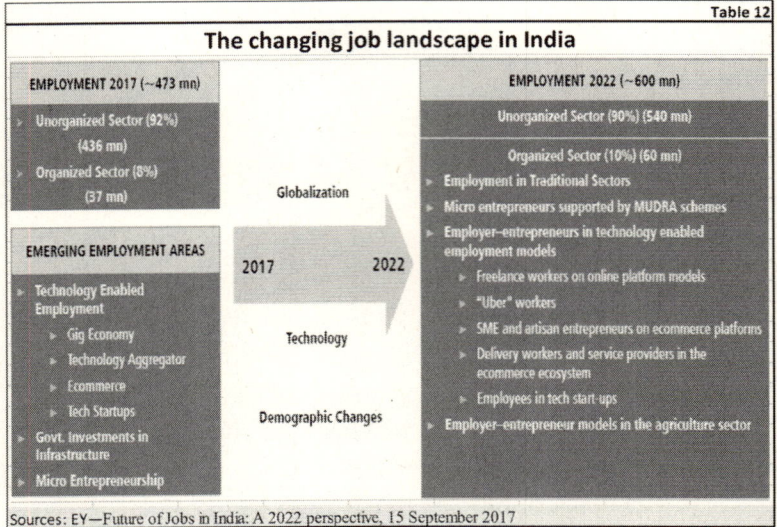

Table 12

The changing job landscape in India

Sources: EY—Future of Jobs in India: A 2022 perspective, 15 September 2017

Industry and commerce will become more competitive because of a reduction in power tariffs by 25–70 per cent. This in turn will make the economy more vibrant. Prime Minister Narendra Modi will then have created the right mood for employment and growth, without subsidies.

Clearly, it is time for India to treat the sun with a lot more admiration and thankfulness.

THREE

Resourceful People

'Our population and our use of the finite resources of planet Earth are growing exponentially, along with our technical ability to change the environment for good or ill.'
—Stephen Hawking

'From the poorest of countries to the richest of nations, education is the key to moving forward in any society.'
—Nelson Mandela

'Animals can be driven crazy by placing too many in too small a pen. Homo sapiens is the only animal that voluntarily does this to himself.'
—Robert A. Heinlein, *Time Enough for Love*

'What we need is not mass production, but production by the masses.'
—Dr Verghese Kurien

'By improving health, empowering women, population growth comes down.'
—Bill Gates

People matter. They can generate huge wealth, but only if the right policies are pursued. This is contrary to what Malthus talked of—that if population growth was not curtailed, there would be food riots and wars.

Most of us have now gotten over these Malthusian fears. Food production can be increased. The fears of water wars too have faded thanks to solar power, which has made desalination very economical—costing less than 2 paisa per litre (never mind the prices state governments are willing to pay to private contractors of desalination projects). Aqua farming has even changed the way seafood can be produced. And hydroponics has made people revise their learnings about agriculture—that you don't need soil or even sunlight for growing vegetables[1] and that this will help you overcome climate change. There has been a similar improvement in poultry farming and hatcheries. China has already discovered a way to grow rice in salt water, which in turn could feed another 80 million people.[2] As for population, one does not have to go the Sanjay Gandhi way to control its growth. There is enough evidence that if people are allowed to climb the economic ladder, population growth automatically slows down.

This is because having more children makes sense when someone is poor or vulnerable. There is strength in numbers. More children allow the family to remain strong in rural areas especially when there is a threat to life. Even beggars know that four pairs of hands begging for alms bring in more money for the family than just two pairs.

---

[1] https://www.moneycontrol.com/news/business/economy/comment-why-hydroponics-could-be-the-future-of-farming-2630781.html

[2] https://www.rt.com/business/442411-china-selectively-bred-saltwater-rice/

But as one begins to look around, one realizes that India's planners have ignored some of the key advantages a large population can offer to the country.

And it does not necessarily have to do with the energy and vitality a young population brings. Having a young population is good, but it can be a liability if it is not educated. As a World Bank official once remarked wryly when he heard an Indian politician waxing eloquent about the demographic dividend India enjoys: 'Even Iran had a demographic dividend during the 1960s,' he muttered. 'But when the young don't have jobs and education, those advantages turn into liabilities.'

Even so, there are other ways in which a large population can be a big boon, especially if there is a visionary who knows how to harness the good out of this resource. For instance, as the previous chapters have shown, more people translate into more dwelling units. Each dwelling unit can become a producer and consumer of electricity using solar power. Since the sources of power production and power consumption are not far from each other, transmission losses are minimal. It is then that one realizes that a distributed cluster-based power generation module can do wonders for the country. It reduces the import of coal and diesel, reduces pollution (hence the expenditure on healthcare services especially bronchial ailments), and gives rural communities an easier way to climb the economic ladder. But for some reason—possibly on account of the clout that state distribution companies (discoms) have and the power of oil companies—such plans have not been pushed earnestly.

People and Milk

Verghese Kurien also saw the immense advantage in large numbers of people. Overnight he created an economic model based on small farmers who could now rear more than two to ten cows per household in their backyards. Most countries would have seen this as a difficult proposition, and would have insisted on amalgamating these small numbers. Not Kurien. He saw in these numbers an advantage unique to India.

His slogan (as explained in the earlier chapter) was: India needs production by the masses, not mass production. By letting small farmers rear their cattle in their backyards, he gave them an additional source of income. By eliminating the three-tier structure the world adopts (where the farmer, the aggregator-processor and the distributor retailer get approximately one third of the market price each) Kurien allowed the farmer to get around 80 per cent of the market price of the milk his cattle produced. All procurement, processing, marketing and distribution related costs were contained in the 20 per cent.

The Kurien model also allowed for expenditure (cost of labour) to become profit because each household took care of its own cattle. Hiring labour was not even thought of. Once again Kurien showed the world how more households could mean greater wealth if only a country had the ability to think innovatively, and self-seeking politicians and bureaucrats were kept at bay because they have the ability to mess up the best of plans. Using this power of numbers, and a carefully honed procurement, processing and distribution strategy, Kurien helped make India the world's largest producer of milk.

Small Can Be Beautiful

All the data collected so far confirm that in India it is the small units that generate more profit and even account for a bulk of employment (see chart on results of census of micro, small and medium enterprises). As the numbers indicate, almost

95.7 per cent of the units in India are from the unregistered sector (see Table 1). These units accounted for almost 88 per cent of the jobs in the country. What is also impressive is that these units often borrow from informal sources—often at interest rates ranging from 24 per cent to 36 per cent per annum—and still generate profits. These units are often referred to as the micro, small and medium sector enterprises (MSME).

Table 1

Summary results of the 4th All-India Census of Micro, Small & Medium Enterprises sector

figures in lakh

Details	Registered Sector	Unregistered sector	Total
Total number of working enterprises	**15.64**	**346.12**	**361.76**
(a) Manufacturing	10.5	104.51	115.01
(b) Services	5.14	241.61	246.75
(i) Number of rural enterprises	7.07	193.12	200.19
(ii) Number of urban enterprises	8.57	153	161.57
Number of women enterprises	**2.15**	**24.46**	**26.6**
Number of enterprises running perennially	**15.14**	**189.13**	**204.27**
Employment	**93.09**	**712.14**	**805.24**
(a) Manufacturing	80.84	239.23	320.07
(b) Services	12.26	472.91	485.17
(i) Male	74.05	610.62	684.68
(ii) Female	19.04	101.52	120.56

Sources: Annual Report, 2015-16, Ministry of Micro, Small and Medium Enterprises, Govt of India

In fact this sector accounts for the poorest default rates either with informal lenders or with banks. It is only now that the government is waking up to the need to make banking services reach out to this critical and vital sector of the Indian economy.

Many of the MSMEs have learnt to grow without seeking any favours from politicians or powerful players.

Money from Waste

Similarly, most planners forget that the biggest advantage that India could harness from the huge numbers of people it has is by creating systems to collect and process human waste in centralized pits. As all excreta is rich in bacterial matter, it can be broken down and processed into gas. As the ubiquitous gobar (cattle dung) gas plants all over India show, even village folk know that dung can be harnessed for methane—the gas that can be used for cooking and even fuelling the engine of a vehicle.

If India can harness human and animal waste, it could generate enough methane to meet the entire import bill of Rs 6 lakh crore (Rs 6 trillion) on account of oil and gas imports (see Table 2). In fact, India could generate wealth worth Rs 18 lakh crore annually. The surplus methane that cannot be consumed immediately could easily be liquefied and sold in global markets. What is even more interesting is that such a move would be synergistic with the government's own objectives of lavatories for all (open defecation free or ODF), Swachch Bharat (clean India) and hygiene.

It is worth mentioning that some of the figures we have computed are on the conservative side. For instance, the average output of human excreta per individual ranges between 400 to 500 grams a day. We have opted for the lower figure.

Unfortunately, these plans have not been given serious thought either because of counter pressures being exerted by the powerful oil and gas lobbies, or plain inertia. It could also have a lot to do with the inability of India's planners to think big.

			Table 2
Big shit spells big money			
Description	Qty/kg/day	Population in mn	Mn Tonnes /year
Human shit	0.40	1,300.00	189.80
Pigs	5.03	11.10	20.40
Cattle	55.47	304.40	6,163.53
Sheep	1.09	71.60	28.45
Agri waste			0.00
Poultry shit	0.12	648.80	27.93
Goat	2.63	140.50	134.92
Other animals	1	2.10	0.77
Total waste per year		-	**6,565.79**
Estimated biogas from each tonne of waste	40	cubic metres	
Total biogas potential from shit	262,631	million cubic metres	
Diesel equivalent (One cubic metre of biogas approximates 1 litre of diesel)	262,631	**million litres or 262 million tonnes**	
Total diesel consumption in India (@)	69	million tonnes	
Total value of biogas potential @ Rs 70/litre of diesel	1,838,420	crore rupees	
Notes: Does not include agricultural waste—wasted vegetables, fruit, dry leaves, twigs, chaff, straw etc.—and food waste.			
Sources: Indian Petroleum & Natural Gas Statistics, 2013-14, Govt of India; 2002, North Carolina Agricultural Chemicals Manual; Livestock manure production rates and nutrient content—J.C. Barker, Biological and Agricultural Engineering; S.C. Hodges, Soil Science; F.R. Walls, North Carolina Department of Agriculture & Consumer Services; http://www.agrienvarchive.ca/bioenergy/download/barker_ncsu_manure_02.pdf.			

Another hindering factor could be the squeamishness of India's so-called upper classes, which would wrinkle their noses at the thought of using methane from dung, especially for cooking. But many small farms all over India have already installed gobar gas plants to meet their cooking requirements. There are two reasons for this. First, it is the simplest types of contraptions to install. Second, India is home to the world's largest population of livestock (see Table 3).

Livestock Population in India by Species

Last updated: 29 February 2012

Livestock Population in India by Species

(in million)

Species	1951	1956	1961	1966	1972	1977	1982	1987	1992	1997	2003	2007 $
Cattle	155.3	158.7	175.6	176.2	178.3	180	192.5	199.7	204.6	198.9	185.2	199.1
Adult Female Cattle	54.4	47.3	51	51.8	53.4	54.6	59.2	62.1	64.4	64.4	64.5	73
Buffalo	43.4	44.9	51.2	53	57.4	62	69.8	76	84.2	89.9	97.9	105.3
Adult Female Buffalo	21	21.7	24.3	25.4	28.6	31.3	32.5	39.1	43.8	46.8	51	54.5
Total Bovines	198.7	203.6	226.8	229.2	235.7	242	262.2	275.7	288.8	288.8	283.1	304.4
Sheep	39.1	39.3	40.2	42.4	40	41	48.8	45.7	50.8	57.5	61.5	71.6
Goat	47.2	55.4	60.9	64.6	67.5	75.6	95.3	110.2	115.3	122.7	124.4	140.5
Horses and Ponies	1.5	1.5	1.3	1.1	0.9	0.9	0.9	0.8	0.8	0.8	0.8	0.6
Camels	0.6	0.8	0.9	1	1.1	1.1	1.1	1	1	0.9	0.6	0.5
Pigs	4.4	4.9	5.2	5	6.9	7.6	10.1	10.6	12.8	13.3	13.5	11.1
Mules	0.1	0	0.1	0.1	0.1	0.1	0.1	0.2	0.2	0.2	0.2	0.1
Donkeys	1.3	1.1	1.1	1.1	1	1	1	1	1	0.9	0.7	0.4
Yak	NC	NC	0	0	0	0.1	0.1	0	0.1	0.1	0.1	0.1
Mithun	NA	NA	NA	NA	NA	NA	NA	NA	0.2	0.2	0.3	0.3
Total Livestock	292.9	306.6	336.5	344.5	353.2	369.4	419.6	445.2	470.9	485.4	485	529.7
Poultry*	73.5	94.8	114.2	115.4	138.5	159.2	207.7	275.3	307.1	347.6	489	648.8

Notes: NC: Not Collected; NA: Not Available * Includes chicken, ducks, turkey and other birds $ Provisional derived from village-level totals

Sources: Livestock Censuses, Department of Animal Husbandry, Dairying & Fisheries, Ministry of Agriculture, GoI; http://www.nddb.org/English/Statistics/Pages/Population-India-Species.aspx.

The harnessing of dung can be achieved, once again, by adopting the decentralized cluster model that was discussed in the chapter on solar power. What this would require is pipes running from each dung collection centre to a central pit. Sweden's Envac[3] has shown how waste can be seamlessly and hygienically transported for distances as long as 3 km. In India the distances between villages and the central pits could be longer. But that is where Indians could adapt the technologies provided by companies like Envac and come up with a waste transportation solution unique to this country. The huge amounts of money that can be made should attract investors to this opportunity, but only if the government created the right enabling policies for permitting them. India would also have to introduce the right type of contract enforcement rules that the world respects and adopts (but more on that later). Once the waste reaches the decentralized pits biochemists could begin their work on introducing the right catalysts to speed up methane generation.

Interestingly, once the methane is extracted, the residual slurry can be dried, diced and then marketed as organic manure. It may make sense to put in desulphonation plants as well; when sulphur is removed, even the stench of excreta disappears. Such plants become economically viable only when the volumes are large. Thus, if the volumes processed are large enough, the sulphonation plant actually pays for itself, because the sulphur can be sold to pharma, pesticide and fertilizer companies (India imports sulphur and its derivatives at the moment).

That in turn would reduce India's import bills substantially. The Rs 18 lakh crore generated by harnessing human and animal waste (see Table 2) could wipe out India's

---

[3]   http://www.envacgroup.com/

oil and fertilizer bills altogether (see Table 4). These remain two of the biggest import items on the government's account.

				Table 4
India's balance of payments				
				figures in crore Rs
	2014–15	**2015–16**	**2016–17**	**2017–18#**
Petroleum, oil and lubricants	842,874	540,505	582,762	--
Fertilizers	45,295	28,593	33,706	--
Total import	2,737,087	2,490,298	2,577,666	2,182,290
Total export	1,896,348	1,716,378	1,849,429	1,441,420
Trade balance	-840,738	-773,920	-728,237	-740,870
Notes: # April–December (provisional)				
Sources: Statistical Appendix to the Economic Survey 2017–18				

Agro Waste

Agro and forest waste can generate even more money—almost four to five times more than human and animal waste.

One of the savvy players in this market is Vinay Kore, erstwhile minister for non-conventional energy with the state government of Maharashtra. He discovered, during one of his meetings with foreign technology delegations, that a great deal of money could be made from agricultural waste.[4]

Since he is in charge of the Warana Cooperative (near Kolhapur in Maharashtra), which is focused on sugarcane—in addition to milk and other items—he looked at this agricultural produce first. He was aware that after the sugarcane had been extracted, the bagasse was usually either used as fodder or burnt as fuel. The good part of the sugarcane went towards making gur (a rural variant of raw sugar) and sugar. Molasses went to distilleries—most cooperatives in Maharashtra that

---

4   http://www.asiaconverge.com/2014/08/india-still-does-not-understand-waste-management/

are involved in crushing sugarcane also have distilleries (either directly owned or owned through association).

But there is a sticky, noxious liquid that is also generated that cannot be used for making sugar or be sold as molasses. This is called spent wash (the local term is bedmass). This liquid is usually burnt. But Kore learnt from the visiting teams that this sticky liquid was rich in microbial content and could be used for generating methane.

So he decided to set up the country's largest digester for processing spent wash. It has a capacity of 22 kilolitres. Instead of using this methane for generating electricity, he does something even better. He knows that producing electricity would fetch him just around Rs 6–8 per litre of methane. But when it is compressed, liquefied and sold in cylinders to the trucking or the restaurant industry, he can make as much as Rs 45–60 per litre. And since the volumes involved are large, he has also put in place a desulphonation plant to take away the foul odours. He sells the sulphur, and thus the plant pays for itself.

Today, the Warana methane digester has become one of the biggest cash cows for Kore.

Initiatives by Sweden

Other companies too have learnt to use bio-waste as wealth generators. Take the case of Scania, the Swedish truck and bus maker, which has a wholly owned subsidiary headquartered near Bengaluru in India. In order to become more relevant to the Indian rural community, it decided, around seven years ago, to import mini digesters, estimated to cost around Rs 2 lakh each.[5] It installed these digesters in rural areas and gave them to the farmers to manage (possibly as part of its

---

5 http://www.asiaconverge.com/2014/11/grundstromer-of-scania-has-big-plans-for-india/

corporate social responsibility or CSR initiatives). Farmers can sell their rotten or unsold vegetables, especially tomatoes, to the digesters' managers for Rs 1 per kilo. The quantities collected each day are so large that enough methane is produced to provide the entire village with a free supply of cooking gas round the year.

The more one looks at agro-waste, the more one realizes that the total value of energy through biomass could be huge (see Table 5 on biomass potential for some key Indian states). In fact, experts say that if the value of agro-waste converted to energy were to be taken into account, the way we have done with excreta above, this value could be at least four to five times more than the value of all energy through dung.

This is something that Tekniska,[6] the Swedish agency in charge of converting waste to energy, also discovered and is today world famous for the manner in which in converts waste to energy. In 2004, in preparation for hosting the Olympics, Sweden decided to clean up its turgid waters and its city as well. It adopted a zero landfill policy for dumping waste. Just that single policy decision propelled policymakers to discover new ways to treat all the waste generated. Dumping it was no longer possible.

Sweden is a cold country, hence it faced two challenges. First, waste converts into methane more effectively in warmer climates. Secondly, during winter, the country needs a lot of heat generation to keep the homes and establishments in its cities warm. So Tekniska Verken[7] came into existence—as a municipal company that creates benefits in the everyday life of approximately 3,00,000 residential and business

---

[6] https://smartcitysweden.com/companies/846/tekniska-verken-i-linkoping-ab/
[7] Ibid.

customers by offering a wide range of products and services in electricity, lighting, water, heating, cooling, energy efficiency, waste management, broadband and biogas. It converted whatever waste it could into methane. Waste that could not be converted into methane was incinerated. Much of the heat from incineration was used to pump warm water through the city's floors (almost all bathrooms and toilets in Stockholm have heated floors). It worked on technologies that would ensure that the emission of pollutants was almost nil. Today Tekniska is so successful in the way it manages waste that it makes decent profits on its operations (see Table 6). Moreover, its success has made it expand its operations to cover other areas in Sweden as well. To do this, it even imports agro and forest waste from nearby countries, notably Norway and the UK.

India, given its size and its agro and forest waste, in addition to dung, could certainly do a lot better.

Table 5
Biomass potential for key Indian states

State	Power Potential (MWe)
Punjab	2,413.2
Uttar Pradesh	1,594.3
Haryana	1,120.8
Rajasthan	1,093.5
Maharashtra	1,014.2
Madhya Pradesh	841.7
Karnataka	631.9
Andhra Pradesh	625.0
Gujarat	457.7
Chhattisgarh	248.5
Kerala	195.9
Total	10,236.7
Assume a similar amount for all other states	18,060.2
Grand total	28,296.9

Sources: Biomass Atlas by IISc, Bangalore, and MNRE website; https://www.bioenergyconsult.com/biomass-india/.

Table 6	
Tekniska manages waste brilliantly	
Converts 1,000,000 tonnes/year (2,739 tonnes/day) of waste into power and heat	
•Biogas	14 million Nm3 - 140 GWh
•Heat	2,100 GWh
•Electricity	680 GWh
300000 regional customers in total - 14000 district heating customers	
•Employees	about 1,000
•Sales	575 million €
•Profit after net interest income and expense	**56 million €**
•Net investment	86 million €
Notes: • Mumbai alone generates 5,025 tonnes of mixed waste (bio-degradable and recyclable) and 2,000 tonnes of debris and silt according to the Mumbai Community Public Trust. • According to the European Environment Agency, Sweden processed 2,146,000 tonnes of MSW in 2010. • Tekniska Verken's figures are for 2013.	
Sources: Tekniska	

Lack of Vision and Will

Yet it is sad to see farmers burning the stubble of their crops after they have been harvested. Had the government helped entrepreneurs set up a digester for every 100 villages or so, it could have allowed the farmers to earn some money from the stubble as well. Such a move would also have enabled villagers in Uttar Pradesh and Bihar to use methane for cooking instead of firewood. Moreover, such a move could have spared Delhi and other parts of north India the smog that afflicts these regions during harvest times. The farmers would get money. The country would reduce its forex outgo. Rural families would be spared the arduous work of collecting firewood. With little smoke from firewood being inhaled, healthcare costs would decline as well.

Similarly, instead of using bagasse as fuel, the government should introduce measures to ensure that it is fermented for generating methane. There is more money in methane generation than in burning this agro-waste. There is also the issue of pollution that must be dealt with.

If one examines the numbers carefully, just harnessing human and animal waste would give India an energy surplus, allowing it to export the oil as well as fertilizers that it produces.

Municipal Waste

In fact, the waste to energy concept has been ignored by most city administrators as well. For example, it is only now that the Municipal Corporation of Greater Mumbai (MCGM) has begun talking of a zero-tolerance policy towards landfills. Most people don't even know that it isn't always necessary to separate garbage into wet garbage and dry garbage either.

Sweden does insist on the segregation of waste. There are separate bins for recyclables, glass and plastics. And should waste be larger than what the bin can hold—old cupboards, pipes, windows etc., customers are advised to bring that waste in their cars to specified storage areas where there are earmarked spaces for each type of waste.

On the other end of the spectrum you have Israel. Its city planners believe that asking customers to separate garbage isn't the most effective way of managing waste. Israel believes in putting all waste into one bin. This is then taken to a central area where it is mixed in water and spun around. Centrifugal forces separate each type of waste, and the separation is largely done automatically. Cameras and manual inspection teams do the final check. All waste that can be fermented goes to one centre. Glass and plastic go to another centre, metal to a third. Odd items like tables or even broken canoes are fished out physically. Building debris, which normally settles to the bottom of the garbage pit, is sorted and resold for construction work. Much of the sorting is also done mechanically. Whatever water can be salvaged is sent for treatment so that the final output can be used on farms. Noxious chemicals are removed at the treatment stage itself.

Sadly, many city legislators have not even bothered to look at examples like Sweden, which has adopted a no-landfill policy since 2004 and has actually become extremely efficient in either recycling waste, or converting it to energy.[8] Sweden has designed toilets for all offices and households that can flush waste without the use of too much water. Today it is so efficient in its waste management techniques that its waste treatment plants are treated as profit centres (see Table 6).

But more serious are instances such as those in Bengaluru where efforts to convert waste into energy were thwarted again and again by a well-entrenched mafia.[9] This mafia ostensibly makes its money by charging municipalities for towing garbage away from the city's boundaries. But it makes more money by selling the monetisable part of the garbage—plastic, rubble for construction, computer peripherals and furniture. The pickings are so big that they would do anything to prevent waste being converted into energy by a private agency.

People often forget that in Bengaluru, more than a decade ago, a consortium of companies led by the Japanese offered to treat garbage at no cost to the municipality, provided it got the land for its waste treatment plant and a concession for

---

[8] http://asiaconverge.com/2016/03/669/
[9] http://www.asiaconverge.com/2014/08/mafia-and-bengaluru-waste-to-energy-story/

thirty years. This proposal too was stalled by the mafia using one excuse or the other to persuade the courts to stay the grant of the tender. Multiple vexatious petitions filed before the judiciary did not allow such a proposal to fructify. The consortium finally lost interest and it seems unlikely that it will bid for the Bengaluru project again.

To sum it up, a large population can generate huge wealth. Waste is just one way in which this can be done. There are other ways too, but only if the government is willing and the legislators enlightened enough.

Remittances

Perhaps one of the biggest advantages India has got from its people is the remittances that Indians send from overseas. Since 2010, India has been one of the top rtecipients of remittances from Indians working overseas. During the past five years— since 2013, it has been the largest recipient of such inflows. Even after the Gulf war began, and there was a subsequent slump in oil prices, which crippled project implementation in the entire Middle East, India's remittance inflows continued to remain strong. They have grown from $12 billion in 2000 to around $65-70 billion currently (see Table 7). Latest figures from the World Bank suggest that they swelled to $80 billion in 2018.

These remittances come from small-time workers— drivers, plumbers, carpenters and the like—as well as from professionals—accountants, financial consultants and lawyers.

All Indians gainfully employed overseas comprise what could be called manpower exports. It does not matter if the work relates to making chairs or advising clients on mergers and acquisitions. Both classes represent manpower exports. For a country that has so many people, India should be encouraging manpower exports even more aggressively.

							Table 7
			What NRIs sent home				
					figures for 2013-14		
Year	Remittances (US$ bn)	India's GDP (US$ bn)*	% of GDP	Remittances source country - 2014	Remittances amount (US$ bn)	Top Remittance Recipients	Remittance amount (US$ bn)
1990–1991	2.1	274.8423481	0.764074	UAE	14.3	India	70.4
1995–1996	8.5	399.7868885	2.1	USA	10.8	China	64.1
1999–2000	12.1	476.6091482	2.5	Saudi Arabia	7.6	Philippines	28.4
2000–2001	12.9	493.954334	2.6	UK	3.9	Mexico	24.9
2001–2002	15.4	523.9685619	2.9	Bangladesh	3.7	France	24.8
2002–2003	16.4	618.3564674	2.7	Canada	3.1	Nigeria	20.9
2003–2004	21.6	721.5856082	3.0	Nepal	3.2	Pakistan	17.1
2004–2005	20.3	834.2150136	2.4	Qatar	2.1	Germany	15.8
2005–2006	24.6	949.1167696	2.6	Australia	1.2	Vietnam	12.0
2006–2007	30.8	1,239	2.5	Singapore	1.1	Spain	11.0
2007–2008	43.5	1224.097069	3.6	Bahrain	0.7	Lebanon	8.9
2008–2009	46.9	1365.372433	3.4	Italy	0.6	Indonesia	8.6
2009–2010	53.6	1708.458877	3.1				
2010-2011	55.6	1880.100141	3.0	Notes: GDP in US$ is as of December each year. Remittances are as of March end. GDP for 2013-14 is as given by the RBI. Thereafter as given by the IMF.			
2011–2012	66.1	1858.744737	3.6				
2012–2013	67.6	1876.797199	3.6				
2013-2014	70.0	1965.7	3.6	India continued to remain the top receiver of remittances in 2017 as well, as recorded by the World Bank in its latest survey on Migration and development brief - Oct 2017.			
2014-15	66.3	2102.392	3.2				
2016*	62.7	2273.556	2.8				
2017*	65.4	2611.012	2.5				

Sources: (i) 24th Report of the Standing Commttee on External Affairs (2013-2014), 15th Lok Sabha Ministry of Overseas Indian Affairs; (ii) http://econ.worldbank.org/WBSITE/EXTERNAL/EXTDEC/EXTDECPROSPECTS/0,,contentMDK:22759429~pagePK:641654 01~piPK:64165026~theSitePK:476883,00.html#Remittances; (iii) http://en.wikipedia.org/wiki/Remittances_to_India; (*) World Bank-Migration and development Brief-Oct 2017 - https://web.archive.org/web/20171115143407if_/https://www.knomad.org/sites/default/files/2017-10/Migration%20and%20Development%20Brief%2028.pdf.

Manpower Exports

It is quite possible that manpower exports will become one of the strategies India will pursue in its quest for global leadership. This is because there is a great likelihood of India, China and Russia becoming the most important players in the world. Should they care to work together, the global axis itself will veer towards these three countries. The numbers suggest that such an alignment may not be totally irrational (see Table 8 on countries and their DNA). This author began pursuing this line of thought in 2009,[10] and subsequent events appear to bear out this line of thinking.

Look at the numbers. The biggest weakness China appears to have is water. It has the least amount of water as a percentage of land mass. That could explain why China decided to consolidate its hold over Tibet in the middle of the twentieth century. Chairman Mao recognized the urgent need for water that China would face. Tibet is the fountainhead of three major rivers in Asia—the Yangtse, Brahmaputra and the Mekong.

Fortunately, thanks to cheaper solar power, the water crisis appears to have become a little less severe. China has begun building desalination plants across its shoreline, and the need to conserve water has made it one of the best recyclers of water in this part of the world. But even that water may not be enough. That is why it is reasonable to expect China to work out a deal with Russia to draw on its water reserves.

Look at the numbers again. Russia has the biggest freshwater reserves in the world. Building a canal from Russia to central China would therefore appear to be the most logical thing to do, and this is precisely what appears to be happening. China has negotiated a deal with Russia to build a canal to draw on Russia's waters.

---

[10] https://www.livemint.com/Companies/wDLWbd3OWUGpp EzYYC0yYO/The-Capitalist--With-increasing-water-needs-will-China-deh.html

Table 8

Countries and their DNA

	India	China	Russia	USA	Bangladesh	Nepal	Sri Lanka	Pakistan
Land Area (sq. km)	3,287,263	9,596,961	17,075,200	3,796,742	147,570	147,181	65,610	881,913
Population (million)	1,324	1,403.50	145	326	163	28.98	21.44	209.97
Density/sq. km	396.2	145	8.4	85	1,106.0	180.0	327.0	244.4
Water (% of land area)	9.6	2.8	13.0	7.0	6.4	2.8	4.4	2.86
GDP $ trn	2.654	11.938	2018	20.199	0.275	0.024	0.086	0.304
Per capita $	1989	8,583	10630	61,687	1660	837	4,020	1,629
PPP per capita $	7,749	16,624	28,918	61,687	4,541	2,573	13,847	5,374
Ratio: PPP per capital/nominal per capita	3.9	1.9	2.7	1.0	2.7	3.1	3.4	3.3

Notes: The table covers four major countries, and four of India's neighbours

Sources: Wikipedia—as on 8 April 2018. The figures are themselves based on other global databases

But the biggest game might lie in the way the three countries use their respective manpower strengths and weaknesses. The numbers show how vulnerable Russia is with regard to manpower. Although it has the largest land mass, it has the poorest density of population. To remain powerful, Russia must generate more wealth from the massive territory that lies within its national boundaries.

Russia knows that it is blessed with the largest reserves of both gold and oil in the world. It may also be the largest repository of rare earths, but that is just a speculation at this stage. It also has large deposits of almost every mineral that the world might need in its move towards newer technologies. Unfortunately, it lacks the manpower resources. Further, given the belligerence of the US and the limited foreign exchange reserves it has at the moment, Russia is not likely to overly depend on Western capital or talent.

So what are Russia's options? It can ask the Chinese to help it exploit its mineral reserves. But history has a lesson— populations from a next-door neighbour can become squatters overnight. It is always safer to import manpower from the country next to the next-door neighbour. Russia might opt to import labour from India, but under strict migration laws (maybe similar to those adopted by most Middle Eastern countries). A closer look at how Russia has already begun using Indian manpower suggests that India-Russia relations could become stronger than they already are.[11]

This appears to be happening already. Russia has been depending on Indian talent from OVL-ONGC for exploiting some of its oil wells. But more importantly, it recently struck a deal with Tata Power to help it exploit its coal mines in

---

[11] http://www.freepressjournal.in/india/rn-bhaskar-india-russia-friends-for-70-years/1051178

Eastern Russia[12] (near Vladivostok) and to build a railway line to the port there. If India negotiates such deals well, it could find a huge market for its skilled manpower in Russia.

This would allow Russia to depend less on Western powers and to cock a snook at the sanctions that tend to disrupt its economic plans. In fact, the West already scored a self-goal when it tried to cut its import of gas from Russia. That prompted Russia to strike a deal with China, which has now become a very important customer for Russia's oil and gas.

The recent government move to mend ties with China[13] so the two counties could jointly help Afghanistan improve its economy is another pointer to the India-China-Russia partnership. It could pave the way for India to work with China as well as other countries to reconstruct war-torn economies—Afghanistan, Syria, Iraq and Libya. This would improve relations with such countries and create a market for India's manpower exports. The recent sanctions on Iran have also made Russia, India and China look for ways to work together, with Iran seeking bilateral relations with all these countries (in addition to ties with EU which has rejected the US move to impose sanctions against Iran).

For China, this realignment of relationships involving Russia and India also means depending less on imports from its eastern coast.[14] And, in any case, China too has a large population, and it has already been deploying its people in

---

[12] http://www.asiaconverge.com/2017/04/making-sberbank-relevant-to-india/

[13] http://indianexpress.com/article/explained/narendra-modi-xi-jinping-india-china-relations-wuhan-summit-donald-trump-doklam-5159123/

[14] Documentary by John Pilger, *The Coming War on China.*

developing mines in Africa, Latin America and Australia. But Russia is likely to remain a market for India, almost exclusively.

Moreover, China (and Russia too) is unlikely to lay out the welcome mat for manpower exchanges with Islamic countries. Both China and Russia have an innate distrust of the rise of Islamic power, though both countries continue to be staunch allies of Iran, Syria and Iran. That is the nature of geopolitics.

The real challenge for India is with regard to how it can work with Russia—and the Middle East—to provide these regions with its manpower. That is where India holds great potential for the entire region. The big hurdle could be the US, which is threatening to draw up a list of 'friends of enemies' and craft more restrictive policies for them. The US has already begun tightening the entry rules for Indians who seek to work there. However, the impact such moves is having on US education enrolments could compel that country to re-think immigration policies.

In this world where the best talent is sought by everyone, the country that loses out on student enrolments might see its best potential discoveries and inventions slow down in the future.

Affordable Housing

There is yet another advantage a large young population gives a country like India. It is the same advantage that Iran saw during the 1980s and finally acted upon around 2005.[15]

When the Iranian Revolution took place in 1979, Khomeini was aware that there were two key reasons behind the success of the revolution. One was disenchantment with

---

[15] http://www.asiaconverge.com/2015/11/housing-lessons-from-iran/

the Western inclinations of Mohammad Reza Pahlavi, the Shah of Iran.[16] That disenchantment reached a boiling point when the Shah agreed to kowtow to US demands and was willing to sign what Iranians call the 'Capitulation law'. The law prohibited any law officer of Iran from trying or arresting any US citizen for crimes that he may have committed on Iranian soil. The best that Iran could do was to send the person to the US to stand trial there. The Iranians refused to succumb to this humiliation that the Shah was willing to accept. That resentment boiled over, leading to the largest ever uprising in Iran.

The second reason was that Iran then enjoyed the same benefits India is believed to enjoy today: a demographic dividend. It had a young population. It was not well educated, though, and Iran could not provide enough jobs. When all the three—lack of jobs, little education, and a large population—come together, you have a potent cocktail that can explode into flames at the slightest spark. And that is what happened with the Iranian Revolution.

To stave off any further revolutions (against Khomeini and his Islamic Republic) the country decided to work on measures that would allow Iran to cope with sanctions the US imposed against Iran and also provide jobs to its people. And it hit upon the strategy of affordable housing.

Khomeini could not translate his vision into reality. But it was taken up by Mahmoud Ahmadinejad (who became president of Iran in 2005) and his successor Hassan Rouhani.[17]

---

[16] https://en.wikipedia.org/wiki/Mohammad_Reza_Pahlavi

[17] http://www.dnaindia.com/analysis/column-policy-watch-house-that-for-a-change-2070936
http://www.asiaconverge.com/2015/03/762affordable-housing-what-india-can-learn-from-iran/

The reasons were simple. Housing is always an urgent need for a young population. It does not require much foreign capital, which was scarce for Iran on account of the sanctions imposed by the West. Iran discovered that labour, both unskilled and semi-skilled, was abundantly available. The raw materials required—land, cement, steel and bricks—could be sourced from within the country. If handled well, creating affordable homes could prevent unrest. It would create jobs and would also meet the aspirations of an upwardly mobile population.

Ahmadinejad and later Rouhani got the government to adopt a 'Future of Youth' scheme, under which the government would contribute 1 million Toman (roughly equal to $1,000 then) to the account of every child that was born. Thereafter, the government would contribute another 10,000 Toman for every 20,000 Toman deposited by the parent into the child's account. The first 'gift' helped create a corpus for even the poorest of children. The second exhorted even the poor to save money for their children.

This money could not be touched, withdrawn or mortgaged till the child was eighteen. At that stage, the child would have a tidy sum and could use it to purchase a dwelling, or even start a business.

To eradicate slums (more on this later), Ahmadinejad announced the 'Meherbani' housing scheme. The government gave lands on the outskirts of each city free-of-cost to developers with suitable caveats on the size of the dwellings and the prices at which they ought to be sold. All 'affordable' houses were to offer at least 700 square feet of living space. Unfortunately, both schemes did not work very well, because of the terrible economic conditions prevailing at that time.

It was finally Hassan Rouhani, the next president of Iran, who went about making these schemes a success. Between 2007 and 2013, almost 4.4 million homes were taken up for construction, of which 1.5 million homes were delivered by 2014.

Thus without any surge in imports, Iran met the two critical demands that the impoverished youth had—food and shelter. It gave the government the breathing space to put into place other measures like education, health and infrastructure. Iran escaped the blight of slums and the danger of civil unrest. It even survived sanctions.

Prime Minister Modi has the right plans when it comes to schemes like Housing for All and Affordable Homes. They would work brilliantly for India. The need for housing has already reached desperate proportions (see Table 9). The figures were compiled in 2012, and today the numbers could have swelled beyond the 25 million mark. But for any plan on affordable housing, or housing for all to succeed, the government needs to construct at least five million houses

Table 9

Distribution of estimated urban housing shortage in India (million)

Factors	As at end-2012
Households living in non-serviceable matcha houses	0.99
Households living in obsolescent houses	2.27
Households living in congested houses	14.99
Households living in homeless conditions	0.53
Total urban housing shortage	**18.78**
I – Economically weaker sections (EWS)	10.55 (56%)
II – Low Income Groups (LIG)	7.41'(40%)
III – Medium and High Income Groups (MIG+HIG)	0.82 (4%)

Notes: Values in parentheses are percentage shares

Sources: Report of Technical Group (TG-12) on Estimation of Urban Housing Shortage 2012, Ministry of Housing & Urban Poverty Alleviation; RBI Bulletin, Jan 2018

a year. If only tens of thousands of houses are built each year, you end up confronting a black market for houses because demand is bound to outstrip supply. It defeats the very objective of affordable housing and housing for all. Unfortunately, many self-serving politicians and bureaucrats have learnt to make money from real estate. Worse, politicians have fattened themselves by creating slums for political reasons (more on this later).

The Fly in the Ointment

But the biggest flaw in all its plans to invest in human capital is the mess the government has made of education.

Consider the following:

- Right from the time India won its independence, the country has defined literacy as the ability to read or write one's name. So if a person's name is Ram, and he can read and write just those three letters, he is considered literate. This definition continues to be used even today. This is quite contrary to global practices wherein a literate person is one who has passed high school. Data based on the limited definition employed in India is used in the census to indicate the country's literacy level. So while the government now claims that the country enjoys a literacy rate of 74.04 per cent, it must be taken with a barrel of salt. Actual literacy rates may be much lower. India has begun to learn the fine art of fudging data.[18] In fact, the government's own data shows that the the poor quality of higher education makes it difficult for the educated to get employment (see Table 10).

---

[18] http://www.asiaconverge.com/2016/12/fudging-education-data-produces-sludge/

A look at the UNESCO figures on literacy puts India clearly below the world average (see Table 11).

	Table 10
The real problem with unemployment	
Educational classification	**Unemployed %**
Not literate	2.3
Primary	3.3
Middle/Secondary/Higher Secondary	3.7
Graduate and above	23.8
Sources: Govt of India, Ministry of Labour & Employment, Lok Sabha, Unstarred Question No. 1385, 5 March 2018	

- Surveys conducted by Pratham, a leading non-governmental organization (NGO), show that actual literacy levels are poorer than what the government would like us to believe. Pratham conducts a survey on education each year under the banner ASER (annual status of education report). In its latest ASER in 2016,[19] it covered 589 rural districts. The survey was carried out in 17,473 villages, covering 3,50,232 households and 5,62,305 children in the age group of three to sixteen years. The survey showed that, nationally, only 42 per cent of the children in standard III were able to read at least standard I level text. This was higher than the 40 per cent in 2014, but still a shameful record.

- The quality of education has collapsed to such an extent that organizations like Nasscom and McKinsey have gone on record to say that barely 25 per cent of the graduates

---

[19] http://img.asercentre.org/docs/Publications/ASER%20Reports/ASER%202016/aser2016_nationalpressrelease.pdf/

they interview are employable. Such a bleak view is further highlighted when one reads between the lines of a recent government disclosure before the Lok Sabha on 5 March 2018.[20] The data submitted by the minister of state for labour and employment confirmed the worst fears most educationists harboured—that unemployment is more rampant among the educated. It is as if the education system has made students unemployable (see Table 10); but this could also be because the states in which the students have studied have not cared to create enough jobs. As things stand now, the government's ability to create jobs is abysmal (see Table 12).[21] There is clear evidence of the government's inability to invest in its people (education and healthcare, causing India's Human Capital Index (HCI) to be the worst in the region except for Pakistan which fares more poorly than India. Its inability to foster capital formation (Table 12 gives the falling rates of Gross Fixed Capital Formation) have contributed to the increasing levels of unemployment.

---

[20] Lok Sabha Unstarred Question No 1385 answered on 5 March 2018 by Minister of State (IC) for labour and employment, Santosh Kumar Gangwar.

[21] https://www.moneycontrol.com/news/business/markets/opinion-do-the-stock-markets-care-for-economic-growth-3073061.html

Unfortunately, all the three suggestions made in this book—rooftop solar, methane generation and affordable housing—have not been pursued aggressively by the government. Had that been done, at least employment could have been taken care of, leaving the government with enough time to look into ways in which education could be upgraded. The beauty of all the three options is that they also trigger industrial growth. Today, the government is firefighting the issue of employment, leaving it with little time to focus on education or the economy.

				Table 11
China trounces India				
Literacy rates: UNESCO's top 10 in 2015				
Territory	**Literacy rate (all)**	**Male literacy**	**Female literacy**	**Gender difference**
Armenia	99.80%	99.80%	99.70%	0.10%
Azerbaijan	99.80%	99.90%	99.70%	0.10%
Georgia	99.80%	99.80%	99.70%	0.10%
Kazakhstan	99.80%	99.80%	99.80%	0.00%
Poland	99.80%	99.90%	99.70%	0.20%
Tajikistan	99.80%	99.80%	99.70%	0.10%
Ukraine	99.80%	99.80%	99.70%	0.10%
Belarus	99.70%	99.80%	99.70%	0.10%
Cuba	99.70%	99.70%	99.80%	-0.10%
Russia	99.70%	99.70%	99.70%	0.00%
Slovenia	99.70%	99.70%	99.70%	0.00%
Turkmenistan	99.70%	99.80%	99.60%	0.10%
World average	**86.30%**	**90.00%**	**82.70%**	**7.30%**
India	**72.10%**	**80.90%**	**62.80%**	**18.10%**
China	**96.40%**	**98.20%**	**94.50%**	**3.70%**

Notes: Some countries like USA, Canada, Sweden, Germany and Switzerland have not been included as they were not registered by UNESCO for its 2015 listing. Figures for Guam have been suppressed because it is a protectorate of the US.

Sources: UNESCO, 2015

								Table 12
Two sides of a flagging employment market								
Not many jobs, really				**Falling GFCF is a cause for concern**				
Age group	Employment		Jobs added					
	2016	2017	2017		2014-15	2015-16	2016-17	2017-18
15–24	53.14	45.92	-7.22	GFCF	30.4	29.3	28.5	28.5
25–64	335.01	346.84	11.83	Of which				
>=65	15.33	12.16	-3.18	Government investment	6.7	7.4	n.a.	n.a.
Total	403.48	404.91	1.43	Private investment	23.7	21.9	n.a.	n.a.

Notes:

Table 1: Jobs - million numbers

Table 2: All figures are percentages of GDP

Sources:

Table 1: Consumer Pyramids Household Survey; CMIE; http://indianexpress.com/article/opinion/columns/pm-narendra-modi-india-job-growth-unemployment-rate-economy-demonetisation-bjp-5157708/

Table 2: Economic Survey; CSO; RBI

- If the school education system has collapsed, the state of higher education is no better. If one were to put all graduates—arts, science, commerce, engineering, medicine, etc.—into one basket, the total pool of graduates would not be more than 3.38 per cent of the population. What is frightening is that half of these graduates are not employable. Thus the country has been able to chug along with only 1.9 per cent of its (employable graduate) population (see Table 13).

- Perhaps the biggest setback to school education was the brazen attempt by the former education minister to permit automatic promotions in schools[22] in the hope that this would increase enrolment numbers at the secondary level overnight. This would have allowed the government to crow about its achievements in the field of education and in meeting the targets set out in the Millennium Development Goals (MDGs). As a result, many school children stopped studying because they knew that the no-detention policy would not hold them back. The poor quality of students in higher classes left good students even more disenchanted. Add to this the poor salaries of schoolteachers and a teacher recruitment policy that favours reservations for special groups irrespective of competence. All these have contributed to the worsening of standards (and numbers) of school education. Thus when India tries to compare itself with China, it is important to note that China focuses on quality education.[23] India's approach is more quantitative, rather than outcome oriented (see tables 11 and 13).

[22] http://www.asiaconverge.com/2010/05/sibals-kiss-of-death/

[23] http://www.asiaconverge.com/2016/04/lessons-education-china-india/

Table 13

Seven decades of messed-up education

Education: Estimated population by age group: 2013 & 14

Age Group	2013	2014	Corresponding Level of Education	Drop in enrolment at each successive stage	
				2013	2014
6–10 Years	130,896	130,648	Primary – Std (1–V)	100.00	100.00
11–13 Years	75,223	74,413	Upper Primary – Std (VI–VIII)	57.47	56.96
6–13 Years	206,119	205,061	Elementary Education – Std (I–VIII)	N.A.	N.A.
14–15 Years	50,244	49,801	Secondary – Std (IX–X)	38.38	38.12
6–15 Years	256,363	254,862	I–X	N.A.	N.A.
16–17 Years	45,085	44,734	Sr Secondary – Std (XI–XII)	34.44	34.24
6–17 Years	301,448	299,596	Education upto Std XII level – Std I–XII	N.A.	N.A.
18–23 Years	140,802	141,046	Higher Education	107.57	107.96

Graduates: barbarians at the gate

	Persons (in cr)	Percentage of total population
Literate without educational level	2.0	1.95%
Below Primary	14.5	14.08%
Primary	14.7	14.26%
Middle	9.0	8.77%
Matric/Secondary	7.9	7.70%
HSC, diplomas, etc.	4.2	4.08%
All Graduates and above (medicine, engg, arts, science, commerce and others)	3.8	3.66%
Literate Population	56.1	54.50%
Total Population	102.9	100%

Data Source (Table 1): Ministry of Human Resource Development, Government of India (website: http://mhrd.gov.in/statist), http://mhrd.gov.in/statist/field_statistics_category_tid=30

Data Source (Table 2): http://www.censusindia.gov.in/Census_Data_2001/Census_data_finder/C_Series/Literates_and_educational_level.htm. Corresponding figures not available in Census 2011

- What compounds the issue is that the government's spending on education has declined as a percentage of GDP (see Table 14). It has been unable or unwilling to introduce an outcome-based grant of funds to schools. And the inclination on the part of the government to mix religion, ideology and linguistic chauvinism with education has diverted attention from the quality of school education being imparted to what is ideologically correct for schools.

Table 14		
India ignores education		
Money spent on education by both central and state governments		
Year	Rs Lakh Crore	% of GDP
2011-2012	2.77	3.2
2012-2013	3.13	3.1
2013-2014	3.48	3.1
2014-2015	3.54	2.8
2015-2016	3.31	2.4
2016-2017	3.95	2.6
2017-2018	4.41	2.7
Sources: Economic Surveys of 2016–2017 and 2017–2018; Vivek Kaul's column at equitymaster.com		

There is another worrisome outcome of poor education and literacy levels. Look at Table 15. Study the figures relating to the skewed gender ratios in India. It is states with low literacy levels (even after adopting the government's own flawed yardstick) that sport the worst gender ratios. These are the states that want to bring in the most regressive diktats (khap diktats). These are also the states that have been the least tolerant and the most vicious about cattle slaughter and barbaric vigilantism. The illiberalism and the intolerance that afflicts the nation come from such quarters.

What is also unfortunate is that sagacious advice that could have come from community leaders has all but disappeared, at least for the majority (Hindu) community. This is the community that ought to have laid down the standards for public discourse and culture. One key reason is that the purse strings of the biggest temple trusts have been nationalized (through the backdoor) by central and state governments. Even the Supreme Court's ruling in favour of temple trusts and against political interference has been ignored.[24]

	Literate Population	Literacy rate (%)	Sex ratio (females per 1,000 males)					
			Total population		Child population (age group 0–6)		Population aged 7 & above	
			2001	2011	2001	2011	2001	2011
INDIA	778,454,120	74.04	933	940	927	914	934	944
Jammu & Kashmir	7,245,053	68.74	892	883	941	859	884	887
Himachal Pradesh	5,104,506	83.78	968	974	896	906	980	983
Punjab	18,988,611	76.68	876	893	798	846	888	899
Chandigarh	809,653	86.43	777	818	845	867	767	812
Uttarakhand	6,997,433	79.63	962	963	908	886	973	975
Haryana	16,904,324	76.64	861	877	819	830	869	885
NCT of Delhi	12,763,352	86.34	821	866	868	866	813	866
Rajasthan	38,970,500	67.06	921	926	909	883	923	935
Uttar Pradesh	118,423,805	69.72	898	908	916	899	894	910
Bihar	54,390,254	63.82	919	916	942	933	914	912
Chhattisgarh	15,598,314	71.04	989	991	975	964	992	995
Madhya Pradesh	43,827,193	70.63	919	930	932	912	916	933

Table 15

Disturbing trends in the Indian northern belt

Notes: Most of the states that have a skewed gender ratio are also states that have the lowest literacy levels. Is there a connection?

Sources: Census, 2011

The concept that religion and politics should be kept away from each other has been forgotten. Politicians have learnt how to create religious leaders who suit their political inclinations. With no financial powers, heads of religious Hindu trusts have watched their authority being whittled down over the years. In the resultant vacuum, new god-men emerge (invariably with a wink and a nod from politicians)

---

[24] http://www.asiaconverge.com/2017/09/should-governments-be-promoting-religion/

and with enough (unaudited) funds to use media to broadcast their limited (sometimes bigoted) vision.[25]

The scenario is thus set for the lumpenization of the majority community, which in turn compels other minorities to degrade themselves as well. It is a sad downward spiral that needs to be stopped if education is to be made meaningful and human capital is to flourish. It is heartening to note that in spite of such lumpenization, at least two communities—the Sikhs and the Parsees—have ensured that not even one of their kinsmen turns to begging on the streets. They—along with some Christian mission schools and those run by sagacious trusts like the Aga Khan Trust the Ramakrishna Mission and Indian corporates—have managed to nurture value systems and educational standards.

Compounding all this is the government's willingness to turn a blind eye to education outcomes at the school level. All these pressures have begun fragmenting Indian society like never before.

If this situation does not improve, India's rankings in the world can be expected to slip. Over the past two decades the number of Indian universities among the world's top hundred has been steadily falling. That alone should set alarm bells ringing. It is unfortunate that few have heeded these indicators seriously.

Already there are reports of Thailand snatching away business from India.[26] Table 8 given above on 'Countries

---

[25] http://www.asiaconverge.com/2017/09/gurmeet-ram-rahim-singh-convicted-rape-haryana-government-protecting-dera-chief-secure-vote-bank/
http://www.asiaconverge.com/2017/09/entrepreneur-godmen-flourish-as-hindu-temple-trusts-nationalised/

[26] http://www.asiaconverge.com/2018/04/india-losing-business-opportunities-thailand-faster-thinks/

and their DNA' shows how Bangladesh is quietly marching close to India in terms of per capita income and per capita PPP (price purchase parity), notwithstanding its extremely high population density. Sri Lanka, which boasts of a better educational system, has already stolen a march over India on these fronts. If India does not get its focus on education right, it could see itself losing out on other fronts. Incidentally, both these countries rank higher than India on the HCI score.[27]

India's Jugaad

While the picture may look dismal, there is something that has always made Indians find a way out. Indians call it 'jugaad'. This is why while the Chinese can rightfully say that their country has grown because of the government, Indians can triumphantly say that their country has grown in spite of the government.

The ability to circumvent the government and still do wonders has been the hallmark of Indian jugaad.

A few examples might be worth mentioning here.

The Unilever Experiment

During the 1970s, Assam was fighting fiercely against the government's penchant for demographic tinkering (more on this later). The government had allowed migrants from erstwhile East Pakistan (rechristened Bangladesh after the 1971 independence war) to enter the state. Indian politicians began playing the one game they are adept at—promising to protect the migrants and to grant them citizenship if they

---

[27] https://www.moneycontrol.com/news/business/markets/opinion-do-the-stock-markets-care-for-economic-growth-3073061.html

voted en bloc for the ruling dispensation. That did not sit kindly with the Assamese and other northeastern tribes who saw in such moves their marginalization and the erosion of their culture. That resentment snowballed into the Assam Agitation, which lasted for six bloody and violent years.

Every 'foreigner' was at risk. Tea gardens that were owned by Bengalis (also considered foreigners) were attacked. Managers were hunted down and burnt to death. It was during these times that Hindustan Lever (or HLL, now Hindustan Unilever) hit upon a brilliant strategy aimed at protecting its managers, its tea gardens and its reputation.[28]

It decided to invite more and more Assamese into its tea gardens and built houses for them. It knew that if the Assamese themselves lived there, the tea gardens wouldn't be burnt down. HLL then started schools for the children of Assamese families and hired the best of teachers to give them the quality of education that only private schools (for the privileged) offered. The company's officials also set up excellent medical centres where the ailing could get quality healthcare.

HLL's shareholders in the UK were livid. They warned the Indian managers that their job was not to provide education but to do business. The managers in India were persuasive enough to make the British shareholders view these expenses from the Indian point of view.

As HLL's tea gardens and managers were spared the wrath that engulfed the entire northeast, the company also

---

[28] This, as yet undocumented anecdote, is based on a discussion that the author had with Susim Mukul Datta (https://www. bloomberg.com/research/stocks/people/person.asp?personId=78 2642&privcapId=40310931) who was chairman of Hindustan Lever Ltd from 1990 to 1996.

discovered something that they had not anticipated. After a few years had gone by, they found that sales of hygiene and toiletry products had begun climbing quite smartly in the northeast. Within a few years, the profits that came in from this growth in business were far greater than the money that they had spent on schools and healthcare.

India learnt once again—much in the same way as Pai and Kurien had during the previous decades—that there is a lot of money to be made at the bottom of the pyramid. This was almost four decades before C.K. Prahalad would make this the theme of his bestseller management theory titled 'Bottom of the Pyramid'.

Since then, more and more astute managers have opted to focus on school (and even college) education so that their own requirements for future managers and workers will not face any sort of constriction. It is also their way of paying back to society what they have earned from it. And more importantly, companies have begun to realize that more money can be made if the people who purchase their goods begin earning more money themselves. Companies that have been doing this [have seen their market shares grow and their reputations soar.

Jain Jugaad

Another brilliant experiment was set in motion by the late Bhavarlal Jain (founder of Jain Irrigation). Since his company had access to large tracts of land in and around Jalgaon, Jain decided to start a school in that part of Maharashtra.

He had a vision. He knew that some of the brightest children often came from poor families, but disappeared from public gaze because they were denied opportunities. So he started a school that would admit only children of poorer families.

He was aware that the demand for good education would be immense. So he set up a system to identify the talented. His people conducted a quiz (a sort of entrance examination) for children who were around ten years old. The brightest children were admitted to the school, but only if they could prove that they were from lower middle class or poor families. The management provided the uniforms (even shoes and socks) and the books. The child had to pay a nominal fee (of around Rs 10 a month).[29] The school building itself was an engineering marvel; it used Indian techniques of cross-ventilation so that the temperature inside the classrooms even at the height of summer was at least 5 to 10 degrees lower than the scorching heat outside.

Predictably, bright children invariably do well. Within a few years, students of this school were winning prizes at state-level contests. As the number of awards grew, so did the demand for admission to this school by children of rich families as well. Jain allowed 10 per cent of the enrolments to comprise students from richer families, charging them higher fees to cross-subsidize the almost-free education provided to poorer children. Then, as the clamour from the rich grew, the quota was increased to 20 per cent and then 30 per cent. Today, more than half the children in the school are from rich families. Nevertheless the quality of education imparted reckons with the best in the region.

What Jain showed was that India lacked a system for identifying the brightest of children. The only such nationwide filter that exists in India is one that kicks in too late—the Joint

---

[29] This is in keeping with a belief among mercantile communities in India that unless a person puts his own skin in the game, the value of a scholarship is often forgotten. What is available for free is often underrated.

Entrance Examination (JEE) for admission to prestigious engineering colleges like the IITs. In fact, India has a lot to learn from the system of filtering talent practised by some of the most progressive of countries, notably Singapore and Israel. The brightest children are groomed for government or defence services, which in turn improves the quality of planning and governance.

If India had the right filters in place to assess children when they reached the age of ten, it could harness and develop the talents of hundreds of thousands of children. But the absence of such a filter, the inability (or unwillingness) of the government to upgrade educational standards of schools, and the corroded state of the entire education architecture have left most of India's children blighted. If they get access to the (substandard) education available, they become unemployable. If they are not educated, they fail to climb the value chain.

Other Instances

One group that has been engaged in human resource development is the Adani group. It has set up schools for children of families who earn less than Rs 6000 a month.

In order to ensure that families do not lie about their incomes, Adani's social connect teams go out and verify the details personally. Today the group has such schools in Ahmedabad, Bhadreshwar (both in Gujarat) and in Sarguja (Chhattisgarh). Collectively, the group educates around two thousand children a year. But even these efforts are too small to meet the huge needs of a country as large as India.

Another example that deserves mention is that of Nanubhai Amin of Jyoti Ltd and his brother Ramanbhai Amin of Alembic. Between both brothers, the family runs several schools, including Tejas Vidyalaya, Alembic Vidyalaya and Navrachna Vidyalaya, among others. All these schools boast academic excellence and admission to them is coveted by the residents of Vadodara. The teachers are well paid, and the students pay high fees. Recognizing that the poorer segments of society also have a right to good education, the management decided to use the existing school buildings and infrastructure to conduct evening classes. Students from poorer communities are admitted to these classes and pay very low, or no, fees. Special teachers are appointed, and the system has become one of the best examples of how a richer set of students can help subsidize education for poorer communities. The quality of education provided in the evening sessions is excellent. India needs many more such schools.

Then there are other schools for the wealthy and privileged that have been started by almost all business groups— Ambanis, Puries, Rais, Munjals and the Mittals, to name just a few. The older business groups like the Tatas and the Birlas have also contributed immensely to the cause of education and continue to do so.

Eventually, the rich and the well-connected can always find ways to groom their children. They can afford private tutors and the high fees that many good schools charge. However, more investments are required to promote schools that provide quality education for the poor.

Government as Spoiler

Unfortunately, all through the years since independence, successive governments have frowned on private investments in the school sector. Thus, the number of schools imparting quality education is extremely small, and the percentage of such schools keeps declining. Many of these schools are often run by Christian missionary sects or groups such as the Ramakrishna Mission or the Swaminarayan trusts.

The government's facile argument is that since education is a state subject, it is for state governments to decide whether private investment should be allowed into primary and secondary education, but the justification does not wash.

The fact is that while education is a state subject, the right to grant tax exemptions and fiscal incentives lies with the Centre. If the government had the vision, and the willingness, it could craft policies that would encourage private investment in the schooling sector. It could also lay down norms for evaluating the eligibility of educational institution managements for tax waivers and/or financial grants. It could also make provisions for the takeover of schools that are not run properly and their transfer to managements that have shown excellence in imparting education. The possibilities are immense. What is needed is commitment and vision. The country has witnessed little of either when it comes to school education.

In the beginning of 2018, the government finally declared that it would allow private managements, under trusts or corporates, to open schools. But the guidelines are missing as are the incentives for opening such schools.

What is also needed is a list of disincentives in order to ensure that substandard education—or needless profiteering— is stopped immediately. The issue of needless profiteering, however, becomes quite attractive when there is a shortage. When the government introduces a licensing system to permit very few schools, a black market is bound to emerge, in one form or another. The malaise continues even at higher levels of education. While private investment in higher education is permitted, there is no system to evaluate outcomes. And crucial educational centres—such as those for medical education—remain under the licensing system. The shortage of seats in medical colleges suits private investors (invariably those connected with politicians) as they can demand huge donations for admission. These donations (also referred to as capitation fees) can be over Rs 1 crore per seat.

Compare this with the cost of medical education in China, where the fee for a five-year course, along with accommodation, in a world-class medical college that imparts teaching in English, is not more than Rs 15 lakh for all five years.

The high cost of (often substandard) private medical education results in high patient fees being charged often for sub-standard treatment and provision of poor equipment at hospitals. The government spends little on healthcare. Most patients pay for medicare out of their pockets. Thus the common man is deprived of decent healthcare. It takes only one major ailment to almost bankrupt a middle-class family (see Table 16).

The answer should be to allow more medical colleges to come up[30] and thus improve the ratio of doctors to population. Today, India has just 0.5 doctors for 100 persons, almost one-third the level that China has (see Table 17).

Sadly, the government's immediate reaction has been to offer bridge courses to convert practitioners of traditional medicine (ayurveds and unanis) and homeopathy into allopathic doctors. The counter suggestion should be why does the government not create a short-term course to convert court clerks into judges, or government clerks into IAS officers? That is a question India's policymakers do not like.

The suspicion is that politicians who run ayurveda and homeopathy colleges want to begin charging capitation fees. Allowing a homeopath or an ayurved to become a

---

[30] http://www.asiaconverge.com/2018/02/budget-2018-and-healthcare/

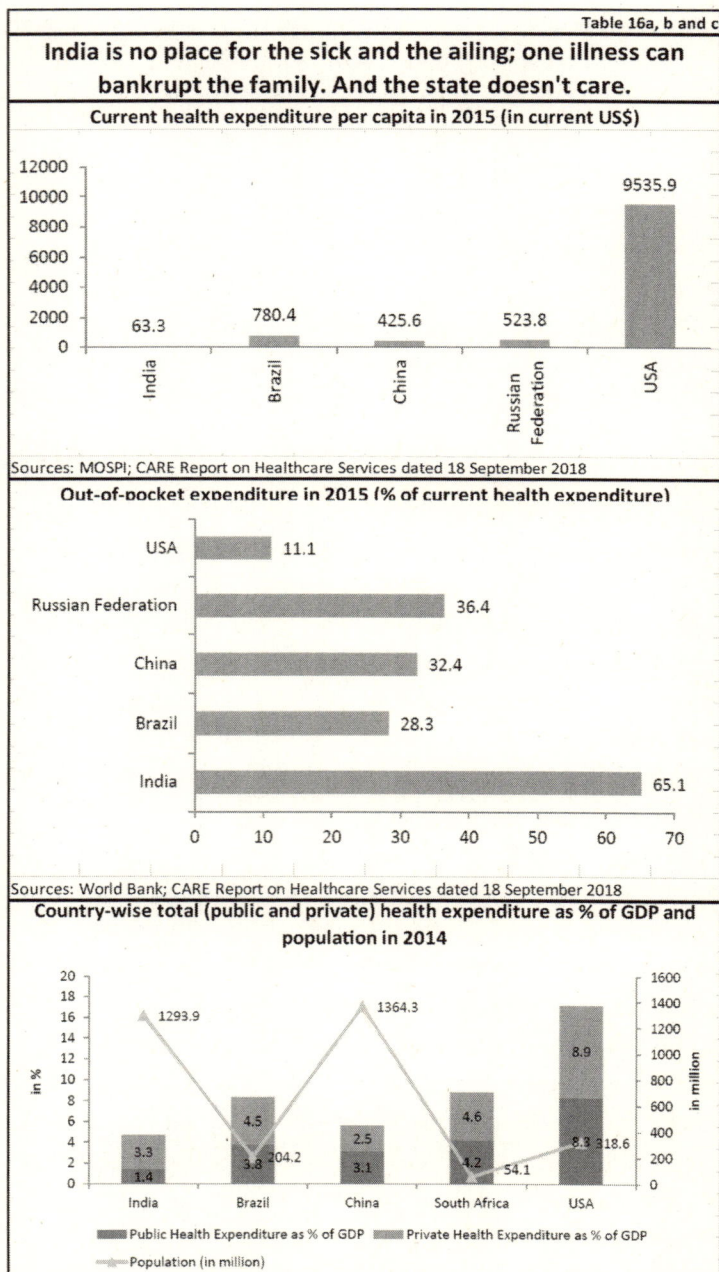

India is no place for the sick and the ailing; one illness can bankrupt the family. And the state doesn't care.

Current health expenditure per capita in 2015 (in current US$)

India	63.3
Brazil	780.4
China	425.6
Russian Federation	523.8
USA	9535.9

Sources: MOSPI; CARE Report on Healthcare Services dated 18 September 2018

Out-of-pocket expenditure in 2015 (% of current health expenditure)

USA	11.1
Russian Federation	36.4
China	32.4
Brazil	28.3
India	65.1

Sources: World Bank; CARE Report on Healthcare Services dated 18 September 2018

Country-wise total (public and private) health expenditure as % of GDP and population in 2014

Country	Public Health Expenditure as % of GDP	Private Health Expenditure as % of GDP	Population (in million)
India	1.4	3.3	1293.9
Brazil	3.8	4.5	204.2
China	3.1	2.5	1364.3
South Africa	4.2	4.6	54.1
USA	8.3	8.9	318.6

Public Health Expenditure as % of GDP   Private Health Expenditure as % of GDP
Population (in million)

Sources: World Bank; CARE Report on Healthcare Services dated 18 September 2018

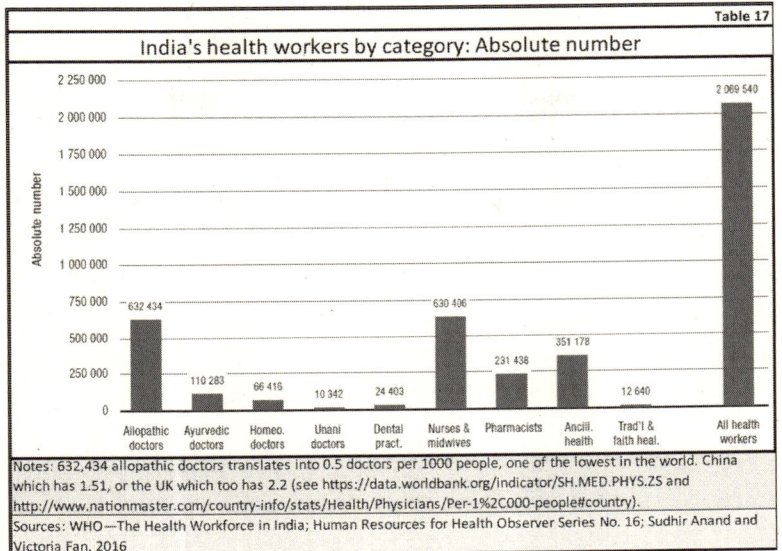

Table 17

India's health workers by category: Absolute number

Notes: 632,434 allopathic doctors translates into 0.5 doctors per 1000 people, one of the lowest in the world. China which has 1.51, or the UK which too has 2.2 (see https://data.worldbank.org/indicator/SH.MED.PHYS.ZS and http://www.nationmaster.com/country-info/stats/Health/Physicians/Per-1%2C000-people#country).
Sources: WHO—The Health Workforce in India; Human Resources for Health Observer Series No. 16; Sudhir Anand and Victoria Fan, 2016

full-fledged medical practitioner would enable the newly certified doctors, the promoters of ayurveda and traditional medicine colleges, and the politicians to make that much more money.

Possibly, in order to deflect responsibility—the Medical Council of India or MCI filed a petition before the Supreme Court against such a decision—the government passed on the buck—for holding bridge courses to enable non-allopaths to become allopath doctors—once again to state governments. Maharashtra—where politicians have a big say in the running of private medical and engineering colleges—is the first to allow homeopaths and ayurveds to become allopaths after completing a bridge course. This move has been challenged by medical associations and the matter is before the courts.

The reason given by government spokespersons is that such measures are needed to cope with the shortage of qualified doctors in rural areas. The reasoning is specious.

If rural sectors are to be covered by medical staff, all one has to do is to issue a temporary order that each medical student has to spend six to eight weeks in a rural posting. True, the student will not know much. But he or she is part of a system where a health problem can be escalated to senior students, or to the professors, and a solution can be found. This would be a short-term measure, because, hopefully, more medical colleges will come up and produce more doctors to improve the ratio of doctors to people.

Devaluing educational standards through bridge courses is an age-old trick politicians have used to degrade education and stunt the tremendous potential of India's manpower. The need of the hour is to immediately end the licence raj for opening medical colleges.[31]

When Grace Becomes a Disgrace

Degrading the educational standards of schools, colleges and institutions of higher learning is something that the government has been adept at. Consider some instances:

1. In any board examination, a teacher evaluates the performance of a student by reviewing the answers the student writes out. The grades awarded are then sent to the local moderator, who decides whether the teacher has been too strict or too lenient. Usually, the moderator will decide on giving grace marks to students who have not performed well. To avoid the charge of bias, the trick is to upgrade (for instance) students who have scored thirty

---

[31] http://www.moneycontrol.com/news/india/budget-2018-focus-on-healthcare-is-good-but-dont-degrade-the-quality-2497317.html

to thirty-five marks. The local moderator's results are passed on to the district moderator, who then applies a similar 'normalization' process, and adds some more grace marks to prop up the number of passing candidates. This is repeated again at the state moderators' meeting. Cumulatively, and quite often, as many as fifteen to twenty grace marks are given to a student. Thus, a student scoring just fifteen to twenty marks is pushed up to pass an examination.

2. Sometimes, state boards try to be clever. One way is to sneak an incorrect question, with incorrect multiple choice options, into the question paper. When there is an outcry, the state magnanimously decides to give five grace marks to anyone who attempted that question. The right way would be to re-compute the marks out of ninety-five and then convert the residual marks out of hundred. The tendency to give grace marks to push up numbers is an age-old practice.

3. Giving marks for physical education, social work, domicile, or some other specious non-academic reason is another method used to prop up poor academic scores.

4. Another way is to say that students are traumatized by the difficult syllabus. The syllabus is made easier, as are the questions.

5. Yet another way is to create rules that allow substandard students to get into highly coveted professional courses like medicine.[32] Media reports on 15 April 2018 highlighted how you can get admission into a medical

---

[32] https://timesofindia.indiatimes.com/india/for-an-mbbs-seat-you-need-just-5-in-physics-20-in-biology/articleshow/63766630.cms

college with just 5 per cent marks in physics and 20 per cent in biology.

The Way Out

Eventually, the solution lies in pushing the government out of evaluation and normalization of results. The other way is to break up the licence raj that still afflicts education, both primary and professional.

The government should link grants and incentives only to outcomes. Clearly, there are other pressures at work, which are powerful enough to jettison even national interests.

Fortunately for India, technology has helped galvanize literacy rates. The mobile phone has enabled input suppliers (fertilizer, nutrients and agrochemicals) to send text messages to farmers on when to plant seeds, when to apply fertilizers or pesticides and when to begin cropping. The farmers' need to read such communication is rapidly transforming literacy levels.

Animal husbandry-related agencies do the same. The milk cooperatives associated with Amul, the largest agricultural brand in Asia, send out SMS messages to farmers telling them when their calves need to be vaccinated, when they are ready for artificial insemination, and when they should be allowed to go dry to prepare them for the next round of insemination. Illiterate farmers receive help from their relatively more literate neighbours until need compels them to learn to read. Consequently, adult literacy has soared, in spite of the government. Mobile aids to education have also helped bolster literacy levels among children. With a little bit of organization and support, such technologies could galvanize a lost generation of children to become more productive.

Consumers Can Still Triumph

There is another blessing that India enjoys because of its large population. In spite of the myopia within the government, the fact remains that people are eventually consumers as well.

The faster they climb the economic ladder, the more they will consume. That is why while smaller countries like Singapore, Korea and Vietnam opted to become economic tigers based on an export model, India can survive and even thrive by exploiting its domestic market. But to do that it must create employability.

The best of India has learnt how to grow in spite of the government. But there is a danger. When islands of excellence are created and the crowds outside resemble barbarians at the gate, there is no telling what the outcome will be. Remember Iran?

Good students from affluent families eventually become managers. Poor children, from economically backward families that could not gain access to good education, end up at lower levels in the corporate hierarchy. This leads to perpetuating the class divide. Education was meant to be the best leveller any society could have wished for. Instead, the government has turned it into a means for promoting inequality.

India's legislators must allow quality to flourish at the school level—for students, teachers and administrators. And they need to ensure that students coming out of schools find jobs quickly, else they will flood colleges even though they do not have an aptitude for higher learning. The government fails to realize that poor quality students entering colleges will only corrode college educational facilities.

Will India be able to do all this? Will India be able to nurture its biggest asset: its teeming millions?

That is a question most India-watchers will be asking themselves for the next decade. It is rise or write-off for India?

FOUR

India's Waters of Life and Livelihood

A retired admiral of the Indian Navy once, quite aptly, described people in the government as being afflicted with sea-blindness.

Behind the caustic remark, there was an understatement. Most people in Delhi did not understand the sea and what it could mean to the people of India. This is because Delhi is landlocked, and somehow a lot of politics in India has been influenced by 'northerners' who also come from landlocked regions. Except for two leaders—Sardar Vallabhbhai Patel and Morarjee Desai (and more recently Narendra Modi)—most post-Independence leaders were from landlocked regions. They were unaware of and oblivious to the tremendous advantages India had because of its 7500-km-long coastline. This benefit alone could push up India's GDP by 1 to 2 per cent year after year, improve its coastal security and create employment for countless millions.[1]

---

[1] http://www.firstpost.com/business/find-out-how-indias-vastly-unexplored-7500-km-coastline-can-generate-millions-of-jobs-3170668.html
http://www.asiaconverge.com/2016/12/coastline-and-waterways-mean-jobs/

Hands off the Seas

For some reason, India's coastline was treated with benign neglect for almost seven decades. Yes, it was used by ships. And yes, India did have a cabotage law in place that reserved coastal shipping rights for vessels sailing under the Indian flag.[2] But it does not have the appropriate laws in place to make the seas vibrant with movement and commerce.

Consequently, India has laws for ships that travel from port to port and from country to country. It has laws for fishing boats and how they should operate. But it has no laws for all those who fall in between and wish to travel from point A to, say, a picnic spot at point B and then to meet a friend at point C and then return to home base. India does not allow this, as yet. But the good news is that moves are being made to rectify this regulatory setup.

True, India does have a navy that makes use of and protects the seas. But the navy has gradually usurped rights over almost everything that sails along India's coast. Citing grounds of security, the navy vehemently objects to the construction of marinas and leisure jetties, or short trips by luxury boats and holidaymakers.

That is why India lost out on the development of coast-based holiday resorts and marinas. The only ones that survived were those that had access by land. Somehow, India's planners forgot, until recently, to pull up the navy and ask its officers to explain how countries like the UK, Sweden, Holland and Hong Kong managed to earn a huge amount of revenue from

---

[2]   This is now in danger of being diluted or even scrapped. Indian shipowners are up in arms against such moves. Shipping Corporation may even have to down shutters. See https://www.moneycontrol.com/news/business/how-great-eastern-and-shipping-corp-stayed-afloat-amid-global-challenges-3130771.html

their limited coastal areas, without stepping on the toes of their respective defence concerns. The UK, for instance, has one of the largest maritime defence fleets in the world. But just travel to places like Portsmouth or Glasgow and you will discover hundreds of leisure boats bobbing up and down on the waters. What the navy does is to post sentries on the naval vessels with megaphones, warning any boat to stay away in case they come within a fixed prescribed distance. Moreover, unknown to most people, there are scores of engineers below the decks of naval vessels scanning the waters for any intruders that seek to approach these vessels from below the surface of the waters.

'Activity,' admitted one naval officer in the UK, 'keeps us alert. The absence of activity would make even our sentries drowsy and careless.'

That lesson was lost on India's planners. There was the myopia of the navy on the one hand, and the sea-blindness of politicians on the other.

But there was an even more discomforting pressure at work.

Self-styled vigilantes invariably find the space to shout down others when it comes to opening a marina or a casino. It does not matter that many car drivers gamble away their earnings every day in the ubiquitous car parks that dot each city. It does not matter that, discreetly, almost every city has gambling joints and prostitution dens that flourish under the collusively benevolent and protective gaze of the police. But anything that seeks to express itself legitimately is suddenly confronted by vigilante moral crusaders. The hypocrisy is nauseating.

The present government hopes to change some of that at least in terms of legally permitting marinas and coastal shipping. What it does not want to clamp down on as yet is the role of vigilantes.

Coastal laws are being modified, and marinas are being built. Cruise ships are being encouraged, and the cabotage laws that do not allow foreign flags to operate on India's shores are being modified for cruise boats and ro-ro boats (roll-on/roll-off boats on which vehicles can be driven on and off).

Moreover, world-class training centres are being opened[3] for skilling people required for maritime and shipbuilding related activities. One such institute is the Center of Excellence in Maritime and Shipbuilding, or CEMS. Such a facility would serve two purposes. First, it would provide skilled manpower for the shipbuilding and maritime sectors. Second, it would boost the ministry's efforts to wean the country away from road transport and focus more on water-based transport, either along the coast or through inland waterways. CEMS is being developed in partnership with Lloyds Register of Shipping (a rare case of the government allowing a foreign body to become a partner in the field of education), which will handhold the institute till it is ready to be taken over by the Indian Register of Shipping.[4]

Sea Blindness

But for these recent developments, whenever it came to India's waterways in the past, everyone turned a blind eye and allowed the ban on maritime activities to continue for seven decades.

---

[3] http://www.freepressjournal.in/analysis/setting-up-of-a-world-class-centre-of-excellence-in-maritime-and-ship-building/1190624
http://www.asiaconverge.com/2017/12/cems-a-world-class-centre-of-excellence-in-maritime-and-shipping/

[4] However, even the CEMS has run into rough weather. Bureaucracy has not allowed it to appoint the people it needs even after a year of coming into existence.

There could be a cultural explanation for this. For thousands of years, the majority Hindu community has been distrustful of the seas. It was considered inauspicious to cross the oceans. Hence if a Hindu did go across the oceans—as did many of India's leaders who went to study in the UK[5] during British rule—he was forced by his community leaders to undergo a purification ceremony (shuddhikaran) on his return to India.

The seas were fearsome, even forbidden. If one studies Hindu mythology, Lord Ram desisted from crossing the ocean to travel to Sri Lanka and rescue his kidnapped wife Sita. He could have taken a boat. He instead chose to pray to the sea gods, and finally on their advice ordered his (monkey) army to build a bridge connecting the southernmost tip of India to the closest northern tip of what is today known as Sri Lanka.

This cultural distrust of the seas could also explain why India did not have a navy for centuries. Yes, there were seafarers—several non-Hindu communities engaged in trade with the eastern coast of Africa and the southeastern territories that are today known as Indonesia, Malaysia, Myanmar, Thailand and Singapore. But except for a solitary incident of a southern Hindu king sending his army across in boats to help a kindred king on the islands of Indonesia, there is no mention of any navy.

India began learning about the relevance of the navy only when the Portuguese, French and, most importantly, the British landed in India. But, almost always, the traders and the seafarers were from non-Hindu tribes and communities. Gradually, as fishing communities were embraced into Hinduism, some of the

---

[5] Among the leaders who went overseas and had to be 'purified' on their return were Lokmanya Tilak and M.G. Ranade. But some like Gopal Krishna Gokhale refused to observe this ritual.

seafarers were Hindus as well. One of them was Kanhoji Angre (1669–1729), who became the first notable chief of the Maratha Navy.[6] He fought against British, Dutch and Portuguese naval interests along the coast of India during the eighteenth century. The British called him a pirate.

Post independence, India began building its own navy. Countries like China, Korea, Japan and Hong Kong had their own navies much before India had even dreamt of one. Not surprisingly, they are maritime forces and ship and boat builders to be reckoned with. India, in comparison, is a recent entrant to the maritime business.

Commerce Ignored

India's planners overlooked the obvious. The country had a 7500-km-long coastline, which could be considered a gift from god. The coastal waters represent a forty-lane highway that the country does not have to construct, or even maintain. That is a huge economic advantage India has overlooked.

It also overlooked the fact that of all modes of transport, water transport is by far the cheapest. While actual costs differ from region to region (see Table 1) and from ocean to sea to river, a broad rule of thumb in India is as follows:

If it costs Rs 1 to transport 1 ton of cargo per kilometre (referred to as per ton kilometre) across oceans, it would cost Rs 3–4 to transport it along India's coastline and along its rivers (inland water transport). It would cost Rs 6–8 to move that cargo on railway lines, and could cost as much as Rs 12 when transported by trucks over land.

---

[6] https://en.wikipedia.org/wiki/Kanhoji_Angre

		Table 1	
Comparison between IWT, Rail and Road			
Parameters	**IWT**	**Rail**	**Road**
Energy efficiency—1 HP can move what weight (kg) of cargo	4000	500	150
Fuel efficiency—1 litre of fuel can move how much freight (tonnes/km)	105	85	24
Intermodal comparative operating costs (Rs/tonne/km)*	1.06	1.41	2.58
Equivalent single unit carrying capacity	1 barge	15 rail wagons	60 trucks
Air pollution	Low	Medium	High
Land acquisition	Low	High	High
Capital required	Low	High	High
Notes: *= inclusive of taxes; HP = horsepower; IWT—Inland Water Transport			
Sources: IWAI, KPMG in India analysis			

	Table 2
Modal share in India	
Sector	**% share**
Road	50.1
Railways	36
Pipeline	7.5
Coastal Shipping	6
Inland Water Transport	0.4
Total	100
Sources: Inland Waterways Authority of India	

Yet, oblivious to these obvious and well-known economic advantages, India opted to focus on the most expensive mode of transport with consequent costs of imported fuel (see Table 2). This ignorance also caused the inescapable collateral damage to human health thanks to pollution. An inefficient transportation system contributed enormously to respiratory ailments and bloated India's oil import bills.

Political Bias?

Some experts allege that there could have been a third, political and commercial, reason that made India ignore water transport. When the British colonized India, they brought in the railways as a means of transporting raw material out of the country and sending finished goods deep into the hinterland. And they saw water transport as a threat to rail transport. Hence, through a series of taxes, licences and diktats, they sought to discourage the use of river transport and focus instead on rail and road transport.

As a result, many of the most prominent Indian cities that were along the banks of rivers began to lose their importance to cities that were next to landlocked railway hubs. Landlocked cities grew in stature, except where seaports and railway terminuses enjoyed a synergy with the commercial interests of the British. Bombay and Calcutta were beneficiaries of this largesse.

Thus, tradition, politics and colonization all combined to make people ignore the waters, which thanks to disuse became putrid and even more unusable over the decades.

It was time for India to shake off these burdens of the past and begin looking at the entire India picture with a new perspective and vision.

Enter Adani

Perhaps no other Indian brought the ports business into focus as Gautam Adani did.[7] True, there were other entrepreneurs

---

[7] http://www.asiaconverge.com/2018/04/gautam-adani-man-change-india/. The article was published in *Log-in*, a DVV Media

who built ports. And there was the central government, which had invested in what are known as major ports in India. But Adani was different. He was an entrepreneur who saw immense economic advantage in ports.

In some ways, he began doing what David Sassoon had done more than two centuries earlier.

David Sassoon (1792–1864) built Sassoon Docks in Mumbai to take care of his

David Sassoon's bust in Bhau Daji Museum, Mumbai

cotton, textile and opium trade.[8] He was a Baghdadi Jew who came to Bombay to escape the anti-Semitic forces that had begun raising their heads in the Middle East. When he arrived in Bombay to trade in textiles from Britain (he had carried on this trade in Baghdad as well), he was seen as an unwelcome competitor by the Gujaratis and Parsees who used what are now Princess Docks and Ballard Pier for their trade. They would not give Sassoon timely berthing space at these docks. So he did the next best thing. He built his own docks. So good

group (https://www.dvvmedia.com/) publication. But the article does not exist online on the DVV Media website.

[8] https://en.wikipedia.org/wiki/David_Sassoon
http://theory.tifr.res.in/bombay/persons/david-sassoon.html
http://www.davidsassoonlibrary.com/index.php?action=history
https://www.haaretz.com/jewish/1864-tycoon-david-sassoon-dies-1.5196948
https://en.wikisource.org/wiki/Sassoon,_Albert_Abdullah_David_(DNB00)

were his designs that the British used them as templates for other docks they built. At the peak of his work in India, he had set up seventeen textile mills, which accounted for more than 60 per cent of employment in what was then Bombay. The docks were synergistic with the cotton he exported to the UK and the textiles he imported from there. The docks were useful for the opium trade from where he, and lots of other Indians and British, made huge sums of money. Later, he decided to use some of the cotton to make his own textiles in Mumbai. When he left Mumbai to settle down (and die) in Pune, he dubbed his son Albert the Landlord of Bombay. The biggest contributor of wealth to Mumbai was Sassoon and his port.

Then there were the Chougules in Goa. But they were content with the port they owned and saw no incentive to expand the ports business further, or to do anything extraordinary.

It was Adani who actually taught Indian planners what merchant ports could mean for this country, and what should be done to make them thriving businesses. Today he is the largest port owner in India and continues to acquire and build new ports in India and overseas (more on this later).

Initially, Adani did not plan to get into the ports business. Thanks to a series of accidents, he ended up owning some land and a jetty that would later become the largest private commercial port in the country.

The accidents that propelled him in this direction were many. First, he was born to a family that had trading interests. His family bought and sold raw material for plastics. Second, he worked as a broker for diamond companies immediately after his schooling. He was compelled to give up his college education because he could not fulfil his attendance requirements and do business at the same time. He completed his graduation years later. Being a diamond merchant helped him hone his financial and trading instincts like few other trades. Merchants have to buy diamond roughs in one currency, process them in India and hence have to be familiar with rupee costs as well, and then export them to a third country with a different currency. Exchange rates, processing cycle-time, and inventory management compel diamantaires to think of exchange rates, interest, currency fluctuations and mark-ups far more quickly than demanded by most other trades.

Third, he got into the export-import business, which in turn enabled him to understand how ports worked, including the fact that ports made much of their money through demurrage and space leasing facilities. Loading and unloading operations at the ports made money, but the big profits came from land-based rental and lease activities.

Thanks to his export and import activities, one of the largest commodity players in the world—Cargill—became interested in him. It wanted Adani to source salt from Saurashtra in Gujarat. When the calculations were done and the price of salt was finalized, both parties wanted to settle on a port from where the salt could be evacuated. Mumbai would be too far. The transportation costs would cripple viability. Kandla, the nearest port, would be a bit cumbersome, but possible.

Not satisfied with using Kandla, Cargill asked for some time to explore other options. Its managers met their counterparts across the world and sought advice. Finally, someone who had access to NASA maps suggested that the best location for evacuating the salt would be Mundra, in Gujarat. Mundra was a small village with a jetty that had been used by fishermen for centuries. Even today, you will find, docking at the old Mundhra jetty, dhows that occasionally traverse the Arabian Sea to trade with merchants in the Middle East.

Since foreign companies were not allowed to own ports, but could be joint promoters of such businesses in partnership with Indians, both Adani and Cargill's managers sat down and decided to form a joint venture to build a modern jetty in Mundra at a cost of Rs 100 crore. Both parties would have had a 50:50 share in the new venture's capital.

That was when a turn of events was to change all plans. The country's forex reserves were quite low, and the government decided to allow 100 per cent equity for foreigners ready and willing to invest in state government owned ports. Till then, all big merchant ports had been owned by the central government (and were called major ports). The nearest to Mundra was the Kandla port, a major port.

As soon as Cargill's managers heard about the policy change, they approached Adani for a reduction in his equity share in the company. They suggested that Adani keep just 11 per cent. The offer was rejected. Cargill's managers then tried appealing to the state and central governments to persuade Adani to change his mind. But that didn't work either. Since the contract papers for a 50:50 joint venture had already been signed, there was little that Cargill could do. The global commodity trader finally gave up, and the entire project was taken up by Adani.

By then the state government had introduced a policy for state ports, where the state would be a partner with a 26 per cent stake.

Adani had learnt from his observations that ports make more money when they have more land. He also knew that the best ports in the world were those that catered to the needs of large coast-based industries as well. Could he persuade industries to shift their plant locations to Mundra?

To ensure that they did, he began acquiring land around the proposed port. By 2007, he had officially acquired over

15,665 acres of land (as given in the IPO prospectus), though many believe that the total land held by the group could be several-fold larger.

He then persuaded the state government to sell back its equity holding in the port company, and paid the state two and a half times the price of the shares. Once he was the full owner of this company, Adani did three things that would stun India.

First, he was aware that a port had no value unless it was linked to the hinterland by road and rail. He knew he could persuade the state government to build a road, as it would be in the state's own business interests to connect the port to other manufacturing hubs. But having rail connectivity was a different matter. It was a monopoly of the central government, and the paperwork and bureaucratic lobbying that would be required would consume a lot of time. Moreover, the nearest railhead (Adipur junction in Gujarat) was more than 70 kilometres away. Speed in setting up a railway line was of utmost importance.

So he took a gamble. He began building, at his own cost and risk, his own railway line that covered a distance of 65 kilometres. Then he went to the railway minister (Nitish Kumar) and told him how a railway line connecting the port to the main railway network would be of immense national importance. He suggested that having a policy allowing all ports to link to the railway network would be in the interests of the country, and would benefit all ports. The minister agreed. A port-rail linkage policy was crafted, which allowed ports to link their terminals to the national railway grid. Adani thus helped the government formulate the first national port-rail linkage policy. It allowed port operators to run their own railway line from the terminals to the nearest railhead.

Adani, in order to further hone his operations, began experimenting with the introduction of double decker cargo trains, which could offer huge savings in transportation costs. In fact, once the dedicated freight corridor (DFC) becomes operational, and the Delhi Mumbai Industrial corridor (DMIC) begins to emerge on either side of the DFC,[9] the full impact of the railway line, the new roads linking Vadodara (a key junction point on the DFC) and the port will all come into play.

Second, Adani built his own airstrip—it is more than 2 kilometres long and thus capable of landing any large aircraft. His reasoning was simple. Sooner or later the port would need international connectivity by air as well. It is the only port in India to have its own airstrip. Currently, it is used for landing his private plane and other chartered aircraft. It can be expected to transform into something bigger later. It is possible that Adani will make it an international cargo/passenger terminal, for high value, low volume goods like diamonds, pharmaceutical and precision engineering products.

But that may not be easy. Globally, almost 70 per cent of cargo is carried by passenger jets. The new wide-bodied aircraft allow more cargo to be carried. Cargo costs are thus subsidized by passenger ticket fares. Industry thus loves the lower costs of shipping through passenger jets. But a new plan that could combine both passenger and cargo might be in the offing.

Third, by acquiring huge tracts of land, Adani began wooing businessmen to co-locate their industries close to the port. Over the past decade his efforts, along with those of the state government, have begun to pay rich dividends. Auto

---

[9] http://www.dnaindia.com/business/report-delhi-mumbai-corridor-will-create-new-best-in-class-cities-1510755
http://www.asiaconverge.com/2011/02/dmic-delhi-mumbai-corridor-will-create-new-best-class-cities/

manufacturers like Honda and Maruti-Suzuki have begun building their plants close to the port. Tata Motors already has a plant in Gujarat. More plants are likely to come up in the vicinity soon.

Maruti-Suzuki has also been using Adani's port as its export base, and this could become one of the largest automobile export hubs in the country. Moreover, Adani has got almost all the oil marketing companies to build their storage capacities close to the port so that oil can be easily imported to Mundra and stored there. A pipeline connecting Mundra to other refineries has made the tank farm assume strategic significance.

Both the airstrip and the land will be immensely valuable to Adani as he starts finalizing plans to set up his defence equipment manufacturing companies.

Today Adani has become the largest port owner in the country, with ports in every coastal state except for Karnataka. According to public information available, Adani has the following ports in India:[10]

1. Mundra, TUNA Dahej, Hazira in Gujarat
2. Murmugao and Vizhinjam on the Western coast in Goa and Kerala
3. Ennore, Kattupalli, Vizag and Dhamra on the eastern coast of India
4. Ports overseas in Australia (Dudgeon Point and Abbot Point) and Indonesia (Bunyu)[11]

The ownership of so many ports across the country (in addition to those held overseas) could propel Adani's desire in towards

---

[10] https://www.adaniports.com/ports-and-terminals
[11] https://en.wikipedia.org/wiki/Adani_Ports_%26_SEZ_Limited

becoming one of the biggest coastal shipping companies in India. By combining ports, ships (he already owns a few ships and has several others on charter) and cargo, and backed by enough land for loading and unloading operations, Adani could offer packages that few could match.

Adani's other interests include edible oil (Adani-Wilmar is the largest branded edible oil company in India today), real estate development, agricultural logistics, power generation, transmission and distribution and now gas distribution as well. But it is ports that will give him the edge that few can match. In fact, as data on ports shows, the private sector has already been growing faster than government-owned ports (see Table 3). Adani's contribution in this sector is immense.

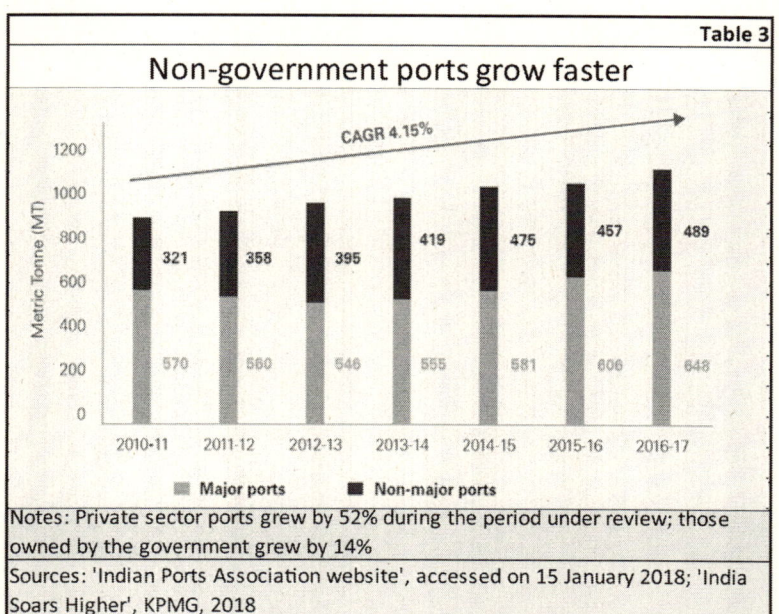

Table 3

Non-government ports grow faster

Year	Major ports	Non-major ports
2010-11	570	321
2011-12	560	358
2012-13	546	395
2013-14	555	419
2014-15	581	475
2015-16	606	457
2016-17	648	489

CAGR 4.15%

Metric Tonne (MT)

Notes: Private sector ports grew by 52% during the period under review; those owned by the government grew by 14%

Sources: 'Indian Ports Association website', accessed on 15 January 2018; 'India Soars Higher', KPMG, 2018

Modi Adds to the Coastal Appeal

Even while Adani was honing his plans for becoming the biggest port owner in the country, Narendra Modi—who was then chief minister of Gujarat—began promoting the concept of coast-based tourism and coastal development.

He first started work on the river Sabarmati that runs through Ahmedabad and managed to make it one of the most attractive riverfronts in western India. He then began promoting the concept of coastal tourism and wanted to make Gujarat's coastline one of the most sought after holiday and business spots.

He was aware that Gujarat had enjoyed the advantage of being a mercantile state for centuries. For over a thousand years, Gujarat has invited traders who have used the jetties and ports that dot its coastline. In fact, of all the states in India, this state has the maximum number of ports and innumerable fishing village jetties. During Modi's tenure as chief minister, almost every port in the state witnessed an expansion in the scale of its operations. Waterfronts were developed, and it was but inevitable that coastal and river development would assume importance when he formed the government at the centre.

Gadkari Unfolds His Plans

Development of ports and waterways was one of the most important portfolios in the government—after finance and home—was given to Nitin Gadkari, who

Playing the role of the moderator at a conference (photo credit, the *Free Press Journal*)

became the new government's Minister for Road Transport
and Highways, Shipping and Water Resources, River
Development and Ganga Rejuvenation.

One of the key decisions Gadkari took was to re-examine
the entire transportation sector. His first focus was on waterways.

As mentioned earlier, India has many rivers that were
allowed to fall into disuse. The biggest question was how
many rivers could be made navigable (see Table 4)? And this
is where ports, inland waterway transport (IWT), roads and
rails began to come together. The plans he chalked out for the
country were breathtaking.[12]

Gadkari structured most of his plans under two heads.
One was Bharatmala[13] which was essentially about the road
network he had planned for India, connecting the country's
villages and towns to cities and to each other. The other was
Sagarmala[14] which was all about the rivers and seas and
making them navigable and to turn them into hubs of thriving
businesses.

First, the government began making plans for a port-led
development programme. It was along the same lines that
Adani had thought of more than a decade earlier. But Adani
owned land, which other ports did not. Therefore, Gadkari
thought of identifying zones that were near ports and declaring
them Coastal Economic Zones or CEZs (see Table 5). Gadkari
too realized that the best model for economic development
would be to co-locate industries near ports so that export and
import became easy. That in turn would ease transportation
on the one hand and reduce inventory holding costs on the

[12] http://www.asiaconverge.com/2016/12/coastline-and-waterways-mean-jobs/

[13] https://en.wikipedia.org/wiki/Bharatmala

[14] https://en.wikipedia.org/wiki/Sagar_Mala_project

Table 4

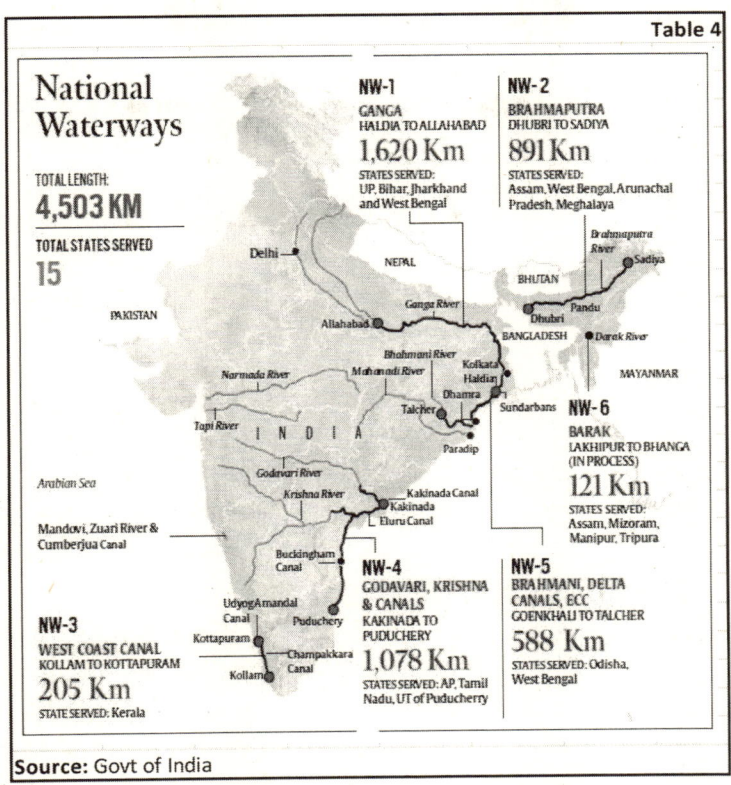

National Waterways

TOTAL LENGTH: **4,503 KM**

TOTAL STATES SERVED **15**

NW-1
GANGA
HALDIA TO ALLAHABAD
1,620 Km
STATES SERVED:
UP, Bihar, Jharkhand
and West Bengal

NW-2
BRAHMAPUTRA
DHUBRI TO SADIYA
891 Km
STATES SERVED:
Assam, West Bengal, Arunachal
Pradesh, Meghalaya

NW-6
BARAK
LAKHIPUR TO BHANGA
(IN PROCESS)
121 Km
STATES SERVED:
Assam, Mizoram,
Manipur, Tripura

NW-4
GODAVARI, KRISHNA
& CANALS
KAKINADA TO
PUDUCHERY
1,078 Km
STATES SERVED: AP, Tamil
Nadu, UT of Puducherry

NW-5
BRAHMANI, DELTA
CANALS, ECC
GOENKHALI TO TALCHER
588 Km
STATES SERVED: Odisha,
West Bengal

NW-3
WEST COAST CANAL
KOLLAM TO KOTTAPURAM
205 Km
STATE SERVED: Kerala

Map labels: Delhi, NEPAL, PAKISTAN, Ganga River, Allahabad, BHUTAN, Brahmaputra River, Sadiya, Pandu, Dhubri, Barak River, BANGLADESH, MAYANMAR, Narmada River, Bhahmani River, Mahanadi River, Kolkata, Haldia, Dhamra, Talcher, Sundarbans, Tapi River, INDIA, Paradip, Godavari River, Krishna River, Kakinada Canal, Kakinada, Eluru Canal, Arabian Sea, Mandovi, Zuari River & Cumberjua Canal, Buckingham Canal, UdyogAmandal Canal, Puduchery, Kottapuram, Champakkara Canal, Kollam

Source: Govt of India

Table 5

CEZ—Proposed locations

Area	State	Area	State
Kutch	Gujarat	Mannar	Kerala
Saurashtra	Gujarat	Poompuhar	Tamil Nadu
Suryapur	Gujarat	VCIC South	Tamil Nadu
North Konkan	Maharashtra	VCIC Central	Andhra Pradesh
South Konkan	Maharashtra	VCIC North	Andhra Pradesh
Dakshin Kanara	Karnataka	Kalinga	Odisha
Malabar	Kerala	Gaud	West Bengal

Source: Ministry of Shipping

other. His office believes that the port-led development exercise will create around 40 lakh jobs, in addition to generation of indirect employment for another 60 lakh people. The timeline for achieving these targets would be within the next three to five years.[15]

But port development will continue for a longer period, and could generate many more jobs. The investment outlay planned for this entire exercise is expected to be in the region of Rs 4 lakh crore (4 trillion). The first phase is expected to be completed by 2020 and the second phase by 2025. Capacity at ports is likely to see a doubling from 1550 million tonnes to around 3000 million tonnes by 2020.

The centerpiece of Gadkari's plans is the development of CEZs. Each CEZ will be attached to one port, either private or government-owned. The government has already identified fourteen CEZs and the process of working on land acquisition has commenced.

Crucial to this programme is community development, without which all the other plans might just crumble. This includes (a) fishery development and (b) skill development. The ministry has conducted studies for twenty-three (of the total of seventy-eight) coastal districts and the remaining studies should be completed by the end of 2018. The study should highlight the specific industries that each coastal district could take up, the investments that may be needed (either by government or by private investors or both), and then a course of action would be put in place for each district.

Almost simultaneously, the government plans to promote coastal tourism along India's coastline and rivers. This includes promoting ocean cruises as well as river cruises. The

---

[15] https://youtu.be/_wTzixAwrt0, a thirty-four-minute interview with Rajive Kumar, secretary, shipping, on the government's plans.

first cruise boat— from Mumbai to Goa—was flagged off in October 2018 and more tourism cruises are being planned. In fact, Mumbai could be the hub of all cruises along the coast of India and even overseas. The figures that have been given out by the ministry are nothing short of breathtaking (see Table 6). During the past three years, in order to ensure that cruise tourists do not face problems with the immigration or customs authorities, several meetings have taken place involving all the four agencies—the ministries of shipping, and of tourism, and key officials from immigration and customs. Most of the contentious issues have been resolved. Digital verification, and e-visas have been introduced along with the provision of a green (domestic) channel for tourists when they are visiting one coastal port to another.

		Table 6
Cruise potential of India and Mumbai			
	Existing (2016)	India's potential (2041)	Mumbai's potential
Number of passengers	200,000	4,000,000	3,200,000
Number of ship calls	166	955	700
Domestic passengers	--	3,000,000	2,400,000
Economic potential (Tax allocated) Rs crore	712	35,500	28,400
Employment potential (No. of jobs)	5,000	250,000	200,000
Source: Mumbai Port Trust			

Development of beaches is also being explored in association with the tourism ministry. In order to give this a big thrust, suitable sections of the existing legal framework relating to cabotage are being modified for specialized vessels like cruise boats, ro-ro boats and ro-pax vessels, which allow passengers to be transported along with vehicles. But cabotage relaxations have already kicked up a storm, because the bureaucracy is rooting for dispensing with all protection of coastal traffic for Indian vessels. Since Indian flag vessels pay GST, income tax on crew salaries (which pushes up employee costs by around 30 per cent) and bunkering which is more expensive than is available overseas for foreign flag vessels, there are fears that such moves could actually hurt Indian shipping terribly.[16]

But the employment potential and that of wealth generation from jetties can be substantial. What people often forget is that jetties and marinas are not just about docking leisure boats. True, they are jetties, but that is only the starting point. Boats need servicing and refuelling. This creates demand for the related infrastructure and skills. With mechanics comes the next stage of boat building. Once the servicing and refuelling aspects of the business are attended to, one realizes that holidaymakers want cafeterias and small hotels as well. That gives rise to new infrastructure and new jobs.

Significantly, Gadkari's vision for development includes the development of waterways.[17] The government has already identified 111 waterways for navigation. Of these, thirty are being taken up for development during the next three years. As many as eight of these are to be developed during 2018 itself. The first five have already been identified (see Table 7), and work along these has commenced. The first container

---

[16] https://www.freepressjournal.in/editorspick/indian-shipping-grows-but-overseas-not-in-india-rn-bhaskar/1382701

[17] http://m.firstpost.com/business/how-a-robust-water-transportation-can-help-india-drastically-cut-its-freight-costs-3116440.html
http://www.asiaconverge.com/2016/11/india-waterways-a-gamechangerrobust-water-transportation-can-help-india-drastically-cut-freight-costs/

			Table 7
National waterways - phase I			
Currently five waterways have been declared as National Waterways (NW) in India			
#	National Waterway	Location	Stretch (km
1	NW1	Ganga-Bhagirathi-Hooghly river system from Allahabad to Haldia	1,620
2	NW2	Brahmaputra river from Sadiya to Dhubri	891
3	NW3	West Coast canal from Kottapuram to Kolam along with Champakara and Udyogmandal canals	205
4	NW4	Godavari and Krishna rivers and canals between Kakinada and Puducherry	1,095
5	NW5	Brahmani river and Mahanadi Delta System along with East Coast Canal	623
Source: Inland Waterways Authority of India			

barge on NW 1 began service in October 2018.[18] It was a container cargo belonging to the food and beverage giant PepsiCo (India). The route was from Kolkata to Varanasi on the river Ganga.

The government is also developing a design for building a 2500-tonne barge that can operate in rivers with a shallow draft of just 2.5 metres (2500 tonnes would be equivalent to an entire freight train).[19] Currently, some of the largest barges on Indian rivers ferry a maximum of 2000 tonnes per barge.

---

[18] https://economictimes.indiatimes.com/industry/transportation/shipping-/-transport/indias-first-container-movement-on-inland-waterways-with-pepsico-on-board/articleshow/66413077.cms

[19] https://youtu.be/_wTzixAwrt0, a thirty-four-minute interview with Rajive Kumar, secretary, shipping, on the government's plans.

More barges would mean more cargo being transported along the rivers. Given the lower costs of river transport, this will help reduce logistics costs for companies located near such waterways. That in turn could help control some of the import costs on account of fuel. It could also help decongest the roads and the railway lines.

Cleaning the Rivers

Rivers are now being used as vital resources for the economy and not just as a means for providing water. Cleaning up the rivers is gaining momentum. The most important project for the government is the Clean Ganga Mission, which aims to clean up the Ganges, one of the most important rivers in India. It is immensely important for religious reasons (myths, prayers and legends surround this river). It is equally important for its water—the Gangetic plains are crucial for agriculture, especially for the backward and highly populated regions of Uttar Pradesh, Bihar and West Bengal. It is also used for navigation.

Unfortunately, religious ceremonies, irresponsible industrialization, apathy and the inability of previous governments to build toilets have all combined to make it one of the most polluted rivers in the country. Half burnt bodies and offerings made to the gods at the innumerable temples that dot the banks of the Ganges all mingle to pollute the river. More serious is the effluent that comes from the towns (human waste and city garbage) and from industries (which emit the most noxious of chemicals). Millions of people use the riverbanks for defecation. Collectively, they make the river water unfit for drinking and bathing.

The Ganga is a perfect example of the blessing that India has in the form of abundant water. Moreover, as the chart, Countries and their DNA (see Chapter III) has shown, this

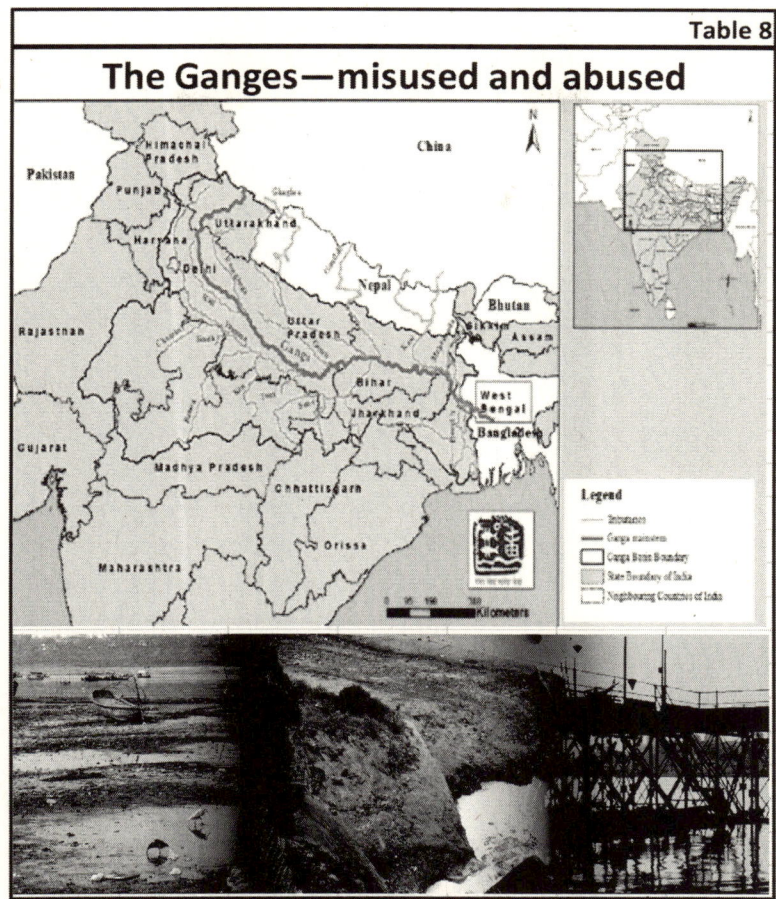

Table 8
The Ganges—misused and abused

Sources: https://nmcg.nic.in/NamamiGanga.aspx and
http://nmcg.nic.in/

country has more water (in terms of percentage of land mass) than all the neighbouring countries—China, Bangladesh, Nepal, Pakistan and Sri Lanka. But India misuses and abuses these gifts.

And Indian planners do not appear to have the vision to remedy the situation. It could be incompetence. But more likely it is greed. The sloth could be whetted by the desire to get more money each year to clean up the river and thus ensure that some of the money is salted away. How else can one explain the fact that in the four years since the National Mission for Clean Ganga (NMCG)[20] was set up, barely 11 per cent of effluent is now treated? As the National Green Tribunal pointed out in July 2017, Rs 7000 crore has already been spent in just two years, but with hardly any improvement.[21]

The problem, say global experts, is that the government has spent the money on cleaning the water, without first stopping the pollutants.

The first target ought to have been industries that pollute the river with noxious effluents. But little action has been taken on this front. It is possible that many of the industrialists are well connected to powerful political families; hence they continue discharging their filth illegally with impunity. The second target should have been cities and towns whose waste should have been sent to sewage treatment plants (STPs).

The cities and towns should have been told that their funds (and the right to collect funds) would be cut off within say two years by which time all city waste should go to STPs. But that would need the support of state governments to freeze fund flows to cities, in case they do not take action. Another way would be to invoke penal provisions of polluting groundwater and national waterways, and send a few industrialists to jail for not complying with the law. But both types of actions require tremendous grit and political resolve.

At the same time, open defecation should be banned, by first building toilets and then ensuring that the waste goes to the city and town STPs. Gradually, and preferably, toilet

---

[20] http://nmcg.nic.in/
[21] https://economictimes.indiatimes.com/news/politics-and-nation/rs-7000-cr-spent-on-ganga-in-2-yrs-without-improvement-ngt/articleshow/59584914.cms

waste along with animal excreta should go to centrally located and connected digesters so that it can be used for methane extraction. Since the Ganges has temples on its banks all along the course of the river, there is a lot of other organic material as well—flowers that are offered to the gods, food that is given as sacred offerings or prasad, clarified butter that is used for lighting lamps. Then there is a lot of food waste from the thousands of kitchens that exist along the river, making food for pilgrims, as alms for beggars and as offerings to the gods. All these are rich in microbial content and can generate methane. The National Mission for Clean Ganga (NMCG) has already begun working on providing special enclosures for bathing, and puja offerings. The water from these enclosures is first cleaned, and then allowed to flow back into the river. But with millions squatting along the rivers, the job is quite arduous indeed!

At the same time, money should be spent on cleaning the Ganges only after these things are done. 'It is cheaper to stop polluting sources, than to allow them to pollute and then treat the waters,' says a global expert.[22]

As things stand today, NMCG has created an STP capacity of just over 259 million litres per day (MLD), which is about 11 per cent of the 2311 MLD the programme seeks to create. Consequently, over 1300 MLD of sewage continues to flow into the main stem of the Ganga. Last year the government decided to hand over charge of this work also to Minister Gadkari. That makes sense, because he is also responsible for waterways, and the Ganges is one of the rivers in his programme.

If all goes well, expect India to see a more vibrant coastline, cleaner and more navigable rivers and the emergence of many more jobs. All this is bound to translate into better economic

[22] http://www.freepressjournal.in/analysis/and-silently-flows-the-ganges/1265081
http://www.asiaconverge.com/2018/04/silently-flows-ganges/

well-being for most Indians. Not surprisingly, these plans are now being described as 'harnessing the waters of life'.

One Little Problem

The plans that the government has chalked out are impressive. But there is one problem. All these plans cost money. And while Gadkari exudes confidence that the money will not be a problem, there are many who believe that it could be an obstacle. They say that the investment climate is just too bad. Gross capital formation is on the decline (see Table 9) as are many other economic indicators.[23] And if there is no appetite for investment, none of these plans may ever be implemented.

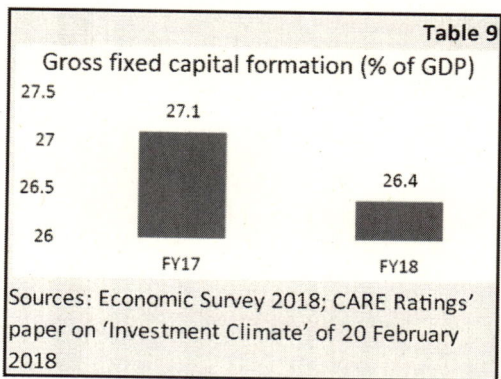

But why is investment slowing down? Well that is another chapter.

---

23 http://www.moneycontrol.com/news/business/comment-from-jobless-growth-to-wary-foreign-investors-the-dark-clouds-on-the-indian-economy-are-here-to-stay-2515845.html
    http://www.asiaconverge.com/2018/02/jobless-growth-wary-foreign-investors-dark-clouds-indian-economy-stay/

FIVE

Hobbled Governance, but There Is Hope Still

'The age of lust is giving birth, and both the parents ask the nurse to tell them fairy tales on both sides of the glass. And now the infant with his cord is hauled in like a kite, and one eye filled with blueprints, one eye filled with night.'

—Leonard Cohen, *'Stories of the Street'*

There is a question that often baffles many: what is the difference between a mafia and a government? The more one examines both, the more one recognizes the similarities. Both collect protection money. The only difference is that the government calls such collections taxes.

But there ought to be a bigger difference. Governments ought to be better at governance and at transparency. Mafias are usually believed to be exploitative. But when one looks around, especially in India, the lines between the two get blurred.

The acid test to check out which is more relevant—government or the mafia—is when one goes to any slum in the country. Ask a person what he would do if his daughter were being molested by a group of boys. Would he, as father, go to the police? Or would he go to the slumlord and ask him to intervene? If the answer is the latter, you know you have a problem. Unfortunately, most fathers in slums would rather go to the local slumlord.

Not surprisingly, the legitimate police force begins to become irrelevant. Conversely, the illegitimate slumlord becomes relevant. And, if you observe closely, most slumlords do not prey on their own parish. This is a community they seek to protect. The policeman is the predator; the spider who wants you to step into his parlour. The police has been transformed into an exploiter.

True, sometimes the role of a protector does involve a bit of threat and even violence. And true, charge sheets do get filed against the slumlord. But for his constituency, the slumlord's reputation grows stronger with each case being filed. He remains relevant as the protector.

Then when the slumlord opts to stand for elections, most of the people in his constituency will vote for him, irrespective of the number of cases the police may have filed against him. He is still the community's protector. And that is how the criminalization of politics begins.

Every political party tries to paint itself superior by decrying the number of candidates with criminal records in other parties. The fact is that all political parties need protectors with their loyalist vote banks in order to win elections. Decriminalization of politics is possible only when the courts—and the law dispensation ecosystem—become stronger.

Why the Courts?

The slumlord remains the dispenser of justice in a society where the legitimate dispensers of justice are not trusted. Thus the legitimate becomes illegitimate, and the illegitimate begins to gain credibility. If the slum-dweller could have been assured justice within hours, with no fear of reprisal, he would have gone to the police. But this would have been possible only if the courts had the power to haul policemen up if they failed to redress the problem. The courts should have the power to punish or even order the dismissal of a policeman if they find that the charge sheets were not filed in time, or that the case papers were written too casually, thus enabling an acquittal of the guilty, or if the police were guilty of acts of commission or omission that hindered the enforcement of law and order and fair play.

This would allow the courts to gain credibility, which in turn would reinforce the image of the policeman as a fair dispenser of law and order.

But the courts can do that only if there are enough judges and magistrates, and if they have the power to identify the corrupt, ineffective or incompetent judges within their fraternity. The courts could do this provided there were no rules that no judge or policeman can haul up a politician or a government servant without first obtaining permission to do so from senior bureaucrats and politicians.[1]

Thus, if the courts could ensure that judicial verdicts are handed over within a few days instead of decades, then the

---

[1] https://www.moneycontrol.com/news/india/opinion-why-corrupt-politicians-and-bureaucrats-can-now-breathe-easy-2822671.html

courts would be both feared and respected. That would keep the police in check. And that would have inspired the slum-dweller to file his complaint at the police station.

More pertinently, it would have removed the need to have a slumlord at all. But that is precisely what the politicians, who are also lawmakers, do not appear to want.

Protect the Powerful and Damn the Rest

The politicians have created an ecosystem that ensures the delegitimization of the lawful which allows them and their nominees to become more relevant. They first ensure that the most powerful implementers of law are kept out of any investigation or prosecution till permission for such action is given by the authorities (politicians or senior bureaucrats whose continuance in office depends largely on legislators. Since July 2018 bankers have been given this dubious ring of protection as well[2]). So you cannot prosecute a government servant, or a policeman or a legislator till permission is granted by the designated authorities. That is the first wall of defence that many predators enjoy.

The second wall of defence is the shortage of adjudicating officials (see Table 1). Each government—it would be unfair to target the current government alone—has tried to ensure that the number of judges or adjudicating officers falls short of the sanctioned strength (which itself is less than the required strength). If this were true of just one department, it could be an accident. Two could have been a coincidence. But more such instances—each with around 20 to 40 per cent of the vacancies left—and a pattern begins to emerge.

---

[2] Ibid.

	Table 1	
Emasculation of the judiciary & law		
Constitutional/Statutory authority	**Sanctioned strength**	**Vacancies**
Supreme Court of India judges	31	7
High Court judges	1,079	403
Chief justices of High Courts	24	9
SEBI Members	9	2
Securities Appellate Tribunal	3	1
Income Tax Appellate Tribunal	126	34
Central Administrative Tribunal	66	24
Central Information Commission		
Commissioners	11	4
Other Staff	160	117
Competition Commission of India		
Commissioners	7	2
Other Staff	197	79
Central Vigilance Commission		
Commissioners	3	1
Other Staff	296	53
IPS (Police) cadre	4,843	938
CBI	7,274	1,656

Notes: It must be clarified that these numbers were probably the same even when P. Chidambaram, the source of these numbers, was himself the home minister and finance minister

Sources: Excerpted from P Chidambaram's column of 4 March 2018 at http://indianexpress.com/article/opinion/columns/minimum-government-maximum-damage-arun-jaitley-bjp-5085043/

All governments since the 1970s have tried to emasculate the judiciary by keeping vacancies unfilled, thus allowing a backlog of cases to pile up.[3] That allows the government to delay the hearing of some cases while expediting the hearing of others.

The third level of defence is keeping all permissions for investigations with the government. With a shortage of staff—both at the level of the judiciary and even at the level of the police force, it is the politician who decides—and informs the judiciary—which case should be fast-tracked, and which should be left idling. This applies to all cases, not just the ones granted with the first ring of defence. Thus, even if a person is found, prima facie, guilty, the government may not give its sanction to prosecute. It is thus the government that decides who deserves to be prosecuted and who does not. The government always has a big say in deciding which charges should be pursued by investigators; consider for instance how the case of auctioning police posts has not been investigated. This is despite a former police commissioner writing about this in the media more than two decades ago.[4] Consider how witnesses turn hostile after ten or fifteen years have passed. Consider how cases get dismissed because evidence was not presented before the courts (the police are not pulled up for this). And consider how an MLC (a member of the

----

[3] https://www.moneycontrol.com/news/business/economy/comment-are-strong-governments-bad-for-the-indian-economy-2528037.html
     http://www.asiaconverge.com/2018/03/strong-governments-bad-indian-economy/

[4] https://timesofindia.indiatimes.com/city/mumbai/Intelligence-bane-of-Mumbai-police/articleshow/147170.cms
     https://www.hindustantimes.com/mumbai/patil-asks-for-report-on-ribeiro-s-letter/story-0LaajRWWkWSBjaZVKVsfEN.html
     https://www.outlookindia.com/magazine/pwa_story_first/221327

state government's legislative council) was given a clean chit, and permission to investigate not granted, even though there was prima facie evidence showing that he was guilty of both tax evasion and human trafficking.[5] And then there is the case of an elected representative beating up a public officer in an aircraft, then bragging about it, and still escaping imprisonment for this act of unwarranted violence.[6]

Of course, there are times when a public interest litigation (PIL) appeal filed before the courts has compelled the courts to pull up the government. Despite the first ring of defence described above[7] the Supreme Court has ruled that sanction to prosecute a public servant is not required if the alleged offence was committed when he was not discharging official duty.[8] This ruling, even though it was given in June 2016, is still to be implemented and enforced by investigation and prosecution officials across the country. But it has rekindled hopes that the rule of law will eventually prevail in this land. As things stand now, a larger bench is examining the issue afresh.[9]

---

[5]   http://indianexpress.com/article/india/prasad-minesh-bjp-mlc-tax-evasion-human-trafficking-krystal-aviation-services-black-money-money-laundering-5149108/

[6]   http://www.thehindu.com/news/national/forced-to-travel-economy-class-shiv-sena-mp-assaults-air-india-staffer/article17608535.ece

[7]   http://www.thehindu.com/todays-paper/tp-national/prior-sanction-must-for-prosecution-of-public-servants-court/article3072078.ece

[8]   https://economictimes.indiatimes.com/news/politics-and-nation/no-sanction-needed-to-try-government-servants-for-illegal-acts-supreme-court/articleshow/53117427.cms

[9]   http://www.livelaw.in/breaking-prior-sanction-mandatory-referring-complaint-public-servant-investigation-u-s-1563-crpc-question-referred-larger-bench/

The most vexatious part of the judicial system is the endless delay caused by the inadequate number of judges, and the swelling number of cases filed before the courts, as well as the tendency of the system to allow for endless adjournments. And as everyone knows, delays only make the oppressor stronger and the oppressed weaker.

The Singapore Lesson

And this is where an anecdote becomes relevant.

For the past couple of decades, a friend's wife has been doing a bit of business in Singapore. She often gets her relatives to send her samples of items that people fancy and purchase from local shops in Mumbai around festive occasions. Armed with this knowledge and with suitable photographs, she then goes to stores in Singapore and asks them if they would like her to source such items for them so that they in turn could sell to the large Indian diaspora in that country.

This business was going quite well for several years till, just once, a local Singaporean owner of a superstore refused to pay for the goods after they had arrived. His grouse: she had sold the same product to a local trader at more favourable prices. She argued that he should not compare prices because the other trader had placed orders at a time when the prices of the products in Mumbai were lower. The superstore owner had placed orders when the prevailing prices were higher. Moreover, she pointed to the contract that both parties had signed. She insisted that he could not renege on the contract. But it was to no avail.

Disheartened, she decided to write off the losses and tried to forget the episode. A couple of months later, instigated by her husband, she finally decided to complain. She wrote to the local authorities. Much to her surprise, she received a court summons within a week, asking her to bring the relevant papers/contracts with her. At the appointed hour she went to the court and presented all documents to the court clerk. The clerk in turn ticked off the appropriate boxes on the summary sheet, flagged the relevant pages of the contract and sent the folder to the judge. The Singaporean owner of the superstore was also there, scowling at her.

The judge called her and the superstore owner into his chambers ten minutes later and asked the storeowner if there was a contract. The storeowner confirmed this, and began to offer his explanations. The judge cut him short and asked him if the contract allowed him to withhold payments. The storeowner said no. The judge promptly ordered that the entire amount be paid to the woman, with interest. He asked the storeowner to work out the details, payment terms and instalments with the court clerk in such a manner that the full payment was made within a specified period. The case was closed in fifteen minutes.

The woman was ecstatic. She had not expected such a quick resolution. She thanked the judge and was about to leave the chambers when the judge called her back. 'Why have you complained two months after the incident?' he asked. She blurted an apology. He retorted, 'Are you trying to make a joke of our judicial process? Do you think that evidence can stay alive so long? Next time, if you make a delayed complaint, I will have to penalize you as well.'

That is something India's policymakers have not learnt. Evidence cannot stay alive for long. The longer the time that elapses before a case is tried, the easier it is for powerful people to doctor evidence and make witnesses retract and turn hostile. Moreover, most folk do not easily remember what happened more than a few weeks ago.

Today, thanks to its ability to adjudicate matters swiftly and effectively, Singapore has become a hub for judicial redressal for countries around the world. The subsequent pages will show how India, with its penchant for finding ways to delay judicial redressal, has a lot to learn from this country.

But let's return to the slum story.

Slums and Demographic Tinkering

In order to make sure that the government in power controls the slumlords—who will later become elected representatives—politicians have mastered the art of playing the slum development game as well. That is why the Iran solution for housing has not taken off in India (see the section on Affordable Housing in Chapter III).

To understand how slums are encouraged, examine some basic data first. See tables 2, 3 and 4. Observe some very interesting numbers.

Watch how the country's population grew and observe the following:

1. India's population grew by 17.6 per cent during 2001 to 2011, during the decade between the two census enumerations.
2. Slums, however, grew at 25 per cent—a tad higher than total population
3. Slum households grew even faster at 37.1 per cent.
4. And children in slums grew at just 11 per cent.

Also watch one more number—the size of households declined from 5.2 in 2001 to 4.2 in 2011. In urban areas, however, the average household in the slums comprised just 0.8 people, and this declined further to 0.5 persons.

			Table 2
Slum Population—some key characteristics			
	2001	**2011**	**Decadal growth %**
Total population	1,028,737,436	1,210,193,422	17.6
Slum Population	52,371,589	65,494,604	25.1
Slum Households	10,150,719	13,920,191	37.1
Household size (persons)	5.2	4.7	
Children in slums	7,576,856	8,082,743	6.7
Scheduled Caste population	9,673,817	13,354,080	38.0
Scheduled Tribe population	1,460,290	2,216,533	51.8

Sources: Primary Census Abstract for Slum, 2011; Office of the Registrar General & Census Commissioner, India

				Table 3
Slum Households				
	Absolute		**Absolute change 2001–11**	**Decadal Growth 2001-11**
	2001	**2011**		
Slums				
Households	10,150,719	13,920,191	3,769,472	37.1
Household size	5.2	4.2	-0.5	
Urban (slum reported towns)				
Households	43,556,155	62,792,741	19236586	44.2
Household size	0.8	0.5		
Urban (all towns)				
Households	55,832,570	80,888,760	25,056,190	44.9
Household size	5.3	4.7	-0.4	

Sources: Primary Census Abstract for Slum, 2011 Office of the Registrar General & Census Commissioner, India

						Table 4
Slum children						
	Absolute		**Absolute change 2001–11**	**Decadal Growth**	**Child Proportion**	
	2001	**2011**			**2001**	**2011**
Urban slum reported towns						
Persons	28,667,504	32,816,316	4,148,812	14.5	12.8	11.2
Males	15,051,769	17,250,108	2,198,339	14.6	12.8	11.4
Females	13,615,735	15,566,208	1,950,473	14.3	12.9	11.1
Sex Ratio per 100 males	905	902	-3			

Sources: Primary Census Abstract for Slum, 2011 Office of the Registrar General & Census Commissioner, India

All numbers have their own story to tell, and the last figure reaches the point of absurdity. But that is how law and order, and democracy works in a country where law enforcement becomes weak.

What the Numbers Tell

Take the first discrepancy. Why did slums grow faster than general population. If one drills own to city demographics one finds the same story. Total population in any of the cities given in Table 5 grew at a slower pace than slum population.

Sociologists will try to explain this as being due to the fact that slum dwellers came to cities in search for jobs. But then so did everyone else. I too would have moved to another city, if I could get a job there. Why did the legal dwelling population not grow as fast as the slum population?

		Table 5
The best and the worst of slum developers		
State	**Proportion of Slum HHs to Urban HHs (%)**	**Population density (persons/sq. km)**
The top five		
Andhra Pradesh	35.7	308
Chhattisgarh	31.9	189
Madhya Pradesh	28.3	236
Odisha	23.1	269
West Bengal	21.9	1029
The bottom five		
Chandigarh	9.7	9252
Gujarat	6.7	308
Jharkhand	5.3	414
Assam	4.8	397
Kerala	1.5	859
Million Plus Cities—the big five		
Greater Mumbai	41.3	21000
Kolkata	29.6	24000
Chennai	28.5	11000
Delhi	14.6	11297
BBMP-Bengaluru	8.5	11371
The next rung of cities		
Greater Visakhapatnam	44.1	2537
Jabalpur Cantt	43.3	478
Vijayawada	40.6	16939
Meerut	40	9200
Raipur	39	4500
Nagpur	34.3	11000
Greater Hyderabad (GHMC)	31.9	18480
Kota	31.8	6135
Agra	29.8	8954
All India	**17.36**	**382**
Notes: HH stands for households		
Sources: Housing stock, amenities and assets in slums, Census 2011; Dr C. Chandramouli, Registrar-General and Census Commissioner, India. Density figures taken from both the Census and Wikipedia		

Obviously, someone encouraged slum dwellers to move to cities. That was the only reason why this set of numbers grew faster than the number for general population. It is then that you realize that the biggest promoter of slums is the politician. He – in collusion with the slumlord – encourages people to gather in large numbers and occupy key areas that are targeted for changing the demography in that district, or territory. Thus the local population gets marginalized, its votes begin to have less relevance, and the new elected representative is not the person that the original natives would like to have elected, but the one whom the newly created slum dwellers have been told to elect. Criminalization of politics begins from here. Where democracy is made a joke. It would be easier to allow politicians to stuff ballot papers into election boxes. The results have been rigged!

Take the second discrepancy. Households grew faster than slum population growth because most entitlements—electricity, water, gas connection rations, etc.—are given to households. Thus in Mumbai, each household can consume up to 200 units of electricity at subsidized rates every month. To get a larger share of these entitlements a family of four shows itself as maybe six households—different combinations for each household. That is how in urban areas, the size of households declines to less than one. That is how the system of entitlements gets misused. The politician, the police, the municipal authorities and the ubiquitous slumlord all share the spoils. The already beleaguered taxpayer pays the price for this as well.

Take the next discrepancy. The growth rate of children was much lower because most parents know that slum development is a game for creating vote banks. It is also a method for grabbing land in the most lucrative of territories. The conditions are squalid. The adults can cope with this.

But they would not like their children to grow up in midst of this squalor. So children are sent back to villages till they grow up and become part of another slum formation exercise crafted by the unscrupulous lawmakers. That explains why the largest slums are in cities where there is a lot of money to be made. Land grab, money for votes, free houses, are all incentives. This is the feeding ground for rent-a-mob schemes for political rallies and violence. And this is where prostitution and gambling is quite rampant. Consider the percentage of the population in cities that are now slum dwellers, and it is then possible to understand how the electoral game gets rigged, and how the most lucrative contracts are then grabbed and managed by the new breed of elected representatives.

And, mind you, this was mostly in towns and cities, which are major revenue generators not just for common folk but also for the government and municipalities. The bigger the revenue pie, the greater the scope for the most lucrative forms of exploitation, be it real estate, or hawker licences or prostitution.

Legislators first create the laws for protection and then use these laws to distort demographics. As a result, Mumbai currently has almost 50 per cent of its population living in slums, though the last census put this figure at 41 per cent.

The pattern is the same everywhere. Squatters suddenly emerge on a piece of government or municipal land. Nothing is done. The crowd immediately puts up a shrine, a statue of Ambedkar, or Shivaji, or some other leader whose name evokes local sentiments, which can then be used to describe any complaint against the squatters as a very sensitive issue and that force should not be used to evict them. If the slum has tribals or scheduled castes residing there, the matter can easily be described as atrocity and bias against these protected people.

A leader emerges from among this motley crowd and demands that water and electricity connections be granted, often for free. Then the legislature seeks regularization of these slums after ten to fifteen years have passed. Then, in the name of cleansing the city, rehabilitation of slums is proposed, and slum dwellers are given free housing in the very place where slums existed so that the eyesore slums can be eradicated. This way the vote bank remains intact in the same territory. Many of these flats allotted to slum dwellers for free are then resold, or given out on rent. Then the slum dwellers move to another slum as guided by their leaders.

Over the years, the message being given out is that if you want to be politically relevant, get your people to squat on public land in large numbers, preferably guided by a person who has the blessings of a political party. Squat there for ten years or so and you will be legalized and entitled to a free flat. Protest a bit more, and a political party will move a resolution to waive, forever, all property taxes for regularized slums. So you get a flat, at no cost, and you don't even have to pay property taxes for it.

Thus, in a city like Mumbai, 50 per cent of the population lives in slums. Around 30 per cent of its people stay in cessed houses where the Rent Control Act still applies, and hence property taxes at market rates are not applied, even if these houses are located in the most expensive of the city's areas. Thus the burden of property taxes falls on just 20 per cent of the population, which has lost the demographic clout to even protest and ask for justice and equity.

As in Jonathan Swift's *Gulliver's Travels*, we have now entered the land of the Yahoos. This is how democracy is derailed. This demographic tinkering is what caused the Assam and north-eastern uprising where politicians tried to game elections by allowing refugees not only the right to settle, but also to citizenship. Even today, the spectre of foreigners is a burning issue in north-east India.[10, 11]

The Assam agitation put into process a set of rules (enshrined under the National Population Register where clear steps are outlined) for identifying people who should be granted citizenship. The story thereafter is a familiar one. Rules are framed and enacted. But action along those lines is not taken. Politicians do not want to give up the tremendous advantage that demographic tinkering allows them. This has resulted in a system so porous that even foreign nationals have at times become elected representatives of an independent India.[12]

But thanks to the Assam agitation, there is a rethink on the entire issue of demographic tinkering. The matter is before the Supreme Court because 2 million alleged squatters in the Northeast are likely to lose citizenship. You cannot evict such large numbers. One solution is to give them work permits without voting powers. This way, they can work—a migrant is invariably a better worker than local residents anywhere in the world. But they cannot alter the voting pattern. If that rule becomes law, it won't be long before the courts may rule that slum dwellers only have the right to work in an area. But voting rights can be allowed only if dwellers have a legal residence. Without voting rights, politicians will lose interest in slum formation. [13]

[10] http://www.caravanmagazine.in/reportage/the-spectre-assam-elections-immigrants-fear
[11] https://www.moneycontrol.com/news/india/comment-the-problem-of-citizenship-and-slum-votebanks-and-the-work-permit-solution-2570637.html
[12] https://www.timesheadline.com/india/foreign-national-using-fake-documents-elected-thrice-telangana-7686.html
[13] https://www.moneycontrol.com/news/india/comment-the-problem-of-citizenship-and-slum-votebanks-and-the-work-permit-solution-2570637.html

It is this tendency to meddle with concepts such as rights for squatters and for freeloaders (and thus penalize the remaining marginalized tax-paying communities), and the abolition of time-tested processes for identifying citizenship that create grounds for great anxiety. People worry about the future of genuine democracy in India.

When Absurd Laws Weaken Values

In March 2011, the former Chief Economic Advisor (CEA) to the Government of India, Kaushik Basu, wrote a seminal paper titled 'Why, for a Class of Bribes, the Act of Giving a Bribe should be Treated as Legal'.[14] In that paper, he argued for simpler laws that would allow corruption to be stanched.

He pointed out that many bribes that were paid were nothing but extortion. Common people cannot get birth certificates, death certificates, get complaints registered with police stations and the like without paying a bribe. At times, it could be clearances to home reconstruction plans. Or it could be getting a driving licence. All these things, listed above, should be given to citizens as a matter of right. But many have to pay a bribe to get them. Surely, the government cannot deny them the right to complain, even if the bribe has been paid.

His argument was simple. You cannot stamp out corruption if the giver of a bribe is as guilty as the receiver of a bribe.[15] To allow for corruption to be reduced, you first need

---

[14] http://www.kaushikbasu.org/Act_Giving_Bribe_Legal.pdf

[15] http://www.firstpost.com/india/bribery-in-india-how-to-minimise-bribe-giving-and-taking-2818398.html
http://www.asiaconverge.com/2016/06/bribery-india-minimise-bribe-giving-taking/

a complainant. Why would anybody complain if he knows that his very admission that he has given a bribe will put him behind bars? And the receiver of the bribe is unlikely to confess before the law enforcement authorities that he received a bribe unless there is compelling evidence against him.

By allowing bribe givers to complain, without first sending them to jail, you create the space for complaints, which can then be recorded. That by itself could be cause to investigate whether the alleged bribe-taker has been living beyond his known sources of income. That in turn could allow the police to register a case of disproportionate assets.

But the government is loath to introduce such laws. It does not even like to discuss this issue. As a result, you find India's corrupt have always found ways to use laws to protect corruption rather than eliminate it.

In July 2018, the government went a step further. It ushered in amendments to the Prevention of Corruption Act.[16] It claimed it had tightened up its Prevention of Corruption Act. But what it did was nothing but the promotion of corruption. It changed the minimum penalty for bribe givers and bribe takers. Earlier it was imprisonment up to three years or fine or both. Now it is a minimum imprisonment of three years, subject to a maximum of seven years, or fine, or both. The new laws make it even more difficult for bribe-givers to complain.

What is worse is that the amendments now do not permit the investigative agencies to launch investigations against bureaucrats, legislators and even bankers, without prior sanction from higher authorities. Thus the three key parties responsible for corruption get protected. The bribe-giver is thus the most vulnerable.

---

[16] An Act to further amend the Prevention of Corruption Act, 1988, Ministry of Law and Justice, Gazette of India, 26 July 2018.

The Need for Arbitration

But it is not only the common citizen who is vulnerable. Small and large corporates also feel vulnerable because they can get caught in the maze of courts and litigation if a business deal goes sour. It is to escape the welter of laws that contradict each other, the delays in judicial redressal and the high costs involved on account of such delays that most businessmen opt for inserting a clause in their agreements that allows them to approach an international arbitral council with a seat outside of India.

The desire to have these hearings in a seat outside of India gained momentum since 6 September 2012 when the Supreme Court decreed[17] that arbitral awards given from seats outside of India could not be reopened for scrutiny by India courts. This decision was taken because many businessmen saw Indian courts delaying the implementation of even arbitral awards.[18] The trigger for this move was a case that began with a dispute that an Australian company had with Coal India Ltd (CIL).

In 1989, White Industries entered into a contract with CIL for the supply of equipment and for the development of a coal mine in Uttar Pradesh. The contract ran into disputes, and in May 2002, the disputes were referred for arbitration before the London Court of International Arbitration. White Industries won an award and CIL was asked to pay them a sum of USD 4.08 million.

---

[17] http://www.asiaconverge.com/wp-content/uploads/2016/08/arbitration-2012-09-06_SC-5-member-bench-bharat.pdf

[18] http://www.moneycontrol.com/news/india/comment-asking-for-investments-is-good-but-can-india-guarantee-speedy-and-fair-grievance-redressal-2489553.html
http://www.asiaconverge.com/2018/01/asking-investments-good-can-india-guarantee-speedy-fair-grievance-redressal/

CIL approached the Calcutta High Court and received a stay on the tribunal award. It did so by seeking shelter under Section 34 of the Arbitration Act, which was originally meant to take up only those issues where the arbitration award went against a country's laws.

Unhappy with the way Indian courts had blocked an international award, White Industries approached the Arbitration Tribunal in London against the government in 1999. When no progress took place in redressing the issue, White Industries moved the Singapore courts against the Government of India, invoking the provisions of the Bilateral Investment Treaty (BIT) that India had with Australia (the BIT allows for grievances being taken up before a Singapore Court). It contended that the damages awarded to it by the LCIA would have been part of its investment portfolio had the Indian courts not frustrated this move. The Singapore courts slapped the Government of India with a huge penalty.[19]

The Government of India was shocked at this development. Backroom negotiations probably ensured that the Singapore court verdict was not given effect. It is possible that White Industries received its payment. But the government is believed to have approached the Supreme Court to immediately review the situation.

On 16 December 2011, the Supreme Court ordered a review of Section 34 of the Arbitration Act. A five-member constitution bench was formed to examine the issue.[20]

---

[19] http://www.dnaindia.com/money/report-judicial-delays-hit-arbitration-awards-1736775
http://www.asiaconverge.com/2012/09/judicial-delays-hit-arbitration-awards/

[20] http://www.asiaconverge.com/wp-content/uploads/2016/08/arbitration-2011-12-16_SC-notice.pdf

On 6 September 2012, the five-member bench stated: 'In a foreign seated international commercial arbitration, no application for interim relief would be maintainable under Section 9 or any other provision, as applicability of Part I of the Arbitration Act, 1996 is limited to all arbitrations which take place in India.[21] Similarly, no suit for interim *injunction simplicitor* would be maintainable in India, on the basis of an international commercial arbitration with a seat outside India. We conclude that Part I of the Arbitration Act, 1996 is applicable only to *all the arbitrations* which take place within the territory of India . . . Thus, in order to do complete justice, we hereby order, that the law now declared by this Court shall apply prospectively, to all the arbitration agreements executed hereafter.'

The constitution bench had ruled that international awards from a seat outside India could not be reviewed or challenged in Indian courts.

For some time the crisis of the government of India having to pay a fine to White and Company appeared to have been staved off. But the government was to be stung once again in a few years' time (see Table 6).

The most damning verdict for the government was in respect of the Devas Multimedia case. Now the government wants to squirm out of such situations because most of the cases involving arbitration disputes have the government as a litigant.

As the Supreme Court observed,[22] the government is a 'compulsive litigant'. The apex court added, 'Mindful of the

---

[21] http://www.asiaconverge.com/wp-content/uploads/2016/08/arbitration-2012-09-06_SC-5-member-bench-bharat.pdf

[22] http://sci.gov.in/supremecourt/2011/30837/30837_2011_Judgement_23-Nov-2017.pdf

Case involving	Penalty amount	Brief background
Three cases, many more headaches		
Ranbaxy		In May 2016, Singapore International Arbitration Centre rules that Malvinder and Shivinder Singh concealed facts from Japanese pharma major Daiichi Sankyo at the time of selling their stake in 2008. It awards damages of Rs 2,562.78 crore. Japan's Daiichi Sankyo had purchased a 34.82 per cent stake in Ranbaxy from the brothers for $2.4 billion in 2008. Despite an arbitration award, full payment to Daiichi has not been made.
Tata-DoCoMo	$1.17 billion	Japan's NTT DoCoMo moved the International Court for Arbitration (ICA) in London in January 2015 after the Tata Group failed to find a buyer or buy back the 26 per cent stake that DoCoMo held in Tata Teleservices. The joint venture (JV) contract had stated that the Japanese company would get Rs 7,250 crore, or Rs 58.045 a share—half its original investment, or the market price, whichever was higher. On 23 June 2016, the London ICA ordered Tatas to pay $1.17 billion to NTT DoCoMo. The Tatas say that the RBI rules do not allow for payment at a pre-negotiated future price, and that payments must be market-driven. On 27 July, NTT moved London's courts to seize Tata assets in the UK to compel it to pay. The order is in NTT's favour. On 28 July, the Tatas move London courts and get a twenty-three-day reprieve. On 29 July, the Tatas pay $1.17 billion to the Registrar of Delhi High court which gives both parties till the end of August to settle matters. On the eve of Prime Minister Narendra Modi's trip to Japan, the Tatas agree to pay DoCoMo. Plans affected after Mistry's ouster from the Tata Board.
Devas Multimedia	$672 million	In 2005 Antrix, the commercial arm of the Indian Space Research Organisation (ISRO), and Devas Multimedia sign a deal. It allowed Antrix to provide 70 MHz of its little-used S-Band spectrum through its transponders to Devas for its digital multimedia services. Devas, in turn, agreed to pay to Antrix a total of $300 million over twelve years. The deal got cancelled by the UPA government on 17 February 2011 in the wake of the 2G spectrum scam becoming public knowledge. Devas then took Antrix and the Government to the ICA in Geneva. Arbitration proceedings began in June 2013. Devas claimed $1.6 billion in damages. Antrix filed an arbitration suit in Bengaluru in November 2015 against the September 2015 order of the ICA asking Antrix to pay damages of $672 million to Devas. The government loses this case as well. Simultaneously, charges of money laundering are filed against Devas under FEMA (Foreign Exchange Management Act 1999), besides accusing it of violating FIPB (Foreign Investment Promotion Board) guidelines. The government is still trying to prepare a criminal case against the promoters of Devas.

Sources: press releases, Supreme Court archives and media reports

phenomenon of the docket explosion and the rising litigation in the country, the Union of India in order to ensure the conduct of responsible litigation framed what is today known as the National Litigation Policy (NLP), to bring down the pendency of cases and get meaningful issues decided from the judicial forums rather than multiple tiers of scrutiny just for the sake of it. The Government, being a litigant in well over 50 per cent of the cases, has to take a lead in not being a compulsive litigant.'

Even the National Litigation Policy (NLP) stated in 2010 that 'Government must cease to be a compulsive litigant. The philosophy that matters should be left to the courts for ultimate decision has to be discarded. The easy approach, "let the court decide", must be eschewed and condemned.'

Almost 50 per cent of the three crore cases pending in the courts across the country are because of the government. Despite the Supreme Court's observation and those of the NLP, the situation has not improved.

It was possibly to protect its own interests that the Narendra Modi government decided to try to amend all the Bilateral Investment Treaties and other agreements that allowed foreign companies to approach an arbitration council with its seat outside of India. It decided to exhort them not to take up any litigation or judicial redressal process outside of India till existing processes in India were exhausted. Naturally, most foreign countries have refused to agree to this.[23]

Then the government decided to set up a first rate Arbitration Centre in Mumbai. But this has done little to encourage foreign companies to take up dispute resolution in India on account of the Supreme Court order, which allows decrees given by arbitration courts in India to be reviewed by Indian courts. The latest salvo to hit the government is the decision of the Asian Development Bank (ADB), which has refused to finance the Metro Rail in Mumbai till the seat of arbitration is Singapore, not Mumbai.[24]

Meanwhile, under great pressure from Japan, which had slowed down its investments in all its major projects in India—the high-speed railway between Mumbai and Ahmedabad, the Dedicated Freight Corridor (DFC) and the Delhi Mumbai Industrial Corridor (DMIC)—the government finally decided to enter into a Comprehensive Economic Partnership

---

[23] https://www.hindustantimes.com/analysis/india-s-bilateral-investment-treaties-once-bitten-57-times-more-shy/story-2d0VyByBuCC55TYz0zDzNK.html
https://thewire.in/economy/deconstructing-indias-model-bilateral-investment-treaty

[24] http://indianexpress.com/article/cities/mumbai/metro-funder-adb-doesnt-want-mumbai-as-centre-for-arbitration-5130906/

Agreement (CEPA) with the country. The CEPA is believed to allow Japan to take disputes relating to its companies to an arbitration seat outside India. However, neither Japan nor India is willing to confirm or deny this. Meanwhile, the government is believed to have asked Singapore to modify the CEPA both countries had signed some years ago, which allows Singapore to opt for dispute redressal outside India. Singapore is believed to have politely and firmly refused. Israel wants a similar provision in its proposed Free Trade Agreement (FTA) with India, but the government has been dragging its feet.

So you have a situation where old and established foreign companies, which seek to further consolidate their position in India, are coming in with large investments. These include players like Vodafone and Maruti-Suzuki. But fresh investments from new companies have slowed down. The only exception appears to be China, which is willing to take the risk and continue investing in India. Large brands like Huawei, Haier and Xiaomi have already drawn up investment plans; some Chinese companies are already financing the building of India's tallest building in Bengaluru; ICBC has already put up its office in Mumbai and Bank of China is waiting in the wings.

Meanwhile, another Supreme Court verdict[25] seems to offer some hope that the arbitration mess could be sorted out soon. After all, the logjam of institutional cases is believed to involve an estimated Rs 2.7 lakh crore (Rs 2.7 trillion).

Judicial redressal is a major reason why the investment mood is not very upbeat. India appears to have forgotten

---

[25] https://economictimes.indiatimes.com/news/economy/policy/
how-a-supreme-court-ruling-may-ease-logjam-in-arbitration-
cases/articleshow/63433608.cms

that judicial delays have a cost for investors. They do not like such situations. If India can ensure speedy dispute redressal, without stay orders and delays, foreign investors may opt for Indian courts. But that will happen only after India has created a track record of efficiency and fair play over a period of time. Currently, the confidence is missing, and understandably so. The government's penchant for bringing in laws with retrospective effect unnerves investors.

It may also be mentioned here, that even though India has managed to jump 23 places to rank #77 in the World Bank's Doing Business 2019 report[26], the fact remains that when it comes to enforcement of contracts India still ranks #163. It ranks #137 on starting a business; #166 on registering property; #121 on paying taxes #108 in resolving insolvency.[27]

This is because, as stated earlier, India has inherited a legacy from Indira Gandhi's time of ramming through judgements that are both unfair and of doubtful legal acceptability, according to some of the finest legal minds. India is known to have overturned past promises with impunity. India saw the abrogation of even a constitutional guarantee to the erstwhile princely states. Having lost the privy purses case in 1969, Indira Gandhi waited till she enjoyed the political clout to change the composition of judges in the Supreme Court. She then proposed the motion to abolish privy purses again, won the case, and the privy purse was abolished.

---

[26] https://www.livemint.com/Politics/GwXhAdltCo1
TCbRTAm5z0H/India-up-23-places-in-ease-of-doing-business-rankings.html

[27] https://www.livemint.com/Companies/qcmaOgYDIUCqo
UKe6MITuM/What-India-can-do-to-better-its-ease-of-doing-business-rank.html

Thus even a constitutional oath was cast aside.[28] That legacy makes legislators believe that they can change laws at their whim. The only saving grace is the Kesavananda Bharati case[29] where the Supreme Court ruled that amendments to the Constitution could be made, provided they did not alter the basic structure of the Constitution. The interpretation of what constitutes the basic structure of the Constitution still vests with the courts, at least for now.

Eventually, investments flow into areas where there is confidence in legal mechanisms. Once that confidence is gone, only high risk capital dares to come in. That comes with very high attendant costs.

Retrospective Laws and Corruption

When it comes to protecting their own ill-gotten wealth, every government in India has tried to usher in laws or postpone the hearing of cases in the courts. This government is no different.

On 14 March 2018, the Lok Sabha passed without any debate—but amid chaotic protests by the opposition parties—twenty-one amendments to the Finance Bill 2018. One of them was an amendment to the Foreign Contribution (Regulation) Act or FCRA, 2010, which bans overseas corporations from funding political parties.[30]

---

[28] Soli Sorabjii and Arvind P. Datar, *Nani Palkhivala: The Courtroom Genius*, available at Amazon, https://www.amazon. in/Nani-Palkhivala-Courtroom-Soli-Sorabjee/dp/8180387542

[29] Ibid and https://en.wikipedia.org/wiki/Kesavananda_Bharati_ v._State_of_Kerala

[30] https://www.outlookindia.com/website/story/foreign-poll-funding-will-no-longer-be-scrutinised/309658

In doing this—and it appears that both the BJP and the Congress parties were party to this manoeuvre—the legislators wanted to circumvent the Representation of People's Act, which lays down rules for elections and bars political parties from accepting foreign funds.[31] The BJP government had amended the FCRA through the Finance Bill 2016 to make it easier for parties to accept foreign funds. Now it has amended it further to do away with the scope for scrutiny of a political party's funding from overseas with retrospective effect since 1976.

Activists like E.A.S. Sarma (former secretary, economic affairs to the Government of India) had anticipated this. In a letter dated 3 February 2018, addressed to the finance minister and to the prime minister's office, Sarma pointed out that 'your government is once again adopting the inappropriate avenue of the Finance Bill to retrospectively amend FCRA, 1976 . . . This, in my view, is not only illegal but it runs counter to the national interest, making a mockery of your so-called campaign of bringing in electoral reforms and enhancing honesty in the electoral system . . . Both FCRA of 1976 and FCRA of 2010 rightly prohibited political parties and their members from accepting donations from foreign sources. The Representation of the People Act echoed these prohibitive provisions. It goes to the credit of the Parliamentarians at that time to have thought about the deleterious implications that foreign donations could have on the political parties and their implications for the national interest . . . I, along with Association for Democratic Reforms (ADR), filed a

---

[31] https://www.moneycontrol.com/news/india/comment-corruption-collusion-and-legislative-filibustering-will-cripple-democracy-2531493.html
http://www.asiaconverge.com/2018/03/corruption-collusion-legislative-filibustering/

Writ Petition [W.P.(C) 131/2013] before Hon'ble Delhi High Court contesting the same. The latter pronounced their judgement on 28-3-2014 upholding the contention in our WP and directing the Union Govt to act against the political parties within six months . . . Instead of complying with that judgement in an earnest and forthright manner, the two political parties, perhaps with the tacit consent of your government, chose to file appeals (SLP 18190/2014 & 32626/2014) before Hon'ble Supreme Court. The appeals of Congress and BJP were dismissed by the apex court on 29-11-2016. Though there was no interim order of the apex court against the High Court direction, the Union Home Ministry, for reasons best known to it, refrained from complying with the judgement dated 28-3-2014 of Hon'ble Delhi High Court. A contempt petition filed by us against the government is presently pending before the Hon'ble Delhi High Court.'

It was coincidental that in another case involving Tamil Nadu, the Supreme Court made the following observation on 15 February 2018: 'The Legislature cannot set at naught the judgments which have been pronounced by amending the law not for the purpose of making corrections or removing anomalies but to bring in new provisions which did not exist earlier. The legislature may have the power to remove the basis or foundation of the judicial pronouncement but the legislature cannot overturn or set aside the judgment, that too retrospectively by introducing a new provision. The legislature is bound by the mandamus issued by the court', said Justice Gupta, who wrote the judgment.[32]

---

[32] https://timesofindia.indiatimes.com/india/cant-overrule-courts-with-retrospective-amendments-says-supreme-court/articleshow/63324303.cms

Corruption May Be Bigger Than Imagined

Corruption is widespread in India, but the truth is that the exact amount of unaccounted or black money are not known. Each time there is a leak and some information comes out—the Panama papers, the Lichtenstein papers—the government promises an enquiry and then nothing comes out of it. Even exhortations from the Supreme Court have not been very effective.

Two incidents show that the figures could be larger than what is known.

										Table 7
Illegal mining continues unabated										
						for all minerals excluding atomic and fuel minerals				
	No. of illegal mining cases registered						Action taken from April '12 to Sept '15)			
States	2010–11	2011–12	2012–13	2013–14	2014–15	2015–16**	FIR lodged (Nos)	Court cases filed (Nos)	Vehicle seized (No.)	Fine realized by State govt (Rs Lakh)
Andaman & Nicobar	n.r.	n.r.	n.r.	n.r.	n. r.	n. r.	0	0	0	0
Andhra Pradesh	13,939	19,913	16,592	7,692	9,379	3,931	2	1	2	1,257
Assam	n.r.	n.r.	n.r.	n.r.	n. r.	n. r.	0	0	0	0
Chhattisgarh	2,017	2,946	3,238	3,996	5,040	2,647	2	13,383	1,138	2,645
Goa	13	1	0	1	0	2	0	0	1	0
Gujarat	2,184	3,485	6,023	5,447	5,716	2,280	240	27	8,941	41,725
Haryana	3,446	2,022	3,517	3,589	5,333	2,288	613	0	0	3,106
Himachal Pradesh	1,213	1,289	n.r.	n.r.	n.r.	n.r.	0	0	0	0
Jharkhand	199	364	663	901	1,162	854	1,891	253	1,346	1,978
Karnataka	6,476	6,691	6,677	8,509	8,464	4,725	620	539	9,720	7,772
Kerala	2,028	3,175	4,550	4,448	4,172	1,459	0	0	0	2,488
Madhya Pradesh	4,245	7,147	7,169	6,725	8,173	6,941	61	28,830	528	14,671
Maharashtra#	34,265	40,642	42,918	36,476	32,717	13,292	13	0	117,848	14,709
Mizoram	0	2	16	21	26	n.r.	1	0	0	2
Odisha	420	309	314	76	104	39	4	4	514	1,225
Punjab	754	314	19	n.r.	n.r.	n.r.	74	0	61	46
Rajasthan	1,833	1,201	2,861	2,953	2,945	1,423	2,258	53	4,235	4,343
Tamil Nadu	277	123	295	1,078	205	25	7,547	1	36,135	11,565
Telangana*	n.r.	n.r.	n.r.	n.r.	3,311	3,129	0	0	2	1,649
Uttar Pradesh	4,641	4,708	3,266	6,777	10,402	4,857	0	0	0	7,903
West Bengal	239	269	479	n.r.	n.r.	575	1,132	0	703	0
Grand Total	78,189	94,604	98,597	88,689	97,149	48,467	14,458	43,091	181,174	117,082

Notes: (a) *Data for Telangana available only after 2015 as it is a newly formed state. Andhra Pradesh data too is only for the bifurcated region after that year (b) n.r. = return not received (c) **Quarter ending Sept 2015. #However, the statement given to the Lok Sabha on 9 March 2017 does not give any value either for the amount of illegal mining material seized or the fines collected for some states, especially Maharashtra.

Sources: (1) Indian Bureau of Mines, Government of India (2) Reply to Lok Sabha on 23 August 2013, Unstarred Question No. 2391 on illegal mining (3) Lok Sabha Unstarred Question No. 2329, on 9 May 2016 on illegal mining (4) Lok Sabha Unstarred Question No. 1503, to be answered on 9 March 2017 on illegal mining

It may be worth rewinding to the turn of this century when illegal mining made national headlines. Two states were targeted: Karnataka and then Goa. Both were BJP ruled states. And both were charged with illegal mining. The governments of both states were accused of receiving political donations from illegal miners.

The unfortunate truth is that the profits from illegal mining can be insanely huge. Consider how, on 13 April 2018, the Odisha government slapped a charge of around Rs 3200 crore on illegal chrome miners.[33] And this is just one of the minor minerals that can be found in abundance in Odisha. Just a month earlier, on 21 March 2018, the state fined another illegal coal miner a whopping Rs 8300 crore![34]

Take another instance. When the Sarada chit fund papers were examined by the Central Bureau of Investigation (CBI), it was found that as much as Rs 1000 crore had been invested in illegal mining in the northeast.[35]

Then look at the government's own data presented before the Lok Sabha.[36] You will then discover that almost every state has indulged in illegal mining. The fines charged are laughably low. Even the trucks seized are not auctioned off. The list shows that Karnataka and Goa are small players compared to states like Maharashtra (it has been

[33] https://economictimes.indiatimes.com/industry/indl-goods/svs/metals-mining/odisha-slaps-rs-3200-crore-demand-notices-on-chrome-miners/articleshow/63747500.cms

[34] http://www.business-standard.com/article/companies/odisha-slaps-rs-83-bn-demand-notice-on-coal-india-firm-for-illegal-mining-118032100594_1.html

[35] http://www.moneycontrol.com/india/newsarticle/news_print.php?autono=10316381&sr_no=0

[36] http://www.freepressjournal.in/analysis/rn-bhaskar-maharashtra-haven-for-illegal-mining-political-funding/1058507 http://www.asiaconverge.com/2017/04/illegal-mining-and-political-funding/

ruled by both the Congress and the BJP at different times). The pickings are huge, and often, some of the money also finances Naxalism and environmental groups to stave off any development work in that area.[37] Invariably such groups operate in territories where illegal mining is rife. The protests against new infrastructure or organized mining projects are orchestrated through tribals, environmentalists and NGOs. But these very organizations have not taken up organized movements against illegal miners, often operating in the very same areas. Strangely enough, there is no information about illegal mining in the Northeast. That territory is notorious for the biggest moneymaking schemes and exploitation in India. Yet there is no data that emerges from the northeast. This is despite reports by the Economic and Political Weekly about illegal coal mining there[38] or pictures about illegal mining in the northeast[39] by Associated Press photographers on the state of exploitation in illegal mines in the northeast, and the Saradha chit fund money being invested there.

There is one more indicator of how much illegal wealth there could be in the country. And this input came from income tax returns filed with the income tax authorities.[40]

---

[37] http://www.moneycontrol.com/news/india/why-protection-from-markets-leads-to-rip-offs-an-example-from-tribal-india-2417491.html
http://www.asiaconverge.com/2017/10/protecting-exploiting-tribal-land/

[38] https://crawford.anu.edu.au/pdf/staff/rmap/lahiridutt/2011/KLD_Illegal_Coal_Mining_in_Eastern_India.pdf

[39] https://www.businessinsider.com/photos-indias-illegal-coal-mines-2012-10?IR=T#but-people-from-all-over-the-country-seek-out-such-work-that-reportedly-pays-150-per-week-this-is-double-the-national-average-of-about-75-per-week-7

[40] http://www.freepressjournal.in/analysis/rn-bhaskar-agri-laundromat-error-or-cover-up/1011862

It all exploded in public view, quite accidentally, in the first quarter of 2016 when a retired income tax officer filed a PIL plea before the Patna High Court. The petitioner asked the court to direct the income tax authorities to release the names of the top 1000 assessees who had declared huge agricultural incomes. According to the petition, the total agricultural income filed exceeded Rs 2000 lakh crore (2000 trillion).

Naturally, almost all publications carried this report, but then they forgot about it. But as one began digging deeper, and began putting together the numbers, it became clear that during 2011 and 2012 alone, around eight lakh individuals filed agricultural income assessment papers with the income tax authorities. If the numbers of assesses was large, the amounts declared were even larger. Just these two years had registered a cumulative income of Rs 874 lakh crore (Rs 874 trillion)—frighteningly large, but not as large as Rs 2000 lakh crore. Divide this number by the largest amount of tax collected during any single year, and you realize that the total incomes declared were a whopping 126 times annual tax collections. The government could declare a tax holiday for Indians for a hundred years! They were eight times India's gross value added (GVA) for that year.

The income tax authorities tried to suggest on 10 March 2016 (Letter F.No. Dgit(S)/Dit(S)-3/Ast/PIL Matter/ Agricultural Income/97/2015-16)[41] that this could be on account of typographical errors. But that would be an impossibility because any person with an income of more than Rs 20,000 is supposed to fill in tax forms (either directly

---

http://www.asiaconverge.com/2017/02/agriculture-as-laundromat-error-or-coverup/

[41] http://taxguru.in/income-tax/verification-agriculture-income-1-crore.html

or through his accountant) electronically. Thus the excuse of a data entry error on the part of tax officials does not fly.

If the individuals had fed in the wrong numbers, they were liable for prosecution because each of them had signed an undertaking that the figures submitted represented a true and fair picture of incomes. The wrong entries would expose them to the charge of providing false information to the tax authorities, which invites severe penalties both in the form of fines and imprisonment.

Now compare this with the amounts that demonetization involved—Rs 15.4 lakh crore. The total currency in circulation was under Rs 20 lakh crore. The agricultural income declared—Rs 874 lakh crore—is several times these levels.

Since agricultural incomes are totally tax-free, they are a great conduit for laundering slush funds. Almost every politician uses this route to justify tax-free income. But never have declarations reached the levels they did in 2011 and 2012, when P.C. Chidambaram was finance minister. Surprisingly, even the Chief Economic Advisor kept silent (Raghuram Rajan held the post then).

The Patna High Court promised to hear the matter in May 2016. It hasn't till now. The case is a hot potato for the income tax department. It can neither accept nor reject these numbers. To reject them, the tax authorities would have to send prosecution notices for supplying wrong information. If it accepts these numbers, the tax authorities and the government would have to declare the source of such income, as even the most fertile piece of land with the most exotic crops could not generate even one-hundredth of such sums.

Somewhere, India's moneymakers must have thought they could get away with this. But the plan did not work thanks to the PIL filed by the retired income tax officer.

So is it possible that the amendments to the FCRA in March
2018 (as described above) were an attempt to sanitize illegal
funds with political parties? Could that be the reason why no
political party raised objections about the passage of these
amendments?? So, is India's black money then more than
eight times its GDP?

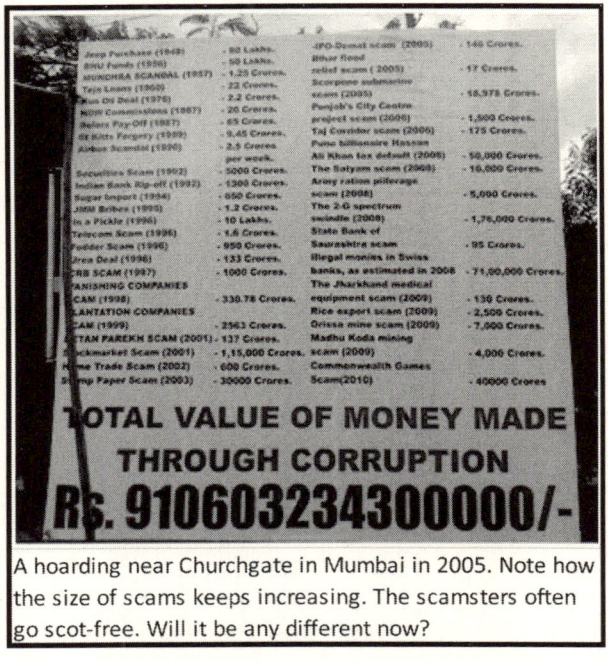

A hoarding near Churchgate in Mumbai in 2005. Note how
the size of scams keeps increasing. The scamsters often
go scot-free. Will it be any different now?

These figures give a totally new perspective to the concept of
black money.

Scams Galore

A hoarding put up in Mumbai almost fifteen years ago
expressed the situation quite succinctly. During the period
1948–2010, India's scams had already accounted for Rs 910

lakh crore—quite close to the Rs 874 lakh crore declared as agricultural income.

Each time a scam takes place, the government brings in new rules, which it says will tighten regulation. Each time, it arms itself with more powers. But each time the amounts get larger, and each time the key players escape.

The examples are many. Nobody even knows where Ramesh Gelli, the erstwhile chairman and managing director of the extinct Global Trust Bank is, or how he was given the first licence to start a private bank. Nobody knows anything about C.R. Bhansali's whereabouts today. He was the scamster who hoodwinked the RBI, market watchdog SEBI and all other regulatory authorities.[42] CRB's merchant banking division handled scores of dubious public issues and went around claiming that it was 'the country's No 1 merchant banker'. CRB's auditors would have been blind not to have read the signs of imminent collapse when they checked the company's accounts.[43] Even the scams of ICICI and other Indian banks will soon become distant memory, never mind the huge amount the Kochars arranged for errant companies, which were eventually declared as non-performing assets (NPAs). A few anecdotes explain how brazen India's policymakers can be, and how frail public memory can be.[44]

---

[42] https://www.indiatoday.in/magazine/economy/story/19970609-c.r.-bhansali-scandal-exposes-ineffectiveness-of-regulators-risk-small-investors-face-831540-1997-06-09

[43] https://www.outlookindia.com/magazine/story/the-anatomy-of-a-fraud/203687

[44] https://www.moneycontrol.com/news/business/comment-lessons-not-learned-indias-scams-amount-to-enemy-action-2550399.html
http://www.asiaconverge.com/2018/04/lessons-not-learned-indias-scams-amount-enemy-action/

When the Harshad Mehta scam took place in the 1990s, everyone came to learn that the source of illegitimate funds was through pledging of fake bankers receipts with banks. Bankers receipts were like treasury bills that could be pledged with banks, and loans could be taken against them. Later it came to be known that because there was no centralized database that could be verified online (the age of the Internet had already dawned), pledging fake bankers receipts, or presenting the same bankers receipts to different banks and taking money several times over was easy game. Banks and the central bank resolved to plug this loophole.

Come 2013, and another financial institution—the National Spot Exchange Ltd (NSEL)—had to be abruptly shut down because warehouse receipts were issued for grains that were supposed to have been stored but weren't actually there. Once again, people realized that without an online database, such scams were bound to happen.

Fast forward to 2018. You have an even bigger scam involving Letters of Understanding (LoUs) that were issued by banks. The RBI had asked banks not to lend against them, but they did. And, once again, there was no central database of the LoUs issued and pledged. Déjà vu!

Even while investigations are ongoing, one of the biggest borrowers was the Essar group. Its loans from Standard Chartered Bank were paid off by selling to Rosneft of Russia the oil refining business under Essar Oil Ltd in India. The Directorate of Revenue Intelligence (DRI) investigation (documented in a 384-page dossier, No. DRI/MZU/CI-11/2013-14 of 11 March 2015) into the manner in which lakhs of crores of funds were siphoned off to tax havens has been gathering dust. Even in the case of Vijay Mallya, a small company in Singapore could get a court decree, attach Mallya's assets and recover some USD 300 million. Employees of Mallya's luxury yacht could get a court order, hock off the yacht and get their unpaid dues. But the Government of India has recovered precious little!

As always, some small fish will be caught, humiliated and sentenced. The big guys will get away laughing.

In Conclusion

India's tainted past would be grist for many scam-based stories. That is one part of the problem. Businessmen know how to deal with scams and how to pay the price for funding corrupt politicians. But they cannot deal with a situation wherein they do not have access to dispute resolution. That is where India will have to make up its mind soon.

Sometimes having a strong party at the centre is bad for business. This is what India's history has shown.[45] But genuine political reform can come either by good mass education—where India has failed miserably—or through a strong judiciary. The latter is the subject of much discussion and attention lately. The eventual aim must be to ensure that people feel more secure and less vulnerable.

If India has to grow, it will have to assure investors that their money is safe, and that they have a right to dispute resolution in any international court. India's biggest challenge will be to create confidence in its law enforcement machinery. If that is set right, all other problems will automatically get tackled. That will be the space many will be watching.

---

[45] https://www.moneycontrol.com/news/business/economy/comment-are-strong-governments-bad-for-the-indian-economy-2528037.html
http://www.asiaconverge.com/2018/03/strong-governments-bad-indian-economy/

SIX

The Seed and the Fruit

No story about India can be complete without discussing agriculture. This is because of several reasons:

First, almost 50 per cent of India's population lives in rural areas and is engaged with agriculture in some form or the other.

Second, agricultural prosperity thus affects at least 50 per cent of the electorate in India and it therefore becomes a major political concern as well. Hence, if the rains fail, or unseasonal rains destroy a crop, it immediately becomes a political issue. Not surprisingly, this is one sector that gets more attention from politicians than any other.

Third, for a variety of reasons, the small farmer remains one of the most exploited categories of people. In contrast, large farmers (who form a very thin crust of this community) remain the most pampered. They play the role that slumlords do in a city (see Chapter V).

Nothing shows this exploitation as starkly as the sectoral share that agriculture enjoys in gross domestic product (GDP). The share of agriculture has plummeted from over 50 per cent of India's GDP in the 1950s to well under

20 per cent today.[1] Table 1 (Sectoral composition of GDP) has older data because the government decided to switch over from GDP to the gross value added (GVA) format since 2011. When 50 per cent of the population contributes to just 17 per cent of GDP, it does suggest that this segment has been marginalized, has been paid little, and even exploited.

Table 1			
Sectoral composition of GDP in India			
Year	Agriculture	Industry	Services
1950–51	53.1	16.6	30.3
1960–61	48.7	20.4	30.8
1970–71	42.3	24.0	33.8
1980–81	36.1	25.9	38.0
1990–91	29.6	27.7	42.7
2000–01	22.3	27.3	50.4
2010–11	14.5	27.8	57.7
2011–12	13.9	27.0	59.0
Sources: Economic surveys			

The GVA Issue

Gross value added can be described quite simply as the total value of all the money that all the stakeholders make through an activity. It does not matter if the activity relates to industry or agriculture or services:

---

[1] Since the government has not introduced a new set of GDP figures with backdata series,, sectoral GDP figures are available only till 2012. But data compiled by the World Bank shows that the share of agriculture to GDP has remained under 17 per cent.

- First, there is money that a government takes away in the form of taxes both direct and indirect. Agriculture is exempt from paying income tax. That is also why agriculture offers the best loophole for powerful politicians and bureaucrats if they want to evade payment of income tax.
- Then there are the workers (who get paid wages and perquisites for the work they do). They contribute to the value-addition by helping convert raw material into a finished product.
- Third is the interest a business pays to the banker or the lender for purchase of machinery or for working capital loans. That is money that the banker collects.
- Some money also goes to shareholders or stakeholders. For enterprises we call this dividends, or share of profit. In agriculture, it is not uncommon for farmers to promise workers a share of their income in the form of crops, thus incentivizing them to produce more.
- Finally, there is money that the entrepreneur or enterprise holds on to in the form of savings (or reserves). That is also part of value added.

These five then become the value added in any commercial activity. Calculations based on the concept of GDP can give rise to a different set of numbers than those based on GVA, as Table 2 will show.

Thus while agriculture and allied activities may have accounted for a 10.5

Table 2
Relationship between Output and Value added
2011–12 to 2014–15

Sector	Average ratio of	
	Sectoral output to total output	Sectoral GVA to total GVA
Agriculture and allied	10.5	17.5
Industry, of which	53.9	31.8
Manufacturing	36.7	17.4
Services	35.6	50.7
Total	100.0	100.0
Sources: CSO data		

per cent share of output (which is very close to GDP), it translates into 17.5 per cent (see Table 3) when the GVA method is used. Whichever method one chooses to use, both point to the same thing—that agriculture gets a smaller share of the GDP or the GVA. What this means is that either farmers will start clamouring for higher prices (this is happening already) or they will move away from agriculture (which too is happening). The first move will cause the GDP/GVA share to increase for the farm sector. The second move will cause the percentage of the population in agriculture to decline to the point when the GDP/GVA share is almost equal to the share of the population. In fact both are happening now.

But this also means that consumers pay higher prices. There are two simple solutions to escape this bizarre situation where either the farmer gets paid less for his produce, or the consumer pays more. The first is to ensure that yields for farmers increase, so that he gets more per acre and thus increases his earnings without increasing prices. The second is by reducing the margins that middlemen get, so that the share to the farmer increases without any end increase in prices.

							Table 3
Sector share of GVA at basic rate at current prices							
Industry	**2011–12**	**2012–13**	**2013–14**	**2014–15***	**2015–16#**	**2016–17@**	**(2nd AE)**
I- Agriculture	18.5	18.7	18.6	18.7	17.7	17.9	17.1
II-Industry	32.5	31.8	30.8	30	29.8	29.3	28.9
Mining and quarrying	32	31	29	27	24	24	25
Manufacturing	17.4	17.1	16.5	16.3	16.8	16.8	16.6
Electricity, gas & water suppl	2.3	2.3	2.5	2.5	2.7	1.6	2.6
Construction	9.6	9.2	8.9	8.5	7.9	7.4	7.3
III-Services	49	50	50.6	51.8	52.5	52.8	54
GVA at basic rate	100	100	100	100	100	100	100
Notes: (*) Third Revised Estimates (New Series); (#) Second Revised Estimates; (@) First revised estimates; (AE) Advanced Estimates							
Sources: Office of the Chief Economic Advisor;							
http://eaindustry.nic.in/key_economic_indicators/Key_Economic_Indicators.pdf							

What Verghese Kurien did (see the chapter on milk) was to ensure both. Yields for farmers was pushed up through education (better cattle feed, better cross breeding and better care), and squeezing out the middleman. There is little evidence that the government has managed to do this for most farmers for the past few decades.

As a result as a recent survey by NABARD shows (see Table 4) the farmer remains impoverished. Although the average all-India monthly income for rural households is Rs 8059, it can be as low as one fourth the amount for marginalized farmers. With such low incomes any talk about doubling farm incomes is just not enough. The farmer must get more—and as Kurien often stated, it should be not less than 50 per cent of the market price.

						Table 4
Average Monthly Household Income by Source of Income						
Source of income	Agricultural households		Non-agricultural households		All households	
	Rs	%	Rs	%	Rs	%
Cultivation	3,140	35	NA	NA	1,494	19
Livestock rearing	711	8	NA	NA	338	4
Other enterprises	489	6	851	12	679	8
Wage labour	3,025	34	3,940	54	3,504	43
Govt/Pvt. Service	1,444	16	2,326	32	1,906	24
Other sources	122	1	152	2	138	2
All sources combined	**8,931**	**100**	**7,269**	**100**	**8,059**	**100**

Notes: The figures presented above highlight that wage labour was the most remunerative source of income for all households contributing a major proportion of roughly half of the total household income, the contribution being higher among non-agricultural households as compared to the agricultural ones. For the agricultural households, cultivation remained the most prominent source contributing roughly 35% of the overall monthly income, followed by wage labour (34%) and government/private services (16%). Among the non-agricultural ones, it was the government/private service which contributed maximum (32%) to the total household income after wage labour, which made up for roughly 54% of the total income.

Sources: Nabard's All India Rural Financial Inclusion Survey 2016–17—https://www.nabard.org/auth/writereaddata/tender/1608180417NABARD-Repo-16_Web_P.pdf

What is equally worrying about the income structure of most farmers is that the amount that they earn from livestock is pathetically low. Rs 711 is extremely low, when just milk output could generate over Rs 3000 per month from a single cow/buffalo.[2] Once again, it points the inability of state governments to ensure that the cooperative movement started by Kurien had spread across each rural district, and that farmers could get a fair price for their produce.

The disparity in farm incomes becomes clearer when one examines Table 5. Also sourced from the Nabard survey, it shows how impoverished farmers can be even in agriculturally progressive states like Jharkhand. As far as Maharashtra is concerned, except for the pampered sugarcane and cotton growers, the state has actually abdicated its responsibility of even providing irrigation to farmers (more on this later).

There is one more fact that needs to be highlighted. Cultivation accounts for barely 35 per cent of even these low

_____
[2] Table 5, Chapter 1 of this book.

Table 5	
States and farm prosperity	
Average Monthly Household Income by States (in Rs per month per household)	
India	8,059
Andhra Pradesh	5,842
Jharkhand	5,854
Uttar Pradesh	6,257
Bihar	6,277
Madhya Pradesh	6,632
West Bengal	6,860
Odisha	7,241
Chhattisgarh	7,272
Telangana	7,811
Rajasthan	8,338
Karnataka	8,383
Sikkim	8,560
Tripura	8,612
Uttarakhand	8,762
Assam	8,880
Maharashtra	8,938
Mizoram	9,491
Manipur	9,679
Tamil Nadu	9,716
Arunachal Pradesh	9,877
Nagaland	10,002
Meghalaya	10,061
Gujarat	10,518
Jammu	10,747
Goa	10,758
Himachal Pradesh	11,702
Haryana	12,072
Kerala	15,130
Punjab	16,020

Notes: Base—All households
Sources: Nabard's All India Rural Financial Inclusion Survey 2016–17—ttps://www.nabard.org/auth/writereaddata/tender/1608180417NABARD-Repo-16_Web_P.pdf

incomes. Clearly, cultivation by itself is not remunerative. The farmer remains exploited in most parts of the country—more on this too a bit later.

There are additional reasons why the government does not want to ignore agriculture, and can supplement those listed out earlier. The first is the need to ensure food security. India was vulnerable at the time it won independence. The failure of rains in a single season could lead to famines, resulting in either deaths or a desperate need to import grain and other items. Sometimes it was both. Thankfully, over the past few decades, mostly on account of better irrigation and more sensible agricultural practices (more on this later), agriculture has become less dependent on the rains, though its impact can still be felt.

The second reason is that agriculture and services offer a country a very high value-added share in any economic activity. This appeals to economists immensely because it points to the additional value that a country can create from the resources available.

Opportunity and Challenges

The focus on agriculture increased when Lal Bahadur Shastri became prime minister in the late 1960s. Aware of how industry had been given tremendous importance by Jawaharlal Nehru (his predecessor), and the shock India had received from losing the 1962 war to China, Shastri began pushing India's planners to take a serious look at both agriculture and defence. He coined the phrase 'Jai Jawan, Jai Kisan'. Ever since then, India's politicians and policymakers have remained fixated on both themes. History has shown that parties have lost the elections when the agricultural sector (and the defence sector as well) is not tended to with care and concern.

In fact, it was Shastri's emphasis on agricultural research that pushed agricultural universities to begin working on hybrid strains of wheat, which then ushered in the green revolution (though the credit for this is often given to Shastri's successor, Indira Gandhi).

The results were startling. As an expert put it, 'The total area under the high-yielding varieties programme was a negligible 1.9 million hectares in fiscal year 1960. Since then, growth has been spectacular, increasing to nearly 15.4 million hectares by fiscal year 1970, 43.1 million hectares by fiscal year 1980, and 63.9 million hectares by fiscal year 1990. The rate of growth decreased significantly in the late 1980s, however, as additional suitable land was not available.'

India had learnt to feed its own people. But it now had a problem of surplus, corruption and callous cynicism.

Notwithstanding the attention agriculture received, its share in GDP and GVA was marginalized (see tables 1 and 3). One reason was that industry grew faster. A second reason was the channelling of funds to industry—never mind the scams and the resultant non-performing assets (NPAs) in the banking sector. A third reason was the rapid growth of the services sector, especially the banking, software and information technology (IT) sectors, which dwarfed even industry.

Agriculture's 14 per cent share in GDP (or the 17.5 per cent share in GVA) poses a big challenge. When 50 per cent of the people contribute only 14 per cent of GDP, there is a mismatch. Something has to give way. One possibility, as mentioned earlier, is for agricultural produce prices to soar till they account for a share of close to 50 per cent of GDP. The second possibility is that people will begin to move away from agriculture because of its poor returns. That way, over a period of time, the population share will come close to the GDP share. Maybe a bit of both is happening right now.

Agricultural prices are rising. And migration to urban areas is noticeable.

But neither is desirable, either economically or politically. A better solution has to be found. That would depend on two strategies.

The first is to increase productivity for each type of crop. The second is to value-add to agricultural produce by integrating it with food processing industries and ensuring better access to markets. There is a third strategy too, which is boosting economic activity in villages so that villages become towns and towns become cities. In this way, the urge to move to urban centres could be controlled. But we shall not discuss this third option here.

The first strategy—increasing productivity—would bring immediate cash to the farmer. The second would ensure stable incomes for the farmer. Proper access to the markets and better methods of price discovery would allow both the farmer as well as the food processing industry to benefit.

Increasing Productivity

Schoolbooks always blame the poor productivity levels of Indian farms on the high degree of fragmentation of land ownership. But that could be a misleading statement. China has more fragmented and smaller holdings. True, as a nation, China has three times India's land mass. But when it comes to arable land, and water, India has a lot more of it than China does.

But what China does better than India is farm management. Its yields are better and its value addition—conversion of agricultural produce into value-added products—is far superior to that of India.

There is another way to look at India's agriculture. India is the world's number one producer of many types of

		Table 6
Agriculture—India and China		
Figures for 2016	**China**	**India**
Total land area—hectares	959,700,000	328,700,000
Arable land—hectares	134,920,900	172,896,200
Irrigated land—hectares	67,141,000	96,457,000
Farm size for every person in rural area in (hectares)	0.156	0.216
Avg. size of household	3.1	5
Avg. farm holding per family*	0.4836	1.08
Farm machines:		
large & mid-size tractors (> 50 HP)	6,454,000	34,597
small-size tractor (upto 50 HP)	16,716,000	474,104
Value of farm output in trillion (Yuan for China and Rs For India)	**5.9**	**8.36**
Rice yield（kg/ha)	**6,862**	**138**
Wheat yield (kg/ha)	**5,327**	**133**
Per capita disposable income of rural residents (Yuan for China, Rs for India)	12,363	111,890

Notes: 1 yuan is approximately Rs 10.5; ha=hectares. When it comes to value of farm output for China, 5.9 trillion is just the value of farm output. Gross output which infludes the value of farming, forestry, animal husbandry and fishery was 11.2 trillion yuan in 2016.(*) The NSSO puts average size of land holding per household at 0.59 ha. in 2017, the World Bank estimates rural population to comprise 66.46% of the total population, or 863 million. It also estimates the average size of rural houseold to be five members.

Sources: Ministry of Agriculture and Rural Affairs and National Bureau of Statistics, Shanghai Institute of International Studies, MOSPI World Bank and RBI's Handbook of Statistics on Indian States 2017–18; India's tractor industry

agricultural items (see Table 7). Some of these are by default because nobody else (or very few others) in the world produces them. This is true of items like buffalo milk, cara-beef (meat from buffaloes) and pulses. But the list of other items is quite impressive indeed.

		Table 7
Crops where India ranks #1		
Fresh Fruit	Okra	Ginger
Lemons and limes	Jute	Chickpeas
Buffalo milk, whole, fresh	Beeswax	Areca nuts
Castor oil seeds	Bananas	Goat milk, whole, fresh
Sunflower seeds	Mangoes, mangosteens, guavas	Pigeon peas
Sorghum	Pulses	Papayas
Millet	Indigenous buffalo meat	Chillies and peppers, dry
Spices	Fruit, tropical	Anise, badian, fennel, coriander
Notes: India does not rank as the biggest cow milk producer. And the recent developments related to the ban on cow slaughter will reduce the cow population further.		
Sources: The Statistics Office of the Food and Agriculture Organisation according to final numbers for 2009		

But when one looks at products that other countries also offer, and then compares yields for those products, India's vulnerability becomes quite visible (see Table 8). One would have thought that a large production base would allow both the government and farmers to work together to make that agricultural product more competitive in the markets. One would have thought that yields would improve. But when you look at the yields in India, and those overseas for the same type of products, you realize how miserably India fares. Just look at buffalo milk, where India is the sole producer. Compare the average yield with the highest yield of milk per buffalo and the inequities in Indian farming begin to show up.

Or take rice. India produces just 3.99 tonnes per hectare while Australia produces 12 tonnes.

Ditto with wheat where India's output of 2.8 tonnes per hectare is dwarfed by the 8.9 tonnes of the Netherlands. India is today surplus in wheat production (more on this later), but it is a very inefficient producer.

Improving productivity is not an easy job for many reasons. First, the seeds used overseas may not be suited for the Indian climate and soil. And there is always a danger of genetic contamination if seeds from other agro-

				Table 8
Major agricultural products in India by value				
	Figures for India		**Most productive country/world**	
Commodity	**Value (US$ bn, 2013)**	**Avg yield (tonnes/ha, 2010)***	**Avg yield (tonnes/ha, 2010)***	**Country**
Milk	46.83			
of which				
Buffalo milk	27.92	0.63	23.7	India
Cow milk	18.91	1.2	10.3	Israel
Rice	42.57	3.99	12.03	Australia
Wheat	13.98	2.8	8.9	Netherlands
Mangoes, guavas	10.79	6.3	40.6	Cape Verde
Sugar cane	10.42	66	125	Peru
Cotton	8.65	1.6	4.6	Israel
Bananas	7.77	37.8	59.3	Indonesia
Potatoes	7.11	19.9	44.3	USA
Tomatoes	6.74	19.3	524.9	Belgium
Fresh vegetables	6.27	13.4	76.8	USA
Buffalo meat	4.33	0.138	0.424	Thailand
Groundnuts	4.11	1.8	17	China
Okra	4.06	7.6	23.9	Israel
Onions	4.05	16.6	67.3	Ireland
Chickpeas	3.43	0.9	2.8	China
Chicken meat	3.32	10.6	20.2	Cyprus
Fresh fruits	3.25	1.1	5.5	Nicaragua
Hen eggs	3.18	0.1	0.42	Japan
Soybeans	3.09	1.1	3.7	Turkey

Notes: Average yield for milk/meat/eggs is per head of species; except for buffaloes where India has no other competitor country, yields are terribly poor; ha=hectare

Sources: Food and Agricultural commodities production/ Commodities by country/India: FAOSTAT, 2013; http://faostat3.fao.org/browse/root_0/commodities_by_country/E; https://en.wikipedia.org/wiki/Agriculture_in_India

climatic regions are planted indiscriminately in India. A lot more work has to be done by India's agricultural research institutes to come up with the right variety of seeds, which can cope with India's soil and climate yet produce more grain per acre.

There are other problems too that are more serious. Indian farmers are not sticklers for good processes. They love taking shortcuts. Then there is the problem of migration of the brightest of minds from villages to towns and cities. They are drawn by the allure of the cities and the growth prospects there. They see little glamour in villages. Go to any farm and talk to young boys playing in the fields. Ask them what they would like to do once they finish school. Each one of them is likely to tell you that if his marks are good, he will migrate to the city. But then who will manage the farm, you ask them. One boy's reply was quite charming, but to the point. He scratched his head, then smiled and said, 'My uncle's son opted out of school in standard V. He can look after the farm.'

This 'brain drain' does pose a challenge. If the brightest of the children are deserting farming—they never give up their ownership of land though, which is immensely valued in India—then how will the not-so-bright understand and cope with the adoption of new technology?

Modi's Solution

When Narendra Modi, who became prime minister of India in 2014, was chief minister of Gujarat, he had realized this problem of most farmers not comprehending new farm technology.

He attempted to address it in several ways.

As access to water was crucial to increasing agricultural productivity, he first lobbied hard for raising the height of the Narmada dam. This allowed water to reach districts furthest away from the river.

He also knew that the water from the river would not be enough to meet the farming requirements of all farmers in the region. He therefore began pursuing other strategies to increase access to water. For one, he began using the MNREGA scheme of the government, which guaranteed a hundred days of employment in a year. He got people to build check dams across the state. The message was simple. Let the water in the river stay in the river, and the water in the ponds stay in ponds. But there is no need to allow the runoff water to go into gutters and into the sea. Over a period of ten years, the state had built some twelve lakh check dams. With rainwater getting accumulated in such dams, more farms had water for crop irrigation. Moreover, it wasn't long before the water tables in the state began rising—Gujarat was perhaps the only state in India to boast of this achievement.

He also began pushing for the adoption of drip irrigation (Table 9).

			Table 9
Drip irrigation			
Productivity gains for select crops (tonnes per acre)			
Crop	**Rain fed**	**Canal/Tubewell**	**Micro-irrigation with fertigation**
Cotton	0.3–0.4	0.8–1.5	2–2.5 (Achieved > 2.5)
Wheat	0.3–0.4	1.5–2.0	2.5–3.0 (In R&D)
Sugar cane	20	25–35	40–80 (Achieved 100)
Potato	NA	6–10	15–20 (Achieved 22+)
Chillies (Green)	5–10	15–20	25–40 (Achieved 45+)
Sources: Industry and farm interviews			

Drip irrigation has the remarkable ability of increasing per hectare yields while consuming less water than conventional irrigation. In order to ensure that more farmers adopted this technique, Modi resorted to three strategies.[3]

First, like almost every other state, he allowed a subsidy of 50 per cent on the cost of the drip irrigation system.

Second, he got appropriate rules passed so that no new agricultural pump connections would be allowed unless the local engineer certified that the farm had installed a drip irrigation system.

The third was even more interesting. He was aware that most farmers need handholding. They need to be coaxed into using technology. So he passed a rule that the subsidy for drip irrigation systems would be reimbursed to the manufacturers of these systems only if they could handhold the farmer-customers for at least a year, with at least one visit each month. While some manufacturers protested against any such move, one Indian company, Netafim India (a wholly owned subsidiary of Netafim of Israel)[4] agreed to do this.

In order to monitor the performance of such drip irrigation manufacturers, Modi set up a company called the Gujarat Golden Revolution Company (GGRC).[5] This company was mandated to check that Netafim's (or any other drip irrigation company's) scientists did visit the farms of each drip irrigation customer and addressed their concerns relating to crops, pests and water

---

[3] http://www.asiaconverge.com/2010/05/narendra-modis-farm-miracle/

[4] https://www.netafim.com/
This company is still headquartered in Israel, though its shareholders are now from other countries.

[5] http://www.asiaconverge.com/2014/01/small-farmers-should-grow-more-with-less/
https://www.news18.com/news/india/forbes-india-gujarat-shows-way-to-green-revolution-335156.html

consumption. Only after GGRC certified that the requisite number of visits had indeed been made could the application for the reimbursement of the subsidy amount be cleared.

Netafim Grows

Such a demand compelled Netafim to employ agricultural graduates and train them on helping farmers understand which crops should be grown given the soil quality, climate and water availability. Farmers were taught how to take photographs of diseased crops on their mobile phones and send them to Netafim. The scientists would then examine the images and shortlist possible pests. So when the Netafim expert visited the farmer, he would already be familiar with the nature of the problem reported and thus also armed with possible solutions.

Modi immediately saw that the expertise of these trained agricultural scientists would be useful to the students of the state's agricultural universities. So he urged Netafim to let a few students accompany each expert. That way, the students would learn about new approaches to crop management that were not taught by their teachers in their classrooms. Modi had begun preparing a new crop of agricultural scientists well versed with new technologies and solutions.

It was these strategies that helped Modi transform agriculture for his state. For the first time, Gujarat bested other states in the country by posting a 10 per cent year-on-year growth for almost ten years, after which growth rates climbed to 12 per cent. This was against the national average of 2–2.5 per cent.

The MP Marvel

Such strategies are now being pursued by Madhya Pradesh, which appears to have bested the growth rates achieved in Gujarat (see Table 10). In fact, Madhya Pradesh got transformed from being one of the sickly states often referred to as Bimaru (an acronym for a group of poorly off states—Bihar, Madhya Pradesh, Rajasthan and Uttar Pradesh). Unlike Gujarat, it has yet to move aggressively into industry and technology. But the first few steps it has taken are impressive (see Table 10).

Netafim and Jharkhand

By adopting both technology and hand-holding of farmers in Gujarat, Netafim's market share for drip irrigation systems in that state swelled beyond 70 per cent. That got the company calls from other states, and new solutions for agriculture in different climate zones and different soil grades had to be found for them as well. One of the brilliant strategies Netafim introduced was in the state of Jharkhand.[6]

Netafim showed the tribal communities of Jharkhand how to convert bare unproductive land in the mountainous region into fertile farms within three to six months. It all began with the state government's desire to improve the lot of tribals who were being seduced into terrorism (Naxalism) because of the lack of opportunities for economic growth.

One problem that exists in India is that tribal land cannot be sold to non-tribals. While this looks good on paper, in reality tribal land becomes something few people are willing to touch. As a result, in and around Ranchi, the price difference between tribal and non-tribal lands could be anywhere between ten and a hundred times. Banks cannot register them as collateral because of their non-bankability.

Thus, most tribals offer their lands to wealthy (and politically well connected) tribals out of desperation. Thus,

---

[6] http://www.asiaconverge.com/2012/09/jharkhand-miracle-netafim-drip-irrigation/

			Table 10
Madhya Pradesh Marvel			
Yields & Technology			
	Figures for 2005–06	**Latest year available**	**Diff between 2005 & now (%)**
ESTIMATES OF YIELD - RICE			
			kg per hectare
Madhya Pradesh	999.0	1,752.3	**175.41**
ALL INDIA	**2,102.0**	**2,400.2**	**114.19**
ESTIMATES OF YIELD - WHEAT			
			kg per hectare
Madhya Pradesh	1,613.0	2,992.5	**185.52**
ALL INDIA	**2,619.0**	**3,034.0**	**115.85**
ESTIMATES OF YIELD - TOTAL FOODGRAINS			
			kg per hectare
Madhya Pradesh	1,130.0	1,940.6	**171.73**
ALL INDIA	**1,715.0**	**2,041.6**	**119.05**
ESTIMATES OF YIELD - OILSEEDS			
			kg per hectare
Madhya Pradesh	1,009.0	841.2	**83.37**
ALL INDIA	**1,004.0**	**968.0**	**96.41**
ESTIMATES OF YIELD - COTTON (LINTT)			
			kg per hectare
Madhya Pradesh	204	544	**266.43**
ALL INDIA	**362**	**415**	**114.64**
PER HECTARE CONSUMPTION OF FERTILISER			
			kg per hectare
Madhya Pradesh	47.1	83.6	**177.47**
ALL INDIA (Average)	**104.5**	**130.7**	**125.03**

Notes: *2014–15 figures; rest 2015–16 figures

Sources: RBI Handbook of Statistics on Indian States 2017–18; https://m.rbi.org.in/scripts/AnnualPublications.aspx?head=Handbook%20of%20Statistics%20on%20Indian%20States

wealthy tribals become more wealthy and powerful by buying up tribal land at highly discounted (and distressed) prices. The dispossessed tribals have little choice but to move to some other rich tribal who can offer money. Recruiters of terrorists are willing to do this. This is how the cycle of deprivation, dissatisfaction and insurrection goes on and on. This is the story in all reserved areas—whether it is land in Sikkim for Sikkimese, or land in Kashmir for Kashmiris or land in the northeast for tribals of that region. Most tribals end up poor, because they cannot get a market price for the land they own. Without price discovery and the ability to get the same price for land that others (non-tribals) get, poor tribals remain vulnerable and exploited.

What Netafim did was persuade tribals to wrest back at least 1,000 square metres (a quarter of an acre) of their own land from their rich brethren. Then the tribals were taught how to create small seed incubators using plastic eggshell trays in which each cup is filled with coco peat (a rich growing medium made from coconut fibre).

One seed is placed in each cup. Within a couple of weeks, the seeds sprout, and each cup has a tiny plant growing in it. Two more weeks and the plant is ready to be transplanted. Coco peat is almost weightless. So when the plant is removed from the cup, it comes out easily (see Table 11). Using mud would have posed a problem because the weight of the moist mud would have weighed down the tender roots and damaged them.

The plant is put into a polypack filled with earth, to get it used to the soil. Four weeks later, the plastic polypack is cut away. The plant, with the earth surrounding it, is then planted in the soil. Using this technique, the mortality rate of seeds has dropped from around 50 to 60 per cent to less than 5 per cent.

Table 11

Clockwise from top left: Cocopeat being filled; one seed per cup; each cup has a sprout; the Sintex tank is ready with drip irrigation; bountiful harvest; Munda, who could have become a terrorist

To irrigate the crops, Netafim designed simple platforms atop which a 'Sintex' tank could be placed. A pump is attached to the tank to fill it up. In the mountainous regions where electricity supply is extremely erratic, this method ensures that even half an hour of electricity can help fill the tank. Then gravity does the rest of the job of supplying water to the plants below through drip irrigation. As drip irrigation doesn't require much water, the water in the tank lasts for several days.

Result? In three months, each tribal household was making a tidy sum of around Rs 30,000. News about the pilot scheme spread like wildfire and the authorities have been inundated with requests for more such support teams ever since.

Netafim continues to grow. It works on a new concept for each project, using its global expertise and crafting it to suit local needs. Already, it is on its way to watching India become its most profitable country-territory. India has begun to dwarf Netafim's operations in the US as well.[7]

Great Stories, but . . .

The Gujarat, Madhya Pradesh and Jharkhand agri-revolutions are great stories. But the success of such strategies also depends on three other factors—market access, price discovery and price stability. All of them have a lot to do with government policy. As the following pages explain, the APMCs (Agricultural Produce Market Committees) that the government created became monopolies and prevented farmer access to markets. The WDRA (Warehousing & Development Regulations Act) was a great scheme which would have empowered farmers, but the wheat and rice lobbies which rooted for government procurement through the Food Corporation of India (FCI) and State Warehousing Corporations did not allow the WDRA or the commodity exchanges to succeed. Commodity markets

---

[7] http://www.freepressjournal.in/business/india-has-become-key-
focus-area-for-netafims-ceo-ran-maidan/1022717
http://www.asiaconverge.com/2017/02/netafim-has-its-sights-
on-india/

would have allowed for price discovery. The WDRA would have worked in conjunction with commodity markets. As for price stability, one needs to look to Kurien—he created a body which ensured imports did not depress domestic prices. Such an agency could work very closely with both the WDRA and the commodity exchanges. Unfortunately, in India, the story invariably ends the same way. Despite the best-laid plans, avarice always appears to overtake good intentions. Unless you have a strong visionary like Kurien (see Chapter 1) or a strong leader like Modi (at least during his chief ministerial days), policymakers and politicians somehow manage to collude at the expense of simple farmers.

In the name of protecting farmers, most states created APMCs where farmers could sell their produce, especially perishables like fruit and vegetables. However, the APMCs eventually became mafias, not permitting any farmer to sell his produce to customers directly. It was not long before the price differentials between selling prices in villages in the catchment area of the APMCs, and consuming metropolises, began spreading to anywhere between five to ten times. Unlike Kurien who ensured that the farmer got 80 per cent of the market price of milk, the APMCs ensured that the farmer got barely 10 to 20 per cent.

Moreover, the APMCs were private associations, run by politicos or by people whom they appointed. They were not audited by government auditors and were not subject to government scrutiny. In Mumbai alone, the APMCs were believed to have earned around Rs 25,000 crore a year.

While a few state governments did try to abolish the APMCs, the agricultural mafia was so strong that the proposals had to be dropped. It was only when Modi became prime minister that he was able to use his political clout to get the APMCs banned across almost all the states in India. But he too achieved limited success.

There was one more way some politicians increased the vulnerability of farmers. That was by denying them water. Much of farming in India continues to be rainfed. To reduce the dependence on the monsoon, state governments were urged (because agriculture is a state subject) to expand the acreage under irrigation. Many states did wonderfully well on this score (see Table 12).

							Table 12
Irrigation and farmer vulnerability							
Top ten Indian farm acreage states							
							thousand hectares
	Gross sown area		% increase	Gross irrigated area		% increase	% of
	1990–91		in sown	1990–91		in irrigated	irrigated to
ALL INDIA	185,742	198,360	6.79	63,204	96,457	52.61	48.63
Uttar Pradesh	25,480	26,147	2.62	14,771	20,965	41.93	80.18
Rajasthan	19,380	24,235	25.05	4,652	10,171	118.64	41.97
Madhya Pradesh	23,880	23,810	-0.29	4,431	10,301	132.48	43.26
Maharashtra	21,858	23,474	7.39	3,319	4,282	29.01	18.24
Gujarat	10,580	12,773	20.73	2,910	6,014	106.67	47.08
Karnataka	11,759	12,247	4.15	2,598	4,186	61.12	34.18
West Bengal	8,663	9,690	11.86	2,492	5,700	128.73	58.82
Punjab	7,501	7,857	4.75	7,055	7,757	9.95	98.73
Andhra Pradesh*	13,193	7,690	-41.71	5,370	3,886	-27.64	50.53
Bihar	10,484	7,673	-26.81	4,192	5,268	25.67	68.66

Notes: All India data are inclusive of Union Territories. Figures for Andhra Pradesh are out of sync, because the state got truncated. This would also apply to Madhya Pradesh and Bihar.
Sources: Ministry of Agriculture and Farmers Welfare, Government of India; RBI's handbook of statistics on Indian states - 2017-18

States like Uttar Pradesh brought 80 per cent of the sown land under irrigation (it had an advantage because much of the land was part of the fertile Gangetic plains).

But watch Maharashtra. Less than 20 per cent of its land is under irrigation. This was probably because politically well-connected farmers used up the waters, whose availability was limited, for water-guzzling sugarcane and cotton. They ensured that other farmers did not get water[8]. Funds for irrigation

---

[8] https://www.firstpost.com/business/ethanol-as-alternative-fuel-why-the-idea-is-bad-and-will-worsen-the-plight-of-sugarcane-farmers-5399791.html

were diverted, even misused. Naturally, the most vulnerable of farmers are those in Maharashtra. State governments over the decades have colluded with powerful political interests to pamper sugar and milk cooperatives, divert money from cooperative banks, and even ignore the distress of farmers. This is now turning into a widespread agitation.

Providing irrigation and banning APMCs is still only part of the solution. The farmers need infrastructure like roads and food storage facilities. They need warehouses linked to commodity exchanges. Unfortunately much of the marketing infrastructure still belongs to politicians, at least in Maharashtra. They own the vehicles and the collection agents, they manage the warehouses and they understand how to supply to the markets and even how to distort prices.

That could explain why the present government is keen to build roads that connect every village. That is also why the government wants to set up small public places where farmers can come and sell their produce. But is that enough?

A Sleeping Warehousing Development Act

Eventually, as does any person who toils for a living, the farmer too expects a fair price for his produce. Kurien knew this. That is why he focused on three things. First, harnessing the productive energy of each Indian family, especially small families who could not afford to own more than one or two head of cattle. Second, ensuring that the cattle owner did not have to face a price reversal. A drop in milk prices would have been catastrophic. It would have disenchanted the farmer and made him invest less in rearing cattle. Third, he focused on the markets. He had to create a mechanism to cater to the demand for the milk that his cooperatives had purchased from the farmers. And he had to guarantee offtake of the milk produced even during the months when there was an abundance of milk. He had to ensure that the surplus milk was converted into powder for use when milk supply was inadequate. And he had to make certain that the milk (and milk products) reached the markets, so that the sale proceeds could then be shared by the farmer. The farmer, for Kurien, was central to all his planning.

In a way, this is precisely what the previous government also tried to do. It created the Warehousing Development Act (WDRA).[9] The body was enacted in 2007. It was meant to insulate the farmer against the vagaries of price, and enable him to store his produce till prices were favourable.

Unfortunately, the government forgot about it and it was notified only on 25 October 2010. There are good reasons to believe that the notification too was pushed through only because the Supreme Court began breathing down the government's neck. The apex court was pained to see grain lying out in the open and rotting because of the shortage of storage space.

The apex court had ordered the government to provide grain free of cost to India's poor rather than allow it to rot. But the government dragged its feet, and eventually did not distribute the rotting grain to the poor, citing one specious reason or the other.

But after one puts all the facts together, one can safely conclude that the government just did not want to let the grain reach common folk. Had that happened, people would have complained about the quality of the grain that was being

---

9   http://www.moneycontrol.com/news/business/economy/the-ghostly-organisation-that-should-have-transformed-indias-food-warehouses-2352429.html
     http://www.asiaconverge.com/2017/08/is-wdra-a-functioning-organisation/

supplied. That would have got the auditors and the assayers into the picture. They would have discovered that someone had paid first-rate prices for second grade grain. The evidence had to be destroyed. The rotting of the grain was a deliberate, callous and collusive act.

But on paper, the WDRA remains a great concept. It could have been a game changer for agriculture.

Surplus Grain, Few Warehouses

The idea was to have warehouses across the country, located so that even the remotest farmer could access them and sell his produce. Each commodity warehouse would be connected to commodity exchanges and to banks.

Typically, most small farmers keep aside some of the grain they produce for self-consumption. The rest they sell in the marketplace. Since the Food Corporation of India (FCI) and State Warehousing Corporations (SWCs) normally procure grain from big or influential farmers, small farmers are often compelled to sell their grain at distress prices.

The warehouses, certified by the WDRA, would take the grain, ascertain its quality and quantity and issue receipts to the farmers. The receipts could be dematerialized as well. The receipt would mention the grade of the grain sold, and the quantity. Any farmer could then walk into any bank and present the receipt. He could then decide whether to sell the grain on the spot markets at the prices prevailing then by surrendering the receipt to the bank and collecting the money right away. Or he could sell in the future markets as well.

Obviously, for the system to work, the warehouses would have to be set up first. To protect the grain from mildew and pests, the warehouses should be designed to ensure proper storage and should have the first-in-first-out processes in place. Second, the warehouses would have to appoint assayers to certify the quality of grain. Third, there would have to be a central registry to track grain deposits and grain purchases and the net unsold stock of grains in the warehouses (failure to have such a central database is precisely what caused the NSEL scam[10]).

Such a system would allow a trader in north India purchase a tonne of grain for western markets, assured that both the grade and the quantity would match with the prices paid. The identification of the grade of grain could be done through commodity markets, which could then supply the desired grade and quantity of the grain to the desired destination by picking it up from the nearest available warehouse.

A properly implemented WDRA would have empowered the small farmer. But that has not happened. The fly in the ointment, once again, is corruption and greed. The WDRA remains almost toothless. It cannot even provide the latest figures on warehousing capacity, hence one has to rely on old data compiled by other agencies.

The Grain Scam

To understand how the grain scam works, one first has to bear in mind that much of the procurement of agricultural products by the government only relates to rice and wheat. Much of the grain politics is the forte of farmers in north India, though the beneficiaries of such fiddles are spread all over the country.

---

[10] https://www.moneycontrol.com/news/business/comment-lessons-not-learned-indias-scams-amount-to-enemy-action-2550399.html
http://www.asiaconverge.com/2018/04/lessons-not-learned-indias-scams-amount-enemy-action/

At one time, the procurement policy made sense as the spectre of famine was always looming large. But today, those fears have eased. However, old practices continue, because they are immensely lucrative—in an unofficial manner.

What the FCI and the SWCs do is simple. They procure as much grain as they can. The modus operandi appears to be to purchase second-rate grain (from well-connected farmers) at first-rate prices. The best way to erase evidence of the fraud is by allowing the evidence of the crop itself to disappear.

That could explain why the government continues to procure more grain than it can store. It procures over 150 million tonnes of grain a year even though the country's storage capacities are almost half that level (see Table 13, More foodgrain, more value destruction). Agronomists like Ashok Gulati have reiterated time and again that the country does not have to maintain a buffer stock of more than 30 million tonnes.

This year, the agricultural output is likely to be higher than before. That could mean more procurement and hence more grain rotting. It is in the light of what has been explained above, that the vulnerability of farmers must be viewed. The absence of irrigation, marketing infrastructure, good warehousing, good commodity exchanges, and good market-makers who ensure that prices do not become major deterrents for farming, have all contributed to farm distress. Cumulatively, they have caused the share of agriculture in India's GDP to remain low.

How to Set Things Right

The first thing to do is to put in place assayers and auditors to vet every purchase made by both FCI and SWC. Gradually, both FCI and SWC's role in procurement should be phased out. All the grain must be sold not to the SWC or FCI but to

					Table 13
	More foodgrain, more value destruction				
	India's woefully inadequate warehousing capacity *(figures in '1000 tonne)*				
As per 2nd Advance Estimates, production of major crops during 2017–18			Covered storage	Cap	Total
Foodgrain total	277.49	million tonnes (record)	**FCI**		
Rice	111.01	million tonnes (record)	Hired	14,430	633	**15,063**
Wheat	97.11	million tonnes	Owned	12,969	2,612	**15,581**
Coarse Cereals	45.42	million tonnes (record)	**Total**	27,399	3,245	**30,644**
Maize	27.14	million tonnes (record)	**CWC**		
Pulses	23.95	million tonnes (record)	Hired	1,295	666	**1,961**
Gram	11.1	million tonnes (record)	Owned	6,844	1,629	**8,473**
Tur	4.02	million tonnes	**Total**	8,139	2,295	**10,434**
Urad	3.23	million tonnes (record)	**SWC**		
Oilseeds	29.88	million tonnes	Hired	9,597	0	**9,597**
Soyabean	11.39	million tonnes	Owned	12,613	140	**12,753**
Groundnut	8.22	million tonnes	**Total**	22,210	140	**22,350**
Castorseed	1.5	million tonnes	**Grand totals**	57,748	5,680	**63,428**
Cotton	33.92	million bales (of 170 kg each)	**Usual procurement***			**101,750**
Sugar cane	353.23	million tonnes	**Expected demand for**			**185,000**
Notes: FCI=Food Corporation of India; CWC=Central Warehousing Corporation; SWC=State Warehousing Corporations. Thanks to the Food Security Act, most farmers will not keep aside some grain for self consumption, as they can buy it for Rs 1-2 per kg. Hence entire production will come into procurement or distress sale			**Current gap in storage**			**38,322**
			Expected gap in storage			**121,572**
* Procurement currently is around 55 per cent of production. Total procurement is thus an estimation.			Sources: Government of India - http://pib.gov.in/PressReleseDetail.aspx?PRID=1521936; Source: India Commodity Yearbook, 2011, NCMSL;Dept of food and public distribution			

WDRA-approved warehouses, which in turn could transfer the desired grade to the FCI/SWC godowns for onward distribution to the public distribution system (PDS) or ration shops. Since the grain has moved through WDRA-certified warehouses, and is now listed on the central database, anyone from anywhere in the country can purchase this grain. If the grain turns out to be substandard, it invites criminal provisions of the law.

Second, any grain that cannot be stored in warehouses must be sold immediately on commodity markets overseas. True, arrival of large quantities of surplus grain might cause the open market prices to slump, but a reduced price for the surplus grain is better than no price for the grain, which will otherwise rot.

Third, high quality, top-loading, bottom evacuation granaries that are world class should be built. That will allow the grain that is first in to be the first out.

Fourth, incentives for setting up more warehouses should be created. The cost of the incentives will probably be less than the cost of keeping the FCI and SWC in business.

Fifth, warehousing should be extended to all kinds of grain, including pulses. This will allow even growers of millets and pulses to find easy access to a market.

Sixth, imports should not be allowed to depress domestic prices. Remember, the pulses crisis in 2016–17? It was triggered by such reckless (unfortunately authorized) imports.[11,12]

Seventh, the functioning of vibrant commodity markets should be promoted. Trade on commodity markets should never be banned. Even in the NSEL case, the scam would not have become a crisis had the markets not been closed and trades frozen. Market closures hurt farmers and set back trading by at least a decade.

All this would promote transparency and give every farmer the ability to sell his produce at market prices rather than distress prices. The farmer could also insulate himself against any potential crash in market prices by selling a part of his produce at prices that he thinks are good even before the crop is harvested.

---

[11] http://www.firstpost.com/business/why-did-the-government-continue-importing-pulses-when-domestic-production-was-growing-3430972.html

[12] http://www.asiaconverge.com/2017/05/how-pulses-imports-drove-domestic-growers-to-the-ground/

Once this is done, the government could then work on a system for storing and processing horticulture produce as well—which would be a bit difficult because such produce is perishable. But if Kurien could do this with milk—a product that has a shorter shelf life than much of horticulture produce—a way can be worked out for other produce as well. What is needed is zero tolerance for corruption and the determination to give a fair deal to the farmer.

Gradually, the job of horticulture purchases should be left to food processing centres. For instance, Jitesh Patel, a potato farmer in Gujarat, has entered into long-term contracts with companies like Pepsico, Balaji and ITC for the offtake of his crop. He grows potatoes to meet the specifications of the buyers.[13]

When farmers enter into such contracts, the cost of warehousing and assaying is taken up by the corporation.

This is what the Jains of Jalgaon do. They enter into contracts with farmers for mangoes. The company provides the know-how for the right kind of seed to be grown, and specifies the manner in which the trees can be grown in clusters so that output remains high without affecting quality. By persuading farmers to grow trees that are shorter, the job of plucking mangoes has been made that much easier. All the mango is then converted into pulp, and 50 per cent of this is sold to Coca Cola. The Jains do the same thing with onions as well. They provide farmers with seeds for the grade of white onions that have a ready market overseas. The farmers grow the crop according to the processes laid down by the Jains, and sell the produce back to the company. The onions are then dehydrated and processed to suit the palates of different markets. With their water content removed, the onions have

---

[13] https://www.youtube.com/watch?v=KgGuGtDUw5w

a long shelf life and are lighter in weight. The Jains export the dehydrated onions to markets all over the world including Europe and the US (where they have processing plants). All contracts are worked out such that if the market prices are higher than the contracted prices, the farmer gets the higher price less 10 per cent. If the market prices crash, the company guarantees offtake at the contracted value. This approach has reduced the risk for farmers and has assured the Jains of a steady and increasing yield.[14]

In effect, the Jains are doing what the government should have done—educating farmers. But with the APMCs quite probably on their way out, and contract farming now becoming legal, hopefully other corporates will also do similar things.

More importantly, the government must educate farmers on how to pool their lands together so that economies of scale can be achieved, and better price realization. This is what happened with farmers in a small village in the north of Gujarat. The farmers there have pooled their land and have begun growing watermelons, which they thought would offer high profit margins. Each farmer gets his share of the revenues earned depending on the area of land he has pooled in. His labour is also accounted for as credits, and revenues allocated for it. Since the watermelon is a ninety-day crop, the farmers divide the cumulative land parcel into ninety equal plots. They sow the watermelon seeds in plot 1 on the first day, in plot 2 on the second day, plot 3 on the third day and so on. After ninety days, the first plot is ready for harvesting. Thereafter it is ready for fresh seeds to be planted as well. Each day, the village sends some of its farmers from Gujarat to Delhi's markets (mandis), where they know they

---

[14] http://www.forbesindia.com/article/breakpoint/bhavarlal-jains-lucky-harvest/17652/1

will get the best prices. This way, each farmer is exposed to the mandis, and the village has fresh produce to sell each day.

Also look at the way Jitesh Patel has pooled land for his potato plantations,[15] or how smaller farmers with barely twelve acres have managed to do well.[16] In all these cases the farmers had studied in agricultural universities and were handheld by corporates. That is a role the government must learn to take up, or at least create a mechanism to ensure that the corporates follow the right practices.

In fact, one of the most promising developments in agriculture is the increasing role of hydroponics.[17] This offers an entirely new way to view agriculture. Conventionally, we were taught that good soil, good water and good sunlight would invariably translate into good agriculture. This is not relevant any more. You don't need earth, or sunlight. All you need is good water with the right nutrients. Instead of sunlight, you use LED lights, because what plants need is spectrum. Different plants need different types of spectrum. Some need blue spectrum, some red, some yellow and some white. And since soil is not used, 80 per cent of pests (which are soil based) become irrelevant. You use less pesticides, less fertilizer. And since the entire cultivation takes place inside enclosures (like a room or a cabin with multi layered shelves with different crops (hence this is also called vertical farming), you can grow 10 times the quantity of crops than can be grown on a field.[18] This may be the best solution to

---

[15] https://www.youtube.com/watch?v=KgGuGtDUw5w

[16] https://www.youtube.com/watch?v=y7btUMpcnRg

[17] https://www.moneycontrol.com/news/business/economy/
     comment-why-hydroponics-could-be-the-future-of-
     farming-2630781.html

[18] https://www.youtube.com/watch?v=VBhTyNbJE6A

an era where climate change causes unseasonal rains and unexpected surges in temperatures which can adversely affect agricultural output. Indians have come up with their own jugaad, on ways to reduce the capital costs of hydroponics.[19] Moreover, the controlled weather conditions in hydroponics allow for a smooth transition to food storage and processing as well. And this is just one of the ways in which agriculture is change.

This is happening in aqua-farming[20] and sea-weed farming[21] as well. They are all new methods which could enhance food supply, provide better nutrition, and still bring more money to the farmer.

Eventually, educating farmers and creating marketplaces is the government's job. Ensuring that agricultural contracts (in contract farming) are enforced is also the government's job. It is non-enforcement of contracts that caused a potato crisis in Uttar Pradesh in December 2017.[22]

But does the government have the will?

---

[19] https://www.youtube.com/watch?v=S21YuRIae2o

[20] https://www.moneycontrol.com/news/business/companies/garware-technical-fibres-could-transform-agriculture-and-fisheries-in-india-3028621.html

[21] https://www.moneycontrol.com/news/india/comment-cultivating-seaweed-could-be-a-massive-opportunity-for-india-2589455.html

[22] https://www.youtube.com/watch?v=icedmsyUbvE

SEVEN

Innovation Is a Wounded Sparrow in India

'They lived and laughed and loved and left.'
—James Joyce

'Innovation distinguishes between a leader and a follower.'
—Steve Jobs

'Corruption is a cancer: a cancer that eats away at a citizen's faith in democracy, diminishes the instinct for innovation and creativity; already-tight national budgets, crowding out important national investments. It wastes the talent of entire generations. It scares away investments and jobs.'
—Joe Biden

'In Israel, a land lacking in natural resources, we learned to appreciate our greatest national advantage: our minds. Through creativity and innovation, we transformed barren deserts into flourishing fields and pioneered new frontiers in science and technology.'
—Shimon Peres

'Innovation is all about people. Innovation thrives when the population is diverse, accepting and willing to cooperate.'
—Vivek Wadhwa

Go to Tel Aviv. Talk with Ron Huldai, mayor of the city, or to Zohar Sharon, chief knowledge officer, Government of Tel Aviv. Both will tell you their biggest anxiety: how to keep Tel Aviv both safe and vibrant. For Israel, security is non-negotiable, but Israel also knows that its growth will come from innovation. And innovation loves freedom—to move around, to discuss, to argue, but eventually to create something valuable.

That is a lesson India is being cajoled into forgetting. The space for discussion and argumentation is being shrunk. Any theatrical performance or movie that could possibly make people sit up and think is being banned on the grounds that it is inimical to public peace. Innovation does not like these walled grounds. It can flourish only when ideas are allowed to jostle around against each other. And laugh.

Israel, on the other hand, has begun to savour the fruits of its conscious move towards greater freedom, making its cities safer and livelier without letting anyone feel insecure. As Avi Simhon, head of the National Economic Council, and advisor to the country's prime minister remarks, 'We have seen the results of this conscious move towards embracing innovation even more fiercely than before 2005. Our debt to GDP keeps falling even while that of the OECD keeps climbing (see Table 1).'

The good thing about innovation is that value-addition begins to soar with 'me-too' solutions. And interestingly, once this atmosphere is allowed to grow, the role of the government begins to shrink, except in matters relating to security. Government expenditure as a percentage of gross domestic product (GDP) begins to ease (see Table 2).

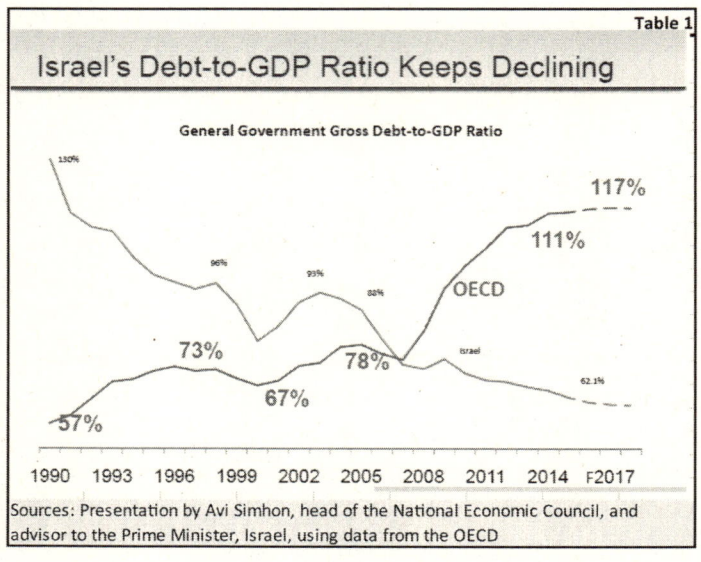

Sources: Presentation by Avi Simhon, head of the National Economic Council, and advisor to the Prime Minister, Israel, using data from the OECD

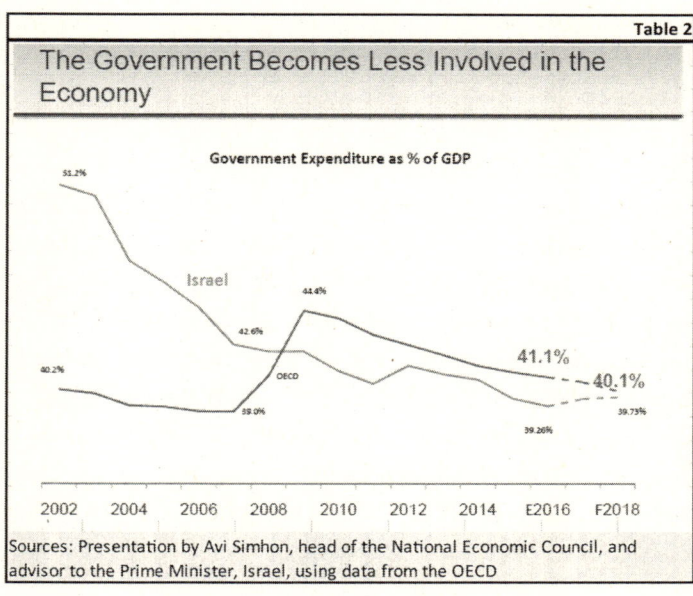

Sources: Presentation by Avi Simhon, head of the National Economic Council, and advisor to the Prime Minister, Israel, using data from the OECD

But in India, government expenditure as a percentage of GDP keeps climbing, and a sense of discomfort is beginning to set in. Instead of feeling safe, the common man is now looking over his shoulder. Couples walk with eyes darting around, fearful that someone will shout a protest.

But it wasn't always this way. As the previous chapters have shown, some of the best innovations in the world have come from India. The Kurien strategy for rural development, in a country where teeming millions threaten to weigh down per capita income, remains incomparable. His method of ensuring that farmers get 80 per cent of the market price of milk has few parallels anywhere. Today, replicating that type of a business model might be a bit difficult as the local mafia is allowed to demand its percentage, part of which is sent 'higher-ups'. The law enforcement and judicial systems must be strengthened to first rein in the mafia. But to do that the political class must first be willing. There is little evidence of that happening. And innovation depends on these little pockets of extortion disappearing.

India and China, Legendary Wealth Generators

Kurien wasn't just a flash in the pan. The pygmy deposit scheme of the Pais, the floating solar project of the Tatas, the educational projects of the Jain and Amin families are all good examples of innovation and foresight. And India, with its teeming millions, should have encouraged many more such projects.

In order to understand and better appreciate the tremendous strengths that both India and China enjoy, one needs to look at a chart based on the data compiled by Angus Maddison.[1]

---

[1] https://www.dnaindia.com/business/column-policy-watch-india-china-will-learn-to-do-more-business-together-1834838

Angus Maddison (6 December 1926–24 April 2010) was an economist who has spent most of his years compiling data to better understand the economic strengths and weaknesses of nations through the ages. He leaves behind the Angus Maddison project[2] which deals with historical economic statistics to better understand the economic history of the world.

The chart that should be of immense importance to anyone studying India and China throws into relief how India and China were two nations that were actually wealth generators without becoming parasites. And this process of wealth generation was evident as early as 2500 BC and continued to the middle of the sixteenth century. Both countries made money from their own territories; they were not expansionist, or even warmongering like so many nations in the world today. Both nations traded with other countries and within their own regions, and generated wealth in such abundance that they together accounted for almost 60 per cent of global GDP since 2500 BC. Both believed in the exchange of ideas, in argumentation, in discourse.

Gutenberg Galaxy

The turning point appears to have been during the sixteenth century and was most probably a direct outcome of the moveable type printing press invented by Johannes Gutenberg. The printing press changed everything.

Yes, there are reports that the Chinese had invented a printing press much before John Gutenberg. But there was a difference. China did not allow the printing press to democratize the written word. Education, like anywhere

---

2 https://www.rug.nl/ggdc/historicaldevelopment/maddison/

in the world during the pre-printing press days, was the exclusive prerogative and privilege of the priestly classes and of nobility. Education, in those days, was unaffordable for common people. The only way they could afford it was by sending one of their children to become a monk or a nun. This was true of all cultures, and all civilizations. Education remained a privilege—reserved for priests and princes (and similar ranks of nobility).

The printing press changed all that. The first book to be printed was the Bible, in German. Ironically, the first crisis took place in the church itself, in Germany, as Martin Luther began nailing on the doors of churches his challenges to the Papal interpretation of Christianity. People who could now afford to purchase a copy of the Bible began to learn how to read and write, and began to realize that what the priests said was not always what the Bible said. The church split and the Reformation was born.

The printing press also led to the age of pamphleteering. Articles and papers on science as well as maps of ocean routes began being printed and distributed. Hence when the steam engine was invented, the maps and the new technology to drive ships led to the age of exploration.

Colonization and Revival

That in turn led to colonization. And that is when both India and China were dragged to their knees. Nothing demonstrates this as clearly as the Angus Maddison chart[3] on the wealth of countries. As money from India and China began reaching the home countries of the colonizers, it began financing more

---

3   https://www.dnaindia.com/business/column-policy-watch-india-china-will-learn-to-do-more-business-together-1834838

science and technology, spurred on by education as well. It wasn't long before both India and China had to bite the dust. Colonization does terrible things to people. It dispossesses them in the first stage, saps them of their vitality in the second, and crushes their sense of dignity in the third.

Fortunately—perhaps it was the Asian DNA that began to assert itself—both India and China began to find their feet after they wrested their independence from their colonizers. But thanks to the nature of Indian politics and corruption, India's sense of nationhood was not as focused as that of China. India could still allow a foreigner to become a citizen.[4] That would be unthinkable in China, or any other self-respecting country. In India a leader asks why he should submit to security checks. In China, Singapore, Israel or the US security checks are mandatory, both for the common man or VIP. In India the powerful demand exceptions to rules; in other countries the powerful submit to rules that make the country strong. In India, the temptation to tinker with demographics had even corrupted the sense of nationhood (see chapter 5). But in spite of this, India has begun to raise its head and has begun to demand that it be counted among the countries that matter in the world.

Conversely—and this could be purely accidental—the biggest financial crises are now unravelling themselves in countries that had learnt to grow on other people's money. Once the easy money from colonization stopped, financial strains began to manifest themselves. This was true of the US as well, which enjoyed the benefits of a reverse colonization for centuries. The Americans brought in slaves and made

---

[4]   https://www.timesheadline.com/india/foreign-national-using-fake-documents-elected-thrice-telangana-7686.html

their wealth. The North did not. Hence they remain wealth generators through creativity and innovation.

Unlike countries which grew wealthy and powerful through money from other countries, both India and China—and possibly the entire Asian region—made money from their own territories. There was no expansionism for colonization.

A Matter of Culture

There was a cultural element to the worldview adopted by Asian countries. A word given had to be defended with one's life, as the Pathans advocated. The concept of honour was supreme—death was preferred to dishonour—as the sepukku tradition of the Japanese affirmed. The world was an illusion that one had to learn to give up—a philosophy almost all the Orient believed in.

Nothing exemplified this belief better than the decision of Chandragupta Maurya, one of the most amazing emperors of India. He built an empire out of nothing, and when he was at the height of his power, he decided to give everything up and wander off into the forests to die, unknown.

A similar story can be discovered about Ghengiz Khan, the emperor wrongly blamed for his brutality. It is an insight that a remarkable researcher—Ravi Boothalingam—can give you, because he was commissioned by the National Geographic team to go to Mongolia and try and locate Ghengiz Khan's grave. He tells you that Ghengiz Khan was maligned because he was perhaps the only great king whose biography was written by the people he defeated. He too decided not to let anyone build a mausoleum after he was dead. He ensured that none of his relatives would know where he was buried. Even today, the best estimate of where he could be buried remains a guess.

India's Heroes

To understand the genius that makes India tick you need
to look at some of its heroes, such as Verghese Kurien and
T.M.A. Pai, whose achievements have been described in
earlier chapters. Then there are giants who were wealth
generators without resorting to using other people's money.
Each of them also believed in paying back to society whatever
they could because they themselves got so much from it.

The author looks at the contributions of three other
personalities from the word of industry and commerce. They
are Brij Mohan Lall Munjal, Venu Srinivasan and Azim Premji.
This selection is entirely the author's own choice, based on
several decades of journalistic exposure and management
studies.

This book deliberately does not mention the Tatas or
the Birlas or other great industrialists who have also left
their stamp on this country. The Tatas remain the most
respected brand in India because of their conscious effort to
remain ethical. Without the Tatas, India wouldn't be where
it is today. They gave this nation its first airline (which was
nationalized), its first textile mills and some of its finest
educational institutions including the Institute of Science.
The Birlas too managed to create several businesses that made
India proud. And at the time when the government's policies
forced India to think small, the Ambanis taught India to think
big. Nobody catalysed the capital markets the way Dhirubhai
Ambani did.

But the author has selected the three because of their
ability to build an empire within a lifetime without seeking
government favours. One of the three is no longer alive. But
the other two still play a very active role in the management of
their respective companies. They have thrived in competitive

markets without the benefit of licensing, or blocking others who sought to get those licences. But, most important, they have tried to give back to society a sense of culture and have tried to sow the seeds of education, which could actually help many other future geniuses to emerge.

Brij Mohan Lall Munjal (1923–2015)

Brij Mohan Lall Munjal was chairman of the Hero Group of companies. This author met Munjal in 1985, at the height of Sikh terrorism, in Ludhiana, at the Hero Cycles factory. Munjal had finally agreed to talk to the media and was willing to be interviewed for a cover story in *Business India*, one of India's leading business publications.

It was during that interview that Munjal talked about his dreams and his plans. He talked about how the company was formed in 1956 to manufacture bicycle components and then moved on to making complete bicycles. He spoke about how the company had grown and how it built its dealership network.

He also spoke about how it had learnt to develop its just-in-time (JIT) practices (even before the Japanese began teaching the world a lot more about JIT). Hero Cycles (even in those days) would have raw material inventory levels of just thirty minutes; finished goods would stay in the factory for just about the same amount of time. He talked about how trucks bringing in raw materials—cycle components, wheels, tyres—would come in through one gate, offload their goods, then pick up finished cycles from another building and proceed to exit through another gate. He spoke about how he had persuaded his dealers to locate their manufacturing units close to his factory if they wanted to do business with him. A location close to the factory would help reduce delivery time, and would allow the Hero group to build an ecosystem that could draw on a pool of talent that lived nearby. He worked with them to fine-tune their business processes so that their output would synchronize with that of Hero Cycles.

He also spoke about how relationships matter—with dealers, with customers and in fact with everybody. This is something that many people often forget about India. In India, relationships come first, processes later. In most countries in the West, processes come first, relationships later.

It was these relationships that allowed Munjal to work with his dealers in a variety of ways to ensure that they both grew together. Yes, the bottom line was always on their minds. But the need to preserve relationships was equally vital. And there were times Munjal would extend himself to accommodate a dealer when hard times befell his family or workplace.

It wasn't long before his company was listed in *The Guinness Book of World Records* as the largest bicycle manufacturer in the world.[5]

Today, Hero Cycles produces over 19,000 cycles a day, and exports many of them to over seventy countries—mostly to Europe, Africa and Asia. It has a network of over 250 suppliers, with around 2800 dealerships and over 7610 employees.

When the government of India began the process of economic liberalization, Munjal agreed to partner with Honda Motors of Japan in 1984. But unlike many Indians who would have been willing to give the foreign collaborator close to 50 per cent of the equity stake in the new venture, Munjal was clear that it would be a Hero company with Honda as a partner. That is how Hero Honda was born.

---

[5] https://www.indiatoday.in/magazine/economy/story/19871015-hero-cycles-makes-guinness-records-as-largest-bicycle-manufacturer-in-the-world-799408-1987-10-15

The company did well. It became the largest motorcycle manufacturer in India. The Munjals worked hard with the Japanese to understand that country's ways of doing things. The key people in the group quickly soaked in as much of Japan's technology and the underlying processes as they could. But the dealership was still largely made up of people who had very strong relationships with the Munjals. Unlike Maruti Udyog (now Maruti Suzuki), the Munjals wanted to increase the share of indigenous content at a pace that did not meet with the timelines the Japanese had set for themselves. For the Japanese, easing the pace of indigenization of vehicles was desirable. They could still make profits through export of components, till such a time when the vehicles could themselves make good profits in India. But the Munjals knew that to be cost competitive, they would have to indigenize rapidly even if it was expensive in the short run.

The strains in the relationship between the two gradually increased. Privately, almost eight years before the split was formally announced, Munjal did admit that the parting of ways was round the corner. The parting eventually took place in 2010, with the formal separation in 2012. The company changed its name to Hero Motocorp and (according to its annual report of April 2018) has already become the largest two-wheeler manufacturer in the world.[6] Today it accounts for a 46 per cent market share in the two-wheeler category.

Brij Mohan Lall Munjal's son, Sunil Kant Munjal, currently runs the group's flagship company, Hero Moto, and he carries on his father's vision and values.

---

[6]   https://www.bseindia.com/bseplus/AnnualReport/500182/5001820317.pdf

Venu Srinivasan

Unlike the Munjals, Venu Srinivasan was part of a family that, as he puts it, 'has automobiles running in their veins'. His grandfather was T.V. Sundaram Iyengar, from whom the TVS group got its name. The group started with a bus service in 1911, in Madurai, under the name Southern Roadways Limited.

As Srinivasan explains in a recorded programme, the group got into processes that looked into preventive maintenance, record keeping, and even techniques to suck up nails and shards that could puncture the tires of the buses.[7] Southern Roadways would roll a 'magneto' vehicle on the roads early in the morning to scoop up pieces of metal that could slow down or make unreliable the quality of service that Sundaram Iyengar wanted to offer.

At its peak, the company had 400 buses, which operated according to a strict timetable, thus endearing this service to thousands.

When Sundaram Iyengar died in 1955, his sons expanded the company with several forays in the automobile sector, including finance, insurance, two-wheelers and three-wheelers, tires and components, housing, aviation, logistics etc.

Today, the TVS group manages around ninety-seven companies that account for a combined turnover of nearly Rs 40,000 crore ($6 billion). TVS Motor Company is the flagship company of the group. It is the third largest two-wheeler manufacturer in India, (sales 3 million units, capacity 4 million) with revenues of over Rs 13,000 crore ($2 billion) in 2016–17.[8] It exports over 4,00,000 vehicles annually.

---

[7] https://www.youtube.com/watch?v=WJvlBfyGOfE
[8] https://www.tvsmotor.com/pdf/Twenfty-Fifth-Annual-Report-2016-2017.pdf

For Srinivasan, the group's name also stands for Trust, Value and Service. To gain trust, he knew the quality of his products had to be good, consistently. He knew that trust came from values and from leadership. Company watchers still remember how in the 1980s when his company was plagued by a labour strike (despite TVS workers being some of the best paid workers in the sector), Srinivasan used to travel in the buses with the workers to assure them that they would come to no harm if they ignored the striking workers and continued to operate the plant.

The TVS group learnt to adopt practices that did not overcharge customers, even during the years when imports were banned, and short-in-supply automobile spares were sold at a premium in the black market. Another automobile group that refused to charge a premium on the overhang of demand over supply (the government in those years did not allow companies to produce more than their licenced capacity) was Bajaj Auto. It was this dedication to values that caused customers to become immensely fond of both the TVS and Bajaj brands.

The TVS group enjoyed such enormous credibility in is dealings that it became perhaps the only group that had a queue of people outside its finance company (Sundaram Finance) to deposit their money. Right from its inception, Sundaram Finance was a brand that people trusted, and knew that their money would be safe with it. They believed that their money was safer with the TVS group than with banks. Some were even willing to wait for years till the company was willing to accept fresh deposits.

In 1962, the group had formed Sundaram Clayton Ltd (in collaboration with Clayton Dewandre Holdings, UK) for the manufacture of brakes, exhausts, compressors and various other automotive parts. The company set up a plant at Hosur in Tamil Nadu in 1978, to manufacture mopeds as well. In 1980, the group brought out India's first moped, TVS 50.

A technical collaboration with the Japanese auto giant Suzuki Ltd resulted in the joint venture between Sundaram Clayton Ltd and Suzuki Motor Corporation, in 1982. TVS Suzuki was born, and commercial production of motorcycles began in 1984.[9]

Like Munjal, Srinivasan also realized that the cost of motorcycles would be much higher than desirable as it depended on imported components. He thus wanted the indigenization of parts to be introduced at a faster pace. Differences with Suzuki also arose on the manner in which fresh capital was to be injected. Finally, in order to take development and innovation into his own hands, Srinivasan approached the University of Warwick and took up two huge warehouses for the development of a new two-wheeler.

With the help of the engineering and industrial design students at that university and with funding from the TVS group, a totally new vehicle with technology owned by TVS was introduced on Indian roads in 1996—Scooty. This author remembers fondly the pride in Srinivasan's eyes as he drove the vehicle (with the author as the pillion rider) through the streets of Chennai at night. The product was an immediate success, with more women opting to purchase it.

That product marked the beginning of the TVS group's shift to designing its own vehicles, producing them almost entirely in India at prices that few could match.

It was obvious that the nineteen-year-old relationship with Suzuki was drawing to a close. In 2001 both companies parted ways and the company was rechristened TVS Motor. It relinquished its rights to use the Suzuki name. There was

---

[9] http://www.moneycontrol.com/company-facts/sundaram-
    clayton/history/SC

also a thirty-month moratorium period during which Suzuki promised not to enter the Indian market with competing two-wheelers.

In many ways, both Munjal and Srinivasan exemplify India's ability to stand on its own, to design and manufacture products on its own, and to adapt Japanese and Western methods of production and business practices to Indian needs. Both groups have invested heavily in education and social welfare. TVS promotes programmes for engineering students to learn new principles of quality management and JIT (just in time). The group has already begun grooming future managers. Srinivasan takes a keen interest in working closely with quality circle groups all over the country, with discussions on engineering excellence and spends a lot of time with management gurus and strategists. He cherishes a vision of India—confident, capable and pursuing a path of dharma.[10]

The group's social commitment is best underscored when one recalls the role it played during the floods in Chennai in 2015. At that time, the TVS group gave out two tonnes of food in the form of packets of cooked rice (6000 food packets) to the National Disaster Recovery Force stationed in Chennai on a daily basis. It worked very closely with the NDRF, because it knew the terrain, and the people, and tried to minimize the hardship that people faced at that time.

Azim Premji

Unlike Munjal and Srinivasan, Premji was not single-minded in his pursuit of any single project. However, like them, his pursuit of excellence was unquestionable. What makes him one of the most unusual and incredible businessmen in India

---

[10] https://www.youtube.com/watch?v=ZNC9TCgRJcM (this video is no longer available)

is his ability to reinvent himself and his businesses, and come out on top.

A graduate from Stanford University, he first entered the family oil business. His father, Muhammed Hashim Premji, incorporated Western Indian Vegetable Products Ltd in 1945, which later came to be known by its acronym Wipro. It was located in Amalner, a small town in the Jalgaon district of Maharashtra. It used to manufacture cooking oil under the brand name Sunflower Vanaspati, and a laundry soap called 787, a byproduct of oil manufacture.[11]

In 1966, upon hearing of his father's death, Azim Premji, who was studying engineering at Stanford, returned to India. He took charge of Wipro. And under his leadership, the company diversified into bakery fats, ethnic ingredient-based toiletries, hair care soaps, baby toiletries, lighting products and hydraulic cylinders. At a time when oil trading was essentially managed by members of a family (because it was largely a cash-based business), Premji professionalized oil purchase and sale.

By the 1980s he decided to further diversify into manufacturing computers, printers and other peripherals to take advantage of the country's move into computerization.

Thereafter the shift to information technology (IT) was a natural progression. Today, he is also known as the czar of Indian IT. *Time* magazine listed him among the hundred most influential people first in 2004 and more recently in 2011.[12] Today, Premji owns 73 per cent of Wipro. He also owns a private equity fund, Premji Invest, which manages his $2 billion worth of personal portfolio.

Just when people thought he would remain content with the IT business, quietly, almost unnoticed, he chalked out big

---

[11] https://en.wikipedia.org/wiki/Azim_Premji

[12] http://www.time.com/time/specials/packages/article/0,28804,2066367_2066369_2066101,00.html

plans in the consumer goods segment as well. In a way, he came full circle. The company's hydrogenated oil and soap business has been growing and expanding since 2005. The revived focus on this market segment possibly began almost a decade ago when the group's fast-moving consumer goods (FMCG) firm Wipro Consumer Care and Lighting (WCCLG) started expanding its footprint.[13] It began with the acquisition of Unza for around Rs 1010 crore in 2007. Unknown to many in India, Unza was a Singapore-based manufacturer of personal care products. After the acquisition, WCCLG's revenues zoomed to over Rs 1500 crore that very year.

Unza brought with it a portfolio of forty-eight brands that were marketed in forty countries. And that included China. Suddenly Premji had access to two of the largest consumer markets in the world—India and China (see Table 3). And while many others found China a difficult market to deal with, Premji went about developing and fine-tuning this line of business.

He was aware that Unza was not doing well in China. Yet he persevered, addressing the variety of issues it faced there. The company appears to have turned around, because last year WCCLG's China business accounted for about $120 million in revenue. Today, China is the third largest market for WCCLG. India accounts for around $500 million and Malaysia for $145 million.

Included in its range of products is Safewash, the liquid detergent brand, which caters to a market worth around Rs 5 billion a year and has been growing at 40 per cent per annum.[14]

---

[13] http://www.forbesindia.com/article/leaderboard/the-other-wipro-and-how-it-tamed-the-dragon/50103/1?curator=alphaideas&utm_source=alphaideas

[14] http://www.business-standard.com/article/companies/wipro-consumer-care-expands-household-products-range-118032000939_1.html

Table 3

Wipro's incredible march towards globalization

Decade	Year	Event(s)
1940's	1945	Establishment of an oil crushing unit at Amalner in Maharashtra
1970's	1970	Manufacturer of Hydrogenated cooking (Vanaspati) medium at Amalner
1980's	1982	For first time in India introduced Flexi packs for hydrogenated cooking medium
	1986	Santoor launched
1990's	1991	Wipro Lighting established; Wipro Baby Soft products launched
2000's	2003	Glucovita acquired; Wipro Safewash liquid detergent launched
	2004	Launch of Furniture Business
	2006	Acquisition of North-West Switches; Acquisition of Chandrika
	2007	Acquisition of Unza - One of the leading companies of South East Asia in personal care business
	2009	Acquistion of Yardley in India & Middle East Asia
2010's	2011	Acquisition of Aramusk; Acquisition of Cleanray, a LED company
	2012	Acquisition of Yardley for UK & Europe (except Germany & Austria); Acquisition of LD Waxson's group - A personal care company South East Asia.
	2016	Acquistion of Zhongshan Ma Er Home and Personal Care Company Southern China

Sources: http://wiproconsumercare.com/about-us/wipro-consumer-care/

As the company mentions in its latest annual report (for 2017-18),[15] WCCL 'is among the fastest growing FMCG businesses in its operating geographies of Asia and the Middle East. Its businesses include personal wash products, toiletries, wellness products, household products, electrical wire devices, domestic and commercial lighting and modular office furniture. It has a strong brand presence with significant market-share segments in India, South East Asia and the Middle East. In 2017–18 . . . it crosses the $1 billion revenue milestone with more than half a dozen $50 million plus brands.' The annual report makes mention of the brands the company has acquired—Unza, Yardley, LD Waxsons which were followed by Ma ER in 2016 (for the Chinese market). In India it continues to sell Santoor and Chandrika brands of soaps, in addition to Glucovita (glucose powder), Northwest Switches, Enchanteur (a female toiletry brand); for special markets it has Safi (halal toiletry), Romano (male toiletry), Carrie (kids toiletry), Pahini (household toiletry) and Garnet (a lighting brand).

Today, the company has a presence in over forty countries with over 8300 employees worldwide. It has eight production plants in India and seven overseas. Besides India, the business has significant presence in Malaysia, Indonesia, Vietnam, China, Taiwan, Hong Kong and Middle East.[16][17]

Incidentally, Wipro Enterprises is the umbrella company that encompasses the three business units of consumer care and lighting, infrastructure engineering and Wipro-GE Medical Systems.

---

[15] https://wiproconsumercare.com/wp-content/uploads/wip-pdf-manager/WEL_Annual_Report-2018_13.pdf

[16] http://wcclg.com/

[17] http://wiproconsumercare.com/about-us/wipro-consumer-care/

Few businessmen have traversed such a vast expanse and generated wealth and profits in each segment. Today, Premji is reckoned to be the second richest person in India with an estimated net worth of $19.5 billion as of November 2017. In 2013, he agreed to give away at least half of his wealth by signing The Giving Pledge,[18] which is a commitment by the world's wealthiest individuals and families to dedicate the majority of their wealth to giving back to society. He started his charitable activities in India with a $2.2 billion donation to the Azim Premji Foundation, focused on education in this country.[19]

A Common Thread

All the three personalities described above have some common traits. They have a zest for innovation, a commitment to winning, and a keenness to give back to society some of what they received in their formative years. All three have been passionate about education and social upliftment. All three have left a mark in India without depending on favours from government licensing or continuous handholding from overseas.

It is worth remembering that it is easier to make money when the government gives you a licence to do something that is denied to others. It is easier when there is the element of regulatory capture, which allows a businessman to persuade an arm of the government to craft rules in such a way that only he benefits and not others. At times, rules are further crafted to exclude others. This is what happened when favoured

---

[18] https://givingpledge.org/

[19] https://www.forbes.com/sites/naazneenkarmali/2013/02/23/azim-premji-donates-2-3-billion-after-signing-giving-pledge/#11202bf24cda

industrialists were allowed to import raw materials which others could not during the days of the licence raj, or when import duties were crafted in such a way that the favoured industrialist benefited, not others. This is what happened when licences relating to new businesses are allowed to be tweaked in such a manner that the favoured players could benefit.

But then if one looks at history, almost 80 per cent of the top twenty taxpayers in India during the 1970s are no longer among the top twenty today. Some have almost disappeared from the corporate pages of Indian newspapers. Many of them were beneficiaries of largesse from the government. Some of them merely inherited wealth. Most of them could not regenerate the wealth and opportunities they had acquired as a favour. Some lost it because of disputes within the family.

None of the three referred to above asked for, or received, such favours. It was sheer will, enterprise and a savvy perception of the markets and managements that made them excel and win. All three are global players today, and all three have squeaky-clean reputations—something that does not come easily in India. It must also be stated here that they are not the only ones to have done this. India is full of such people. These three are only representatives of a class of industrialists that has learnt to think innovatively, and grow without government support. The list is extremely long, and some of the names that come easily to mind are Cyrus Poonawala who has become the world's largest vaccine producer, or Dilip Shanghvi of Sun Pharma, or Dr Pratap Reddy of Apollo Hospitals who was bold enough to launch the first (five-star) hospital to approach the capital markets, or the lesser known Warke family behind Hi Media which is reckoned to be among the largest producers of biological media for pharmaceutical and food industries. All of them have done India proud

As mentioned earlier, all of them have been innovative. Munjal had to be innovative to transition from making spares for cycles and then to making entire bicycles, in much the same way that the TVS group too had to transition from making spares to making the moped and then the Scooty. Premji remains a serial entrepreneur, constantly reinventing himself, but seldom abandoning any business that he created, nurtured and developed.

All three players flirted with foreign collaborations to acquire technology, but gradually found the terms restrictive and decided to blossom on their own. All three have taken up social causes to pay back to society and thus nurture the roots of the environment in which they grew. Above all, each of the three has tremendous personal integrity.

Thou Shalt Not . . .

The more one looks at India, the more one realizes that it is not the lack of a spirit of innovation, but the creation of absurd rules that makes being innovative quite difficult. Consider some instances.

The world of telecommunications blossomed in the US and in Europe because governments there allowed common citizens to play around with frequencies that were open for use by anyone. Naturally, free-to-use frequencies soon get clogged as students and communication geeks begin to pump their data to others through these channels. That is how people begin to invent ways to shut out the 'noise' on the network and allow a particular stream of data to be transmitted almost uninterrupted and without distortion.

The human ear works in much the same way. Try talking to a friend in the midst of a noisy crowd, and you will discover that your friend can hear you, and you can hear him despite the noise around. This is because the human ear has the ability to filter out those frequencies that are not relevant and focus instead only on those that are. Telecommunications works the same way, using filters and algorithms.

India is a land where most people are gifted with a sense of numbers. It has produced geniuses in mathematics and statistics. India too could have come up with its own filters and algorithms, if only the government had allowed people to use free-to-public frequencies. Instead, the government bans the use of any frequency without a licence and makes it extremely difficult to acquire such licences. It is this dog-in-the-manger approach that has stifled innovation in India.

Consider a second example. Drones are now becoming popular and are being put to a variety of uses, such as mapping agricultural harvest. And to interpret pictures taken from a drone, or to filter out certain colours to highlight certain aspects of a picture, extensive use of software programming and algorithms is required. But flying drones is not permitted.[20] [21] The welter of rules and conditions is intimidating. How can India learn to use new technologies or harness them to suit its needs if the government does not allow Indians proper access to them? How will India be prepared for a new world of transportation and surveillance if it does not even care to allow its youth to discover ways to tweak technology?

---

[20] http://www.moneycontrol.com/news/business/economy/comment-killing-innovation-threatens-to-be-fatal-for-modis-make-in-india-2509453.html
http://www.asiaconverge.com/2018/02/killing-innovation-threatens-to-be-fatal-for-modis-make-in-india/
[21] https://www.livemint.com/Technology/sBsvTm7uepIDHk2OsNt5oJ/The-dos-and-donts-of-flying-drones-under-new-regulations.html

In August 2018, the government finally brought in a new set of rules governing the use and flying of drones in India.[22] But they continue to be intimidating, and the heavy breathing of law enforcement agencies can always be felt by anyone keen on experimenting with this technology.

What Indian bureaucrats have learnt to do is what some call the hammer approach. The phrase comes from an apocryphal idiom, which states that when you think you have a hammer, every problem looks like a nail. Since the government has the power to ban, it thinks any problem can be solved by merely banning it. Never mind the deleterious effect of such a ban. If the policeman or the bureaucrat does not understand a bit of technology, instead of finding ways to learn more about it, he opts for the simple solution—ban it. If the problem isn't there, why worry about the solution?

Take a third instance. Consider how the government has banned crowdfunding. What was needed was proper supervision and swift punishment for those who misused crowdfunding and diverted funds. But when a bureaucrat finds himself inept and incapable of dealing with a situation, the solution is a ban. It has obviously been forgotten that innovation and crowdfunding often go hand-in-hand.

The deleterious effects of such an approach can be seen everywhere. In fact, some of the best innovations have taken place in areas where the government was yet to create laws to regulate (and stifle) an industry.

A good example was the way Kurien drafted his own rules for the milk industry. Today, starting a cooperative isn't easy. Dealing with the office of the Registrar of Cooperation (for cooperative societies) can be quite vexatious. Look at the magnanimity of the registrar of cooperatives when it

---

[22] Ibid.

comes to errant practices by the politically powerful. Yet try approaching this office for a cooperative housing problem, and the exercise can be quite unnerving. This is one office that refuses (at least in Maharashtra) to accept registered letters, even though refusal of such letters by any arm of the government is patently illegal, punishable by even dismissal.

And the ubiquitous presence of extortionists (they go by various names) make the climate for doing business in India quite difficult.

At times, innovation gets derailed by special benefits to preferred groups. It is what some call the smothering effect. It is similar to the way the tribals got smothered with the laws that prevented the sale of tribal land to non-tribals (see chapter 6). But more on this aspect a bit later.

Contagion through Government

The contagion is not confined to milk or agriculture. Look at software. This industry did not require anything from the government. There was nothing that the government could licence. Y2K (the change in code required at the turn of the century that would convert two-digit year endings into four-digit dates) was an opportunity for Indian coders. The IT industry grew from there, spurred by enterprise that harnessed genius free from government controls.

Then came 100 per cent tax breaks for software which in turn triggered a big market for money launderers. Remember Satyam?[23]

The IT industry had done quite well for itself all along. It was not tainted by scams. That changed when the

---

[23] https://www.livemint.com/Opinion/QlmPLTT0JkWewueh DnLTcM/Nuts-and-bolts-of-Satyam-saga.html

government thought it could guide the future of the industry. True, governments need to create policy. But when a policy gets misused, shouldn't it have been rectified immediately? And why was no policy-maker penalized for introducing half-baked policies?

This is what happened to the diamond industry as well.[24] It grew well so long as it could manage without government favours. But once it decided to persuade the government to tweak the laws to favour one class of diamond cutters and merchants over other classes, the industry's downward spiral began. The government was used by organizations to push their own agenda at the cost of Indian interests.

Similarly, the moment the government stepped in to manage quotas for garment exports, there were licences and opportunities being offered to people who could curry favours from politicians. Talent and competitiveness took a back seat. Today, Bangladesh exports almost ten times the garments (in value terms) than India does.[25]

Leather exports[26] were doing quite well, and so were beef exports, till the government stepped in with its half-baked laws. Today both sectors are struggling to regain their balance in global markets.

---

[24] http://asiaconverge.com/wp-content/uploads/2015/12/2015-02-05_Govt_Book_4-2-15_Low_Res.pdf

[25] http://www.firstpost.com/business/jobs-at-risk-is-india-prepared-for-huge-unemployment-or-is-it-blissfully-sleeping-3353496.html
http://www.asiaconverge.com/2017/03/is-your-job-at-risk/

[26] http://www.firstpost.com/politics/milk-is-key-to-up-and-so-is-leather-will-cow-vigilantism-spoil-the-party-for-bjp-3197238.html
http://www.asiaconverge.com/2017/01/uttar-pradesh-elections-budget-2017-and-milk-leather/

It was to overcome stifling government regulations that all the three top exporting industries—leather, diamonds and garments—opted to fragment themselves into small units, each employing less than twenty people. That way, restrictive labour laws did not apply. Bangladesh on the other hand allowed the garment industry to grow—some units have as many as 40,000 workers under the same roof. Not surprisingly, India's garment exports have remained stunted at around $1 billion, while those of Bangladesh have grown beyond $26 billion.

More than ever before, the government needs to step aside and allow people to discover new ways of doing things. That is what the small and medium enterprises have been doing all along. They try and stay out of the way of the government. And they account for almost 90 per cent of jobs in India. They also remain profitable in spite of borrowing money at over 30 per cent interest per annum (see Table 1 in Chapter 3).

Look at the world of finance as well. The government's job was to regulate, not to advise bankers on who they should lend money to. Today, you have the unfortunate situation where public sector bank (PSB) managers (even those who have retired) are being hauled over the coals for lending money imprudently. Not one charge sheet has been filed against the politicians and bureaucrats who asked bankers to lend money to favoured borrowers imprudently. Moreover, unlike PSB managers who were pulled up, the authorities looked the other way when it came to private sector bankers who were handled with kid gloves. The principle of one law, and abjuring conflict of situations do not apply to them.[27]

---

[27] http://www.freepressjournal.in/analysis/go-chanda-kochar-please-go/1269603
http://www.asiaconverge.com/2018/05/chanda-kochar-must-go/

Look at consumer finance as well. Much of consumer finance in India is actually akin to secured lending—loans are given only against assets and counter guarantees. And yet banks incur bad debts. Preposterous! Then who will engage in unsecured lending? A lot of innovation is possible here as well, because so much more needs to be done.

There is a lot of innovation possible in the gold markets. This is one sector which employs over 3 million people. India is the largest consumer of gold in the world (see Table 4). Of course there are some years when China moves to No 1 position, and India slips to No 2. But for most of the years, India remains the largest consumer of gold.

							Table 4
India's gold lust: sources of supply							
							estimates in tonnes
	2012	2013	2014	2015	2016	2017	Year-on-year % change
Supply							
Gross Bullion imports	974.5	959.4	994.8	1,065.0	648.3	991.7	53.0
of which doré[1]	23.2	36.9	84.1	229.0	141.9	250.6	77.0
Net bullion imports	842.8	876.4	898.6	913.6	557.7	917.7	65.0
Scrap	118.0	95.8	92.5	80.2	79.5	88.4	11.0
Domestic supply from other sources[2]	10.0	9.6	9.9	9.2	9.9	8.8	-11.0
Total supply[3]	970.8	981.8	1,001.0	1,003.0	647.1	1014.9	57.0
Notes:							
1 Volume of fine gold material contained in the doré							
2 Domestic supply from local mine production, recovery from imported copper concentrates and disinvestment							
3 This supply can be consumed across the three sectors—jewellery, investment and technology.							
Sources: Metals Focus; World Gold Council							

The government itself admitted this in the Lok Sabha in March 2017[28] that '[even though] there are no firm statistics on estimated demand and availability of gold in the country . . . as per rough estimates gold demand in the country is 800–900

---

[28] Lok Sabha unstarred question no. 4842 on 31 March 2017.

tonnes per annum'. And the trade will tell you that almost 100 tonnes of this is smuggled into the country each year.[293031]

Yet short-sighted regulations first drove the industry underground (through the Gold Control Act), then was allowed to move to the smugglers because of a very high import duty of 10 per cent plus other cesses. Everyone in the trade knows that gold is a high value, low volume product. It can be smuggled in very easily. It is used to buy illegal opium from India—through the porous India–Pakistan border and the equally porous northeast borders. There are many ways this gold import duty can be streamlined to reduce smuggling, and make the trade blossom. Reports have been sent to the government,[32] but either the policymakers want to abet gold smuggling, or they do not understand how to make the gold industry flourish. So you have Japan brilliantly promoting gold tourism in Kanazawa, while India's jewellers tremble at the havoc government officials would cause through their intrusive and crafty ways.

Take ecommerce too. For the healthy development of any industry you need a mechanism to resolve disputes. You cannot have transactions at lightning speed, with a few clicks,

[29] http://www.moneycontrol.com/news/business/economy/why-indias-part-illicit-love-affair-with-gold-will-sizzle-on-2324155.html

[30] http://www.moneycontrol.com/news/business/economy/duties-taxes-corruption-how-the-government-abets-the-smuggling-of-gold-2324877.html

[31] http://www.moneycontrol.com/news/business/economy/this-is-how-government-can-clean-up-gold-trade-and-make-it-both-healthy-profitable-2327393.html

[32] http://www.asiaconverge.com/wp-content/uploads/2015/12/AConverge-Gold-booklet-ALL-low-res.pdf

and not have an ecommerce regulator in place.[33] Worse, instead of keeping ecommerce under the RBI (because it is an extension of the financial market and the banking industry), the government has chosen to keep it under the charge of the Information Technology ministry (MEITY) whose concern is bandwidth and IT infrastructure. Is the government waiting for another scam to take place? Already, you have the beginning of a scam with quasi government bodies issuing receipts for utility without including service charges paid to third party IT partners. Thus, your bill and receipt mention one amount, the debit to your bank specifies another amount.[34]

The government is equally misguided on interest rates. The government conveniently ignores the fact that the cost of doing business with small and unsecured borrowers is higher because the attendant risks are greater. But when the government directs banks to clear loans to MSMEs within 59 minutes, and at subsidized interest rates, even when they represent increased borrowing risk,[35] you distort the meaning of innovation, and queer the pitch for good banking.

Higher interest for higher risk is always the principle behind microfinance. Yet, when it began hurting politician-backed moneylenders, the government banned microfinance. So, was it protecting moneylenders? Good justifications often conceal the wickedness of intentions. That too kills innovation. The only kind of innovation such approaches

---

[33] http://www.moneycontrol.com/news/business/economy/how-off-the-book-e-payments-to-government-bodies-open-the-door-to-huge-scams-2382859.html

[34] http://www.moneycontrol.com/news/business/economy/how-off-the-book-e-payments-to-government-bodies-open-the-door-to-huge-scams-2382859.html

[35] https://www.moneycontrol.com/news/business/the-smoke-signals-about-the-economy-could-be-misleading-3147771.html

spawn is that of creating new ways to cheat. At a larger scale they become scams.

The worlds of finance, manufacturing and energy are likely to get skewed further. The age of disruption is likely to create problems that few have anticipated.[36] Old jobs are at risk, and it won't be long before India will have to cope with the challenge of finding jobs for everyone. The country will need innovative approaches to ward off the coming economic turbulence. Yet, the government is unwilling to do so. Consider its refusal to modify laws relating to power distribution and transmission (see Chapter 2).

Innovation is required in creating new jobs for new markets in this world of disruption. But that needs education—it needs decent levels of literacy and good quality higher education. If we are to go by the government's own admission before the Lok Sabha on 5 March 2018, it is the educated who aren't finding jobs (see Table 12 in Chapter 3). Unemployment is rife in this category. It could be because not enough jobs are being created. But it could also be because the educated have become unemployable because of the deplorable educational standards even at the school level.[37] The quality of education also affects the quality of innovation.

The uneducated find it easy to get jobs because there is a demand for unskilled labour. But what happens when the unskilled aren't required any more? India needs to revamp its school education urgently. That will improve the chances

---

[36] https://www.youtube.com/watch?v=2b3ttqYDwF0

[37] https://www.moneycontrol.com/news/india/comment-the-governments-jobs-problem-is-serious-but-there-are-solutions-at-hand-2567017.html
https://www.asiaconverge.com/2018/05/governments-jobs-problem-serious-solutions-hand/

of tomorrow's workers to learn new skills quickly. Without quality school education, the coming disruption will be hugely painful for India.

Some of the most innovative of jobs will come in through tourism. The market will require a variety of skills—tour operators, taxi drivers, mechanics at jetties, waiters, marina managers—the list is long.

In some ways, the government is taking some serious steps. It has begun promoting coastal tourism. It has begun to streamline the processes at ports in such a manner that foreign tourists are not hassled at each coastal city they visit. In one of the rare moves that suggest good governance, the government brought in the home ministry, tourism, customs and immigration officials together and worked out processes that should ease the problems for tourists. Tourism will create jobs, but that is the good part. The other part is the need for security and instilling a sense of safety. Shrill cries of intolerance do not inspire safety and security. The absence of speedy redressal of tourist grievances can also be a dampener for tourism. Taken together, both scotch any innovative approaches in this sector.

Eventually it comes back to dispute redressal, tolerance and education.

India has the spirit of innovation. It just needs to get the government to focus on things that are its domain—primary education, law and order and the removal of the licence raj for education. Just these will allow the spirit of tolerance and experimentation to triumph once again. Leave the rest to the markets and to entrepreneurs.

The government must get out of religion. It must put an end to the politics of vulnerability—for transvestites, homosexuals, prostitution and temple trusts.[38] The world

---

[38] http://www.firstpost.com/india/courting-god-the-supreme-court-attempts-to-rescue-indias-temples-2730860.html

is complicated enough without someone tweaking rules all the time.

In conclusion, India has three advantages—its history of dharma, tolerance and coexistence; its zest for innovation spurred by inexhaustible curiosity; and its willingness to laugh at itself and its gods.

There is one more huge advantage India enjoys. It is— along with China—the world's biggest consumer market. Combine all these advantages and you have a force that few other countries can match. Combine this with the geopolitical advantages of working closely with China and Russia,[39] and well, you could even see the course of history change for good.

---

[39] https://www.dnaindia.com/analysis/column-policy-watch-can-modi-and-xi-reshape-eurasia-2082715

Epilogue

It is as suggested in Nani Palkhivala's story. India grows in spite of the government.

In fact, the government needs to realize that there are always a variety of perspectives, and that each perspective can be right, as in the fable of the blind men and the elephant.

One story that highlights this remarkably well is the story of the world according to the precepts propounded by five Jews. Each one of them changed the way people thought. Each was followed by another Jew who debunked the words of his predecessor. Yet each of them was right. . . in his own way.

Somehow, India has to find an answer for its own problems. Viewing everything from a Western worldview may be unhelpful.

The first Jew exhorted people to think. He told his people that if your reasoning is right, everything will be right. He was a wise man. He was Solomon.

The second Jew talked about the coldness of the mind. The mind was sterile. Love is what mattered. Caring for people is what made life move on. And that is why Jesus said, love thy neighbour.

The third Jew was neither amused nor impressed with either of his predecessors. He dismissed all talk about the head and the heart. What matters, he said, is the stomach. Fill it and the world is good. Leave it empty and you will make an animal out of a man. Thus said Karl Marx.

The fourth Jew merely smiled when people talked to him about the mind. Or the heart. Or even the stomach. The biggest force in life is what lies between your legs, he said. Sex is what makes the world go round, explained Dr Sigmund Freud.

Nonsense, chuckled the fifth Jew. Everything is relative, said Albert Einstein.

Acknowledgements

This book owes immensely to many people:

My editorial colleagues and friends who heard me out, helped me hone my concepts and encouraged me. In particular, I am thankful to (in alphabetical order)

o Ashok Advani, publisher, Business India Group of publications, who helped me grow as a journalist and nurtured my skills;
o Swaminathan Anklesaria Aiyar who brought me to the Express Group of publications, where I grew and spent twelve years of my career. Under him, I learnt the art of studying numbers relating to both the Indian and the global economy;
o Homi Bhabha, my advisor of last resort. He simplified things for me, when nothing made sense;
o Abhijit Bhattacharjee, group head, public relations and corporate communications of NDDB, who was always willing to clarify issues relating to milk, dairy farming and even vegetables and fruit;

o　Marezban Bharucha, senior lawyer and friend, whose insights into the working of courts and policymakers were extremely useful;

o　Sucheta Dalal and her husband Debashis Basu are old friends with whom I have spent hours discussing concepts;

o　Dhaval Desai, senior fellow and vice-president, Observer Research Foundation, who has been a friend and a willing participant for undertaking research on projects that are of immense economic relevance. He has constantly encouraged me to write more on issues that are both economically and socially relevant. I also owe thanks to his team at ORF which has never failed to get me to interact with a wide section of people;

o　Dr Surendra Dhelia, my family doctor, friend, colleague on the Society for the Right to Die with Dignity, and my mentor when it came to understanding the way businessmen think;

o　The EIW and the Online Media teams. The list is long, but without the interactions I had with them, I would have lost a great deal;

o　Bajrang Eriwal, chartered accountant, who is amazing with his knowledge of tax laws and precedents;

o　Louis Fernandes, friend, colleague and currently attached to educational institutes in Australia and South Korea;

o　The *Free Press Journal* editorial team which has always been around when I needed advice or some research inputs;

o　Viveck Goenka, chairman of the Express Group, who steered me into various positions of honour and responsibility—Editor – *Express Investment Week*, Executive Editor – *Financial Express*, Associate Editor – *Indian Express* and Chief Operating Officer of the

Indian Express Online Media Ltd. It was during these years that I took a harder look at the economy, and began analysing economic policy;

o   R. Jagannathan, colleague, editor and friend, with whom I discussed story ideas, and even economic strategies. Even today we traverse through interests which both of us cherish and support;

o   Anay Joglekar, former journalist, researcher and currently in-charge of media relations at the Israeli Consulate who has an amazing understanding of water, agriculture and politics in Maharashtra;

o   Ajay Jugran, senior lawyer and friend, with whom I discussed innumerable issues, especially arbitration, for hours on end;

o   Rahul Joshi, editor-in-chief, Network18, who saw talent in me, welcomed me into the Network18 fold, which in turn allowed me to further pursue policy analysis;

o   Abhishek Karnani, director, *Indian National Press*, publishers of *Free Press Journal*, for letting me bring out policy booklets which further sharpened my understanding of policy-related matters;

o   Gautam Kirtane and his wife Shaheeda, who inspired me with their focus on social concerns—whether it was related to the cleaning up of the Mithi river, or FGM, or even urbanization;

o   Latha Venkatesh of CNBC, senior journalist and friend, who has always been willing to help friends out and encourage them in the pursuits they choose. I have been a beneficiary as well;

o   Radhika Marwah and her wonderful editorial team, who helped me shape this book, modify my tables and charts, and redo some jottings. Without their immense help and support, this book would not have seen the light of day;

o   Jawahir Mulraj, friend, philosopher and guide, my guru, whom I have used as a sounding board, and has helped further develop my ideas. At times he has disdainfully tossed away a concept I propounded, and at times encouraged me;

o   Santosh Nair, editor, Moneycontrol.com, who has been a constant support in my editorial pursuits at Network18, and with whom I have discussed many of my concepts before putting them down for publication;

o   The Network18 team, especially Debdatta Das who introduced me to Penguin Random House, and to Rajat Dev who helped me with design inputs. Both were invaluable;

o   Chandan Parmar, chartered accountant and friend, who helped me understand how informal businesses work and even think;

o   Chetan and Vinay Parikh—two incredible brothers with an amazing gift for numbers and whose analyses of industry after industry for *Express Investment Week* helped me understand the Indian economy better;

o   Ajit Ranade, economist, and a constant source of inspiration for me. His views on the Indian (and global) economy have educated me immensely;

o   Anthony Raj, friend, and once a colleague-journalist, was responsible—along with Deepak Raja—for ushering me into journalism during the 1980s. I owe them a great deal for my growth in this profession;

o   Deepak Rohra, a very old friend, whom I run to for advice and help each time there is a problem that I cannot easily comprehend;

o Mitesh Shah, chartered accountant and friend, whose advice on financial structures and taxation has always helped me clear the cobwebs in my mind;

o Sandeep Sharma, banker, investment manager, and friend, who has often encouraged me to continue meandering in the thickets of wild concepts;

o Utpal Sheth, friend, and CEO & Partner, RaRe Enterprises, for always being around to discuss things with me;

o Shardul Shroff and his amazing wife Pallavi, both very senior lawyers and dear friends, who made me explore the legal minefield through which all policies must traverse. They have sat with me for hours on end, clarifying for me issues that baffled me. Shardul was one of the first people with whom I began discussing issues relating to milk and adjudication which helped me further develop my concepts with the additional clarity that I now enjoy. He has been a friend, philosopher and guide, whose views and support I have valued, and cherished;

o Shankar Sitaraman, friend, and currently editor-in-chief, *National Herald*, who encouraged me to write on policy matters for Moneycontrol.com. He appointed me as consulting editor with Moneycontrol and encouraged me to write about radical concepts;

o P.R. Somasundaram, friend, and currently managing director, World Gold Council, whose inputs were extremely helpful while understanding the market for gold and the interplay between gold and the economy, politics and even society. It was through him that I began looking at how different countries treated gold in their respective territories.

o   Bahram Vakil, senior lawyer and friend, who helped
    me understand the Insolvency and Bankruptcy Code;
o   Sandip Vimadalal, lawyer and friend, always available
    with a hand of support;
o   Liu D Zongyi, Senior Fellow, Institute for International
    Strategic Studies & Center for Asia-Pacific Studies,
    who has always been around for advice, research
    assistance and with a hand of friendship.

A lot is owed to my colleagues (and their families) at the
educational centres with which I have been associated.
Among them are the Ghuryes, the Havanurs, Pritti Kumar,
the Pathalams and T.J. Ravishankar. Interactions with them
have also contributed to my understanding of social equity
and the Indian economy.

The list is long, and the names above are just some of the
innumerable people who have helped me grow. To all of them
I owe a lot.

Consular officers who helped me understand policies in
their respective countries. Given below are (once again in
alphabetical order) some of the many names of those who
helped me out.

o   David Akov, former consul general of Israel in
    Mumbai, who was always willing to spend time with
    me to connect me with people in Israel and learn more
    about the innovations in that amazing country;
o   Nimrod Assouline, former deputy head of mission at
    the Israeli consulate in Mumbai, who introduced me
    to scores of Israelis travelling through Mumbai and
    helped me learn about their innovative concepts;

o K.C. Damodaran, former head, Indo German Chambers of Commerce in Mumbai. He often accompanied me on my trips through Germany, and helped me with a better understanding of the industry and policies of that country;

o Ya'akov Finkelstein, consul general of Israel in Mumbai, who has continued the good work that David Akov and Nimrod have been engaged with;

o Yoshiaki Ito, former consul general of Japan in Mumbai. He brought me close to Japan's companies and concepts;

o Masood Khaleggi, consul general of Iran in Mumbai;

o Soung-eun Kim, former consul general of South Korea in Mumbai;

o The late Dr Guenter Krueger, director general of the Indo German Chambers of Commerce;

o Chung Lin Ying, former consul general for Singapore in Mumbai. I could spend hours with him trying to understand how Singapore shaped its policies;

o Ali Mohammedi, former consul general of Iran in Mumbai;

o Zheng Xiyuan (former consul general For the People's Republic of China in Mumbai, and current consul general of PRC in Manchester, UK) and his charming wife Li Fanghui who have always been patient with me while helping me understand so many policies relating to China. Both husband and wife got me introduced to some of the best academic bodies in China, where I delivered a few lectures;

o Andrey Zhidkov, vice-consul, Russian Consulate in Mumbai, for helping me understand a bit more about Russia.

Once again, the list does not include the scores of people I visited in various countries who also helped me appreciate the way their respective governments handle policies to empower and enrich their people. The list above also does not include the (many) other consular officers who have helped me navigate the world of policy and commerce.

Industry captains—some of whom are mentioned in this book—who helped me think in terms of strategy. Some of them include (once again, in alphabetical order)

o   Gautam Adani, who was willing to spend hours with me on several occasions to help me understand the business of ports and coastal development;
o   Badnarayan Barwale, the late chairman of Mahyco, who was one of the first to explain to me, almost thirty years ago, the concepts behind hybrid seeds and how they could be used to galvanize agricultural productivity;
o   Bhavarlal Jain, the late chairman of the Jain group of industries, who remained bound to his roots in Jalgaon, even as he traversed business sectors ranging from PVC pipes, to agriculture to education. His approach to agriculture was enormously educative;
o   Aleksei Kechko, managing director, SBERbank India, for offering me insights on investments that Russia was keen on, and the way it views India;
o   Verghese Kurien, who was perhaps the biggest inspiration for me, in appreciating how strategic advantages are identified, nurtured, and then exploited;
o   Brij Mohan Lall Munjal, who let me become the first journalist to write about the Hero Group when it was headquartered in Ludhiana, Punjab. He discussed

with me, over several days, the options he had first in tying up with Japan's Honda Motor Company, and then the inevitability of finding his own path;

o   Nani Palkhivala, the amazing jurist, who was among the first people who helped me make sense of a long list of figures given in the country's budget papers. His analyses, anecdotes and critiques made more sense to me as I grew older. The lessons were invaluable;

o   Deepak S. Parekh, chairman, HDFC Ltd, an incredible banker who has always been around to advise and to guide lost souls in the maze of finance and industry;

o   Dilip Piramal, CMD, VIP Industries, who took a keen interest in promoting policy-based panel discussions while he was president of the Indian Merchants' Chamber;

o   Mukund Rajan, former (and first) Brand Custodian of the Tata group, and member of the group executive council of Tata Sons. He likes to describe himself as corporate strategist, liberal thinker and entrepreneur. He took interest in the work I do, and helped me clarify some thoughts I harboured;

o   Suresh Senapaty, currently director with Wipro, who was for several years my travel companion on the crowded trains of Mumbai, and who used to discuss product strategy with me more than thirty years ago;

o   R.S. Sodhi, MD, GCMMF, who made me appreciate the crucial relevance of the Amul brand for India and even for Asia. He and his team—which included Jayen Mehta—helped me better appreciate the factors that make the milk industry in India so unique, so amazing, and so rewarding;

o   Ratan Tata, who explained to me the decisions he had to take as the chairman of the Tata Group when he took charge. One of my most memorable interactions was during a flight from Delhi to Mumbai on a Sunday morning, when we could speak undisturbed for almost two hours—a priceless experience with amazing insights;

o   Venu Srinivasan, chairman, Sundaram Clayton Group, who explained to me the way he got the Scooty designed and manufactured to become a better vehicle than what Suzuki had offered to the Indian markets. I still remember—with immense warmth—the night when he took me for a ride down the streets of Chennai (then Madras) to make me appreciate how great a vehicle the scooty was.

Once again, the list of industrialists, corporate honchos and entrepreneurs from whom I learnt a lot is very long—partly because I had the opportunity of interviewing them as a journalist, and also because each person had his own little strategy that he worked on, almost tenaciously. Together, they reshaped almost every concept I had, modified my views, sometimes made me reject them, and quite often build on them.

–   Finally, there is my family—especially my daughter Dharini who prodded me on to write this book

Without them this book might not even have emerged from the labyrinths of my mind.